LAOS

The Research Institute on Contemporary Southeast Asia (IRASEC), based in Bangkok, Thailand, is a member of the network of research centres of the French Foreign Ministry. IRASEC calls on specialists from all academic fields to study the important social, political, economic and environmental developments that affect, together or separately, the eleven countries of the region (Brunei, Burma, Cambodia, Indonesia, Lao, Malaysia, the Philippines, Singapore, Thailand, Timor Leste and Vietnam). IRASEC's research output consists of academic studies written and designed to be disseminated not just to specialists, but to the wider public. To that end, IRASEC has developed a number of series with a variety of publishing partners.

Mekong Press was initiated in 2005 by Silkworm Books, Thailand, and the Creativity & Culture Division of Rockefeller Foundation's Southeast Asia Regional Office in Bangkok, to encourage and support the work of local scholars, writers and publishing professionals in Cambodia, Laos, Vietnam and the other countries in the Greater Mekong subregion. Books published by Mekong Press will be marketed and distributed internationally. In addition, Mekong Press intends to hold seminars and training workshops on aspects of book publishing as well as help find ways to overcome some of the huge challenges for small book publishers in the region. Mekong Press is funded by the Rockefeller Foundation's Learning Across Borders in the Greater Mekong Sub-region progam.

LAOS

FROM BUFFER STATE
TO CROSSROADS?

by
Vatthana Pholsena
Ruth Banomyong

Translated by
Michael Smithies

MEKONG PRESS
Chiang Mai, Thailand

This publication is funded by The Rockefeller Foundation.

Originally published in French by IRASEC in 2004 as
Le Laos au XXI siècle: Les Défis de l'intégration régionale

Published in English in 2006 by
Mekong Press
6 Sukkasem Road, T. Suthep, Chiang Mai 50200, Thailand
E-mail: info@mekongpress.com
Website: http://www.mekongpress.com

ISBN-13: 978-974-94805-0-2

Original cover photo © 2006 Bryan Watt
Copyedited by Gael Lee, bonyfish, Singapore
Typeset by Silk Type in Janson Text 10 pt.

Printed in Thailand by O.S. Printing House, Bangkok

5 4 3 2

CONTENTS

LIST OF MAPS, FIGURES AND TABLES

LIST OF BOXES

ACKNOWLEDGEMENTS

We would like to thank Adirson Semyaem, Grant Evans, Christopher Goscha, Andrew Hardy, Vincent Huynh, Kajit Jittasevi, Hans U. Luther, Sophie Quinn-Judge, Paul Reddicliffe, and Judith Stowe for their help, advice, and suggestions. In Laos, we must express our gratitude to the Ministries of Communications, Transport, Postal Services and Construction, Foreign Affairs, and Trade for their help and collaboration. Lastly we would like to thank the Asia Research Institute of the National University of Singapore which gave financial support to our research.

This book is dedicated to Roong, Rujikorn, and Ruthira.

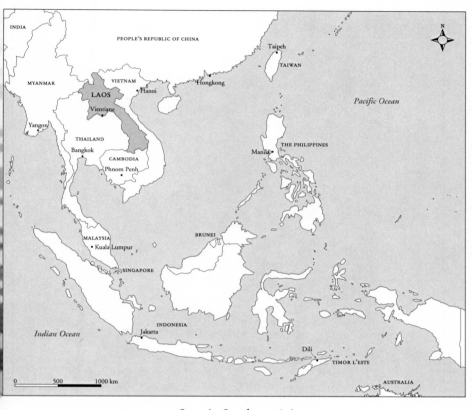

Laos in Southeast Asia

Laos: provinces and capitals

INTRODUCTION

The function of a buffer zone implies, by definition, the existence of political and military forces on both sides likely to collide if they were in direct contact. The geographical area today occupied by the Lao People's Democratic Republic represents the reduced territory of the kingdom of Lan Xang, formed in 1353 by Prince Fa Ngum, who returned from exile in Cambodia to Laos as a conqueror. Its formation was helped by the decline of Sukhothai, another Tai kingdom established in 1292. What was to become Laos could prosper and retain its stability by benefiting from its neighbors' problems. Dai Viet, literally "Great Viet", and Burma were regularly convulsed by internal power struggles, whilst Cambodia inexorably declined, and Ayutthaya, the future Siam, did not really hinder the development of its northern neighbor. Even at its highest point in the seventeenth century, Lan Xang always remained "the land in between" (Evans 2002) which soon splintered in an almost synchronized process of self-destruction and retreat before enemy conquests. In the eighteenth century, the Siamese and Vietnamese, greatly aided by the bickering among the pretenders to the Lao throne, clashed through vassal states created from the territory of Lan Xang, incited by the need for living space on the one hand, and fear of conquest and extermination on the other (Toye 1968, xiii).

It was already a question of survival and the opposition of two worlds, one more marked by Indian religious influences, the other by China. Two and a half centuries later, a troubling similarity was to occur in the middle of the Cold War, in an attempted balancing act, whose failure would have meant the end of the country. At the price of a partial loss of its political and territorial sovereignty, Laos, taking the place of the defunct Lan Xang, saw its territory serve as a buffer zone for outside powers, a "domino" which should not fall (for capitalist Thailand and its allies, especially the United States), and a "rear base" for others (communist Vietnam and its mentors, China and the USSR).

Now the time for expansionist policies, military threats, and even ideological battles has passed. This is a good time to reevaluate the position of Laos. Is the framework of historical analysis still valid to understand the position and function of the country in the post-Cold War period? Laos, along with Vietnam and Cambodia, joined ASEAN in the 1990s. Indochina, as envisioned by the French colonial rulers and the Vietnamese communists, has effectively ceased to exist. Thailand and Vietnam, former enemies, have become trading partners. "Business" certainly does not efface all the wounds of the past. If history is the key to understanding the present, it does not necessarily control its future. Overriding national frontiers and the state authority, new rules in international relations, fresh stakes and challenges all need to take account of past mentalities and reasoning, but at the same time current strategies and parameters. In short, to what degree is it justifiable to define contemporary Laos as a buffer state, at a time when international players favor the region, indeed the world, as the framework of action, competition, and also cooperation?

What has never changed, from Lan Xang to Laos, is the absence of an outlet to the sea. The accounts of European explorers who in the seventeenth and eighteenth centuries did not travel beyond Siam, already spoke of the "little known" Lan Xang, a "country in the interior", described as a "great and powerful kingdom", but at a month's traveling time north from the Siamese capital, and "very difficult to reach" (Stuart-Fox 1998, 100). This relative isolation (the first European accounts of Lan Xang date from the 1640s; at this period the kingdom of Ayutthaya already had a reputation for cosmopolitan trading and military prowess), explains in part the political, territorial and military stagnation of the kingdom, which was unable to profit by the exchanges resulting from maritime trade, or to benefit from the transfer of military technology from the European powers.

What is Laos today? The opening up of the country has become a priority of the government and international institutions, in particular the Asian Development Bank (ADB). The intention is to change the image and reality of the country, from being land-locked to land-linked, bringing together all the countries in the Greater Mekong sub-region. The possibilities of this evolution give rise to the hope of changing contemporary Southeast Asian geopolitics. Laos could even become in the third millennium what it was five centuries ago, the center of the region, a crossroads of all the regional trading routes (Stuart-Fox 1995, 179). This is the possibility this book seeks to examine.

1 GEOPOLITICS OF A BUFFER STATE: FROM THE PRE-COLONIAL PERIOD TO THE COLD WAR

Between the regional empires of Siam and Vietnam

Lao historiography, whether communist or otherwise, presents the Buddhist kingdom of Lan Xang (the kingdom of a thousand elephants), which reached its zenith in the seventeenth century under King Sourinyavongsa, as the glorious past of the present Lao People's Democratic Republic. Upon the death of the ruler in 1695, the kingdom, rent by internal divisions, was progressively broken up and became the object of struggles for influence between its two powerful neighbors, Siam, present-day Thailand, and Dai Viet, present-day Vietnam.

From the eighteenth century, the political and territorial unity of Lan Xang was unable to overcome these internal power struggles. It split apart and was divided into three principalities: Luang Prabang in the north, Vientiane in the center, and Champassak in the south. One could also add a fourth division, with Xieng Khouang (Muang Phuan) intermittently liberating itself from the tutelage of Vientiane.

Greatly weakened, the old kingdom was the object of Siamese expansionism a few decades later, and in 1779 the three political entities became vassals of the Thonburi king Taksin. In 1827, after reprisals following the uprising of Chao Anou, the last king of Vientiane, Siamese forces sacked the city and conducted a massive population shift to the Khorat plateau, the northeast of present-day Thailand. The last attempt by Chao Anou to give the Lan Xang kingdom its autonomy and reconstitute its unity was blocked by the annexation of Vientiane and Champassak by Siam. Only Luang Prabang retained some semblance of sovereignty, paying tribute to both Bangkok and Hue, and to Peking for good measure. The political expansionism of Siam was then confronted by the ambitions of another empire, Vietnam, and its "movement to the south" *(nan tien)*, at the expense of Lao and Khmer territory.

The political and administrative fragmentation of the old kingdom of Lan Xang increased Vietnamese influence over Lao territory to the east of the Mekong. During the advance of Siamese troops, the local chiefs turned to their other powerful neighbor to seek support and protection. From the beginning of the nineteenth century, the territory of the present-day provinces of northeast Laos, Hua Phan and Xieng Khouang, recognized the suzerainty of Hue.[1] But the destruction of Vientiane and the appearance of the Siamese military inside Lao territory caused the Vietnamese and Siamese forces to enter into direct confrontation for control of the Lao and Khmer political entities. A series of confrontations between the two powers, that stretched for nearly half a century, ended only in 1847 with the signing of a treaty establishing co-suzerainty over Khmer territory and, subsequently, over the Plain of Jars.[2]

This respite was short-lived. With the arrival of the colonial period, the political and territorial framework of the Lao principalities was to undergo another disruption.

Between the colonial powers—Britain and France

The arrival of the French gave the Lao territories new geographic boundaries and a new political framework. On October 3, 1893 a treaty signed between the French and the Siamese forced the Siamese to cede to France their territories on the east bank of the Mekong. The French were never to reconstitute the old kingdom of Lan Xang. Instead, they redrew the territorial frontiers according to geopolitical considerations inspired by a particular concept of Indochina, which in fact only accorded reduced importance to Laos, simply seen as an extension of what was to become Vietnam.

The Lao territories were to be modified subsequent to negotiations, pressure and horse-trading between the French and the British, each trying to block the advance of the other while maintaining its own possessions in mainland Southeast Asia. Thus in the decade following the 1893 treaty, France had the opportunity of trying to extend Lao territories and include the whole of the Khorat plateau, annexed by Siam in the eighteenth century. But Britain stopped this,

A French view: Siam's annexation of the right bank of the Mekong and colonial rivalry

Only the outright annexation of Siam, apart from expanding our colonial empire, would have allowed us to hold in check the English and the Germans, our trading rivals.

For a long time, the Siamese had said "The day when we shall be forced to retreat, we will only leave land, water and the wild beasts in the forests." And, in fact, it was almost to the letter that this maxim was applied by them, in 1827 and 1840, when, fearing Annamite reprisals on the left bank, they removed their train to the right bank, even as far as the valley of the Menam, both people and cattle…They lacked only the time to carry out their sinister project, but they left us with a depopulated, devastated land, and kept for themselves the Laos of the right bank and the rich provinces of Angkor and Battambang, that is, well-populated and fertile lands, never having experienced, unlike French Laos today, several invasions in less than a century.

The hesitation in the Bangkok court, when the ultimatum was delivered, as well as its attempts to keep the territory on the right bank of the Mekong above the 18th parallel, clearly showed, once more, the interference of Britain, which, though not obvious, had never ceased to make its influence felt throughout all these negotiations. This hidden influence was aimed at retaining its dominance in the Phan Na [Sipsong Panna] and as it was already ruling over the kingdom of Ava [Burma], of facilitating the realization of its projected railway in the direction of S'Semao and Yunnan-Sen [in southeast China].

Lucien de Reinach, *Le Laos* (1901, 28–29)

anxious to maintain Siam as a viable and independent buffer state between British India and French Indochina. At the beginning of the twentieth century, the French no longer sought to expand the limits of Indochina, and consequently, the opportunities to expand Lao territories were not all taken. The last important territorial modification took place in 1904 with the annexation of parts of the west bank of the Mekong (Saiyabouri in the north and a part of Champassak in the south). Two months later, France and Britain signed the Entente Cordiale by which they explicitly recognized their respective zones of influence. Political expansion ceased. With the treaties of 1893, 1904 and 1907 (the last, between France and Siam, confirmed the present frontiers of Laos), France finally obtained what it sought, the "reconstitution of Cambodia, a strategic hinterland in Laos, 'rounding out' their Indochinese empire, control of the Mekong river and relatively well-defined frontiers" (Stuart-Fox 1995, 121).

In reality, on both the economic and strategic levels, the French authorities perceived of Laos to be a mere prolongation of Vietnam, the latter considered as the keystone of its colonial effort in Indochina. In a recent study, the historian Christopher Goscha (1995, 154) demonstrated how the French colonial project in ex-Indochina was guided by the desire, even the will, to transform a vast political area into a palpable and concrete entity. The Vietnamese were seen as the indigenous base for this project. The French authorities encouraged Vietnamese immigration into Laos (as well as into Cambodia) with the aim of supplementing administrative personnel and increasing the labor in the mines and plantations. Laos was not considered by France as a political entity sanctified by history. The different regions, instead of being unified, were governed with a dual structure: the kingdom of Luang Prabang acquired the status of a protectorate, while the rest of the Lao lands were administered by the colonial regime.

Resulting from both geopolitical strategy and the French conception of an Indochinese empire, the French only acquired a part of the former kingdom of Lan Xang. Without the Khorat plateau, France only had an under-populated part of the old kingdom of Lan Xang. The Lao nationalist movements would adopt these frontiers, and not those of the kingdom of Lan Xang, as the geopolitical limits for the struggles for national independence. But the concept of a national ideal had to be created. The dual French administration of the Lao territories prevented the creation of a unified political entity. The view that the modern state of Laos is a French creation is thus flawed. It was only in 1899 that upper Laos (extending from the northern limits of Khammouane province to the southern limits of Luang Prabang) and lower Laos (from the southern limits of Khammouane province), administered by senior officials, respectively based in Luang Prabang in the north and Khong in the south, were regrouped into a single administrative entity established at Savannakhet, then from 1900 in Vientiane. However, the kingdom of Luang Prabang remained under the direct administration of King Sisavangvong of Laos.[3] The declaration of independence, and at the same time the unity of Laos, was proclaimed on September 15, 1945, allowing the rest of the world to consider Laos as a political entity distinct from the other components of French Indochina.

Another view of Lao political identity

If Muang Lao did not exist, after 1711, as an empire in the political sense of the word, it nevertheless survived, because of its great homogeneity and its peoples and by the form of its political and administrative organization, a unified nation. This nation could be termed many-headed, because it was governed by several rulers of the same dynastic origin, each exercising his temporal power within the boundaries of his tiny state, but all having real moral and spiritual authority within the whole country which, from this viewpoint, could be considered, in spite of its apparent dismemberment, as remaining still in its unified form, until the day when a great prince, a person of talent and incontestable and uncontested merit, would come and rally around himself all the minor rival state leaders and regroup them once again under his rule. In sum, a sort of masked and potential confederation of states, unknown in international European law...

France was confronted by this many-headed nation, this potential confederation of states which was Lan Xang, when it intervened in the upper and middle Mekong valley towards the end of the nineteenth century.

Had it been better informed, France could have either reestablished this confederation to the benefit of one of the ruling Lao kings at that time, or boldly assumed itself the confederation's leadership. Unfortunately it did nothing. Lao unity was sacrificed once more, and would only reappear, as will be seen, half a century later.

Katay D. Sasorith [Prime Minister of Laos 1954–56], *La Laos, son évolution politique, sa place dans l'Union française* (1953, 46–47)

The Cold War and civil war: Laos in the turmoil of the Indochinese wars 1945–1975

The Lao independence nationalist movement split between the Lao Issara and the Pathet Lao

On March 9, 1945 the Japanese interned what remained of the French colonial administration in Indochina and encouraged the Cambodian, Lao and Vietnamese authorities to declare independence under their umbrella. Laos did this on April 8, 1945, in spite of the opposition of King Sisavangvong, who refused to collaborate with the Japanese and in addition distrusted the political ambitions of the other members of the Lao aristocracy. Prince Phetsarath, the king's nephew and viceroy in Vientiane, took over as prime minister. He established a provisional government in Vientiane and created, on August 8, 1945 the grouping of Lao Issara (Free Lao), which was to become the kernel of the future government. Two of his brothers, princes Souvanna Phouma and Souphanouvong, as well as other members of the Lao upper bourgeoisie and aristocracy, joined this new grouping. This first Lao nationalist movement, Lao Issara, was born in the immediate post-war period and at its head was an elite, all of whose members were ethnically Lao.

But the return of French troops after the capitulation of Japan in August 1945 led to conflict between King Sisavangvong and Prince Phetsarath. The king, replying to the demand of the prince to reaffirm the unity of Laos, informed him on the contrary of the abrogation of the declaration of independence of the country and its return to French protection. On September 15, Prince Phetsarath, in a gesture of defiance, proclaimed the independence of Laos and at the same time the integration of all the country's provinces (and thus the fusion of the regional authorities of Luang Prabang, Vientiane, and Champassak) under his sole authority. But the position of Prince Phetsarath and his supporters soon became untenable with the reoccupation of the country by French troops. The prince resigned his office on October 10, 1945. On March 21, 1946, at Thakhek, in the center of Laos, Sisavangvong was once again crowned king of Laos. On April 24th French forces entered Vientiane. A constitution was adopted on May 11: Laos became a constitutional monarchy within the French Union.

During this period, members of the Lao Issara in Bangkok continued their activities as a Lao government in exile. Some of them did not, though, reject the idea of a compromise with France. Profoundly conservative and anti-revolutionary, they conceived of the French as the best, or perhaps the least harmful solution which would permit some stability and preserve Laos from the communist threat (Christie 2001, 117). A split was to become increasingly apparent in the ranks of the Lao Issara between the adversaries and partisans of cooperation with France. Before this crucial choice, Prince Phetsarath and his brothers were to take diverging paths. Phetsarath adopted a long term and inflexible policy which would lead to ten years of exile in Thailand. Opposing all foreign intervention in Lao political affairs, he favored strict Lao neutrality in relation to France and Vietnam, a strategy and an objective which the country would never be able to apply or achieve. Souvanna Phouma, on the other hand, returned to

Vientiane when the Lao Issara government in exile dissolved itself on October 25, 1949.

But Souphanouvong had already made clear his refusal to accept the new political direction in Vientiane by resigning from the movement in early 1949.

The first congress of Lao communist leaders took place on August 13, 1950 in Tuyen Quang in North Vietnam. With strong support from the Vietnamese communists, the congress proceeded to elect a new Lao resistance government, with Souphanouvong at its head as prime minister. A second meeting, again in North Vietnam, took place in November 1950. It added to the Pathet Lao a new political movement, the Neo Lao Issara (the Free Lao Front). This outlined a brief political program which called on all Lao, regardless of ethnicity, to form a united front against the French and the abolition of unfair taxes (Fall 1965, 178). The partisans of the Souphanouvong faction only represented a minority within the Lao nationalist movements, so the support and mobilization of the numerous non-Lao ethnic groups would be essential to the survival of the Lao communist movement.

Neutrality, an impossible alternative

After the Geneva agreements of July 1954 (barely two months after the French defeat at Dien Bien Phu on May 7), Laos was turned into a political, then military battlefield, between North Vietnam and China on the one hand, and on the other, Thailand and its ally the United States. Laos occupied an extremely important strategic position: it is surrounded from west to east by Thailand, Burma, China, Cambodia, and Vietnam. When Vietnam was divided by the 17th parallel following the Geneva Agreements, Laos found itself the de facto border of both North and South Vietnam. Furthermore, the country was henceforth neighboring two socialist countries in the region, the Chinese People's Republic and the Democratic Republic of Vietnam, as well as the "neutral" states of Cambodia and Burma. Lastly, Laos had, with the Plain of Jars in the northeast, an extremely important strategic zone from where air bases could cover the whole of South China and mainland Southeast Asia.

From 1955 the primary objective of the Americans, who replaced the French in Indochina as the dominant Western power, was to control as much of Laos as possible. The country was seen as a "domino" which could save Thailand, and the whole of Southeast Asia from the "communist menace".[4] The drama of Laos was then less in its traditional divisions than in the internationalization of its internal politics. Its neutrality would have been respected if the parties involved, in particular the external powers (Thailand, the United States, and the Democratic Republic of Vietnam) had accepted it. But the neutrality of Laos was constantly to give way to the rivalry between these powers. On the one hand was the Pathet Lao supported by the Viet Minh and the communist bloc, with China at its head, and on the other were the anti-communists of the Royal Lao Government supported by Thailand and the United States; between the two camps were the neutralists, somewhat to the left of the political chessboard. In 1958 the government of Souvanna Phouma, then that of Phoui Sananikone, might well proclaim that the Geneva agreements of 1954 were carried out by Laos, which signified in other words that the country had no need of foreign support to settle its internal affairs. But this vision was firmly rejected by the Democratic Republic of Vietnam, which in a declaration that same year by its then prime minister Pham Van Dong, indicated that the solution to the problems of the three former Indochinese states, such as they were outlined in the Geneva agreements, "were one and indivisible" (Evans 2002, 121). The breakdown in 1963 of the Geneva agreements reached the previous year, which affirmed the neutrality of Laos and the collapse of the second coalition government, sealed the fate of Laos.

In the 1960s, the escalation of the Vietnam War made any attempt to leave Laos outside the battlefield of the Cold War illusory. From 1964,[5] the United States supported the South Vietnamese regime militarily, which implied, amongst other things, the necessity of neutralizing North Vietnam and opposing communist infiltration into the south. A terrible vicious circle began: military confrontation increased, the great powers (the United States, China, and the USSR) became more involved, and the stakes for Hanoi rose. Laos and North Vietnam shared a common frontier of 1,130 km and the land route through eastern Laos was the best for the communist troops to reach South Vietnam. Consequently, helping Pathet Lao with both words and arms, the Viet Minh labored for its own survival. On the other side, the Americans used the airfields in the north of Laos and in northeast Thailand to bombard North Vietnam. They also heavily bombed the northeast (the Plain of Jars) and the east of Laos in order to attempt to halt the advance of the Lao and North Vietnamese communist forces supplying communist troops to South Vietnam

The Lao tragedy

The tragedy for Laos was that the kind of settlement the Geneva Agreements tried to create in Laos had been overtaken by events long before the final arrangements were made in mid-1962. By 1962, the insurgency in South Vietnam was already seriously threatening the survival of the regime there. The "Ho Chi Minh Trail" through the mountains of Eastern Laos was firmly established, and the main priority for the North Vietnamese patrons of the Pathet Lao was the maintenance of firm and exclusive control of the eastern provinces of Laos. In return, the North Vietnamese were tacitly—not openly— prepared to acquiesce in effective American control of the Mekong river area in Laos—an area that was seen by the United States as strategically vital for the security of Thailand.

Between the strategic priorities of the United States and North Vietnam, as they geared up for full-scale conflict in South Vietnam, the Laotian neutralists were squeezed out of existence. Laotian neutralist politicians and their armed force units gradually slid either into the Royal Lao or the Pathet Lao camps. In the same period (1963–64) the coalition government once again broke up, and the condition of de facto partition and civil war was resumed. Against his inclinations, but bowing to the irresistible realities of the Indochina situation, Souvanna Phouma now presided over a Royal Lao government that was, in all but name, an American protectorate. Conversely, the Pathet Lao regime, particularly the "Ho Chi Minh Trail" area, had become a strategic adjunct of North Vietnam's war effort. The fate of Laos—that "Shangri-La" for those who had witnessed its unearthly beauty before it had fallen victim to ideology and geopolitics—would now be decided by the outcome of the Vietnam War.

Clive J. Christie, "Laos and the Vietnam War", in *Southeast Asia in the Twentieth Century. A Reader* (1998, 226–27)

from the North through the famous Ho Chi Minh trail (which in reality was a network of tracks through the mountains and forests).

The intensification of American attacks on the "trail" led to a generalization of the war in the east of Laos. The objective was clear: at the same time to prevent Pathet Lao and Viet Minh forces from rallying the rural population, which could provide them with support and shelter, and to ruin the social structures created by the Lao communists and the North Vietnamese in these areas.

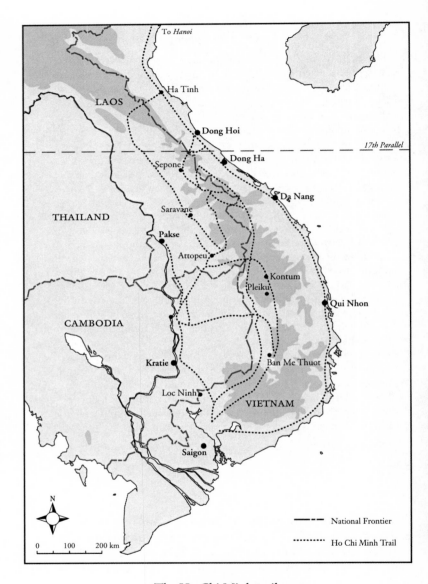

The Ho Chi Minh trails

The degree of internationalization of the civil war in Laos was such that any resolution of the conflict progressively escaped its political leaders, in spite of attempts to form coalition governments (1957–58, 1962–63). On the ground, the advantage at the beginning of the 1970s was largely seized by Pathet Lao forces and those of their ally North Vietnam. In 1972 the "liberated zones" already covered three-quarters of Lao territory and more than half its population. But the evolution of the American-Vietnamese war would be still more decisive for ending the confrontation. The progressive retreat of American forces from South Vietnam from 1969, in parallel with the "Vietnamization" of the conflict, would be complete by March 29, 1973. Le Duc Tho and Henry Kissinger signed the Paris agreements on January 23, 1973. The departure of the Americans from ex-Indochina dealt a fatal blow to the armed forces of the Royal Lao Government. Without their massive military and financial support, they rapidly disintegrated. Less than a month later, on February 21, 1973, a ceasefire agreement was signed in Laos. The entry of the Khmer Rouge into Phnom Penh and the seizure of Saigon by North Vietnamese troops, respectively on April 17 and 30, 1975, precipitated the end of the regime. The Lao People's Democratic Republic was proclaimed on December 2, 1975.

Socialist solidarity threatened by the third Indochinese conflict

A period of reconstruction: the short-lived "neutralist" policy

The seizure of power by the Pathet Lao placed Laos firmly in the socialist camp. The foreign policy of the country after 1975 logically followed the communist ideological canons, that is, being guided by "proletarian solidarity" between the socialist states and the belief in the ultimate global victory of socialism in its struggle against capitalism. More prosaically, this solidarity went hand in hand with an integration into a hierarchy dominated by the Soviet Union and its ally, Vietnam.

The bonds, already very close, between the new Lao leaders and their Vietnamese companions in arms in the "thirty-year struggle" against the "imperialists" and their "lackeys" were further reinforced, to such a degree than some observers did not hesitate to denounce the total stranglehold of Vietnam over its neighbor. The American scholar Arthur Dommen even predicted in a work published in 1985 that Vietnam and Laos could in the future form a union, on the model of the Soviet Union, composed of distinct republics led by a single party, of course controlled by the Vietnamese party (Dommen 1979, 124). Dominated, controlled, even exploited, Laos would be reduced to the ranks of a "satellite state" in the Vietnamese orbit, and the Vientiane government a puppet of Hanoi (Dommen 1979, 201). The young Lao People's Democratic Republic would only have very limited or even no margin for maneuver, and its foreign policy would be entirely subjected to Vietnamese national interests, at least in the early years of its existence (Stuart-Fox 1991, 187). Observers' comments left no room for doubt. Yet, into this schematic picture of a master-apprentice relationship[6] has to be introduced some nuances concerning the facts and the necessity of a cyclical perspective. In other words, Lao foreign policy after 1975 was not just an ideological relationship exclusively Vietnamese in direction, and cannot be understood without reference to geopolitics and history.

Once installed in power, the Lao communists hardly had time to profit from their victory. Laos was exhausted by the war. The new leaders had the enormous task of reconstructing a country severely damaged by bombardments[7] and whose economy had been artificially kept afloat by American aid—more than 500 million dollars between 1964 and 1975 (Stuart-Fox 1997, 153). Furthermore, the military situation remained troublesome, especially in the early years after the change of regime. The new government had to confront in the north and south of the country resistance guerrillas led respectively by anticommunist Lao groups using Thailand as a rear base, and by the Hmong,[8] some of whom had been recruited by troops trained by the CIA in the American-Vietnam war to fight Pathet Lao and North Vietnamese troops. In addition Kaysone Phomvihane, the first leader of the new Lao People's Democratic Republic, escaped more than one assassination attempt in 1976. Faced with an uncertain situation, and well aware of their fragile hold on power, the Lao leaders sought to consolidate their base; they reinforced ties with Vietnam as an inevitable choice for the survival of the regime. The "special relationship"[9] which linked the two communist movements before 1975 then became a special bilateral relationship between two sovereign states.

After reciprocal visits and exchanges of delegations between party members and state officials of the two countries in 1976, important agreements covering political, military, economic, and cultural cooperation were signed in Vientiane in July 1977. The Treaty of Friendship and Cooperation, valid for 25 years, was the most important of these. Article 2 (there were six in all) of the treaty drew attention to foreign policy, with both states agreeing to help and support each other mutually and unreservedly in the conduct of close cooperation with the purpose of reinforcing their defensive capacity, preserving their independence, sovereignty and territorial integrity, and in their struggle against the maneuvers and acts of sabotage caused by the imperialists and reactionary foreign forces.[10]

In the circumstances, the treaty was already preceded by the facts. It legitimized the Vietnamese military presence on Lao soil. The exact number of these forces is difficult to establish. It varied between 24,000 and 30,000 at the end of 1977, to rise to between 50,000 and 60,000 at the height of the third Indochinese war, from 1979 to 1983 (Evans and Rowley 1990, 63; Brown and Zasloff 1986, 246). The Lao authorities did not deny this military presence, which was incidentally very useful to Vietnam (Dommen 1985, 127). Article 2 of the Treaty assured Vietnam of a buffer zone separating it from China, and removed the threat of possible encirclement of its frontiers by pro-Chinese forces. However, Vietnamese interests were not the only considerations, and there was something in this for the Lao leaders. Laos has little defensive capacity. It needed military assistance to protect its frontiers. In 1976 and 1977 anti-government guerillas were still active and tensions with Thailand re-emerged in the frontier areas.

The worrying economic situation (a serious drought occurred in Laos in 1977) and concerns about internal security increased the desire for close relations between the two countries. It was also probable that the years 1975–77 reinforced the conviction of the Vientiane government that the survival of the regime depended on the Vietnam-Laos axis, supported by the Soviet Union. The Lao Communist Party, in the early years of the regime, was split between, on the one hand, the need to remain in power and suppress armed resistance, and, on the other, the urgent need to reconstruct and develop the country (Thayer 1982, 252). The first of these priorities required a foreign policy which would consolidate links with socialist countries and in particular Vietnam; the second rather called for multilateralism suitable for a climate of appeasement and essential for rehabilitating the regime in the world. In fact the "special relationship" between Hanoi and Vientiane did not stop the Lao leaders from developing a multilateral foreign policy, particularly in regard to other socialist countries, and especially the Soviet Union. This soon became the most important donor country for Laos. Between 1975 and 1985, it granted aid estimated at 450 million dollars (not including military assistance, which was also substantial), or three times that offered by the Socialist Republic of Vietnam in the same period, a sum coming annually to 13 million dollars (Stuart-Fox 1991, 197).

More curiously, Laos was the only one of the three former French Indochinese countries to have maintained its diplomatic links with the United States, even if they were reduced to a minimum. Relations with China were cordial if distant (at least until the Vietnamese troops' invasion and occupation of Cambodia). With a certain historical continuity, relations with Thailand were ambiguous in the second half of the 1970s. But this agitated relationship was often affected by factors independent of the geopolitical context, because it was greatly affected by events relating to internal Thai politics, which were particularly frenzied in this decade. The indestructible link between Thailand and the United States during the two Indochinese wars logically led to reinforcing the traditional suspicion of the Lao leaders of their southern neighbor. However, in April 1976 a new government, led by then Prime Minister Seni Pramoj, was democratically elected. The advent of a moderate government was to assist a relaxation in bilateral relations. Trade and political agreements between Thailand and Laos were signed the same year to mollify their relations. But this good augury was short-lived. On October 1976 Thanin Kraivichien was put in power following a military coup. Thanin's foreign policy regarding Laos quickly led to a sharp deterioration in relations between the two countries. The new government imposed trading restrictions and drew up an eccentric list of 273 strategic products (including petrol, cement, medicines and bicycles) whose export to Laos was forbidden. These hostile measures weakened the already fragile Lao economy. Repeated frontier incidents reinforced the tension between the two countries and led to recriminations on both sides; while one renewed accusations of a communist plot, the other spoke of "provocation" and a desire to overthrow the socialist government.

Then Thai internal politics were again reversed. In October 1977 the government of Thanin was in turn overthrown by General Kriangsak Chomanan who, unlike his predecessor, was in favor, like Seni Pramoj, of easing tension between Thailand and its communist neighbors.

The vicissitudes of Thai internal politics in the second half of the 1970s were not the only matters affecting Thai-Lao relations. During the Cold War years, ideology and historic antagonism played a primordial role in the foreign policy of the two nations. Each suspected the other of evil intentions and cozying up to foreign powers with the sole purpose of adversely affecting the national security of the other. On the one hand, Laos accused Thailand of allying itself with China with a view to helping the Lao and Cambodian anti-government guerillas who were still active after 1975. On the other, Bangkok saw Vientiane as a mere puppet of Hanoi and their proximity a threat.

One could say that until 1979 the Lao government was trying to implement a balanced foreign policy without jeopardizing socialist solidarity. Whilst maintaining friendly relations with neighboring states, and favoring those of the socialist bloc, Laos did not spurn economic aid from Western countries (including the United States) and multilateral organizations. In short, its rulers tried to pursue, though very timorously, a diversified foreign policy. They knew that Laos was a minor diplomatic partner and could not influence the deterioration of relations between Hanoi and Phnom Penh or Beijing. China viewed askance the extension of the Soviet sphere of influence in Southeast Asia. Not only did Vietnam reject its traditional stance of tributary country, but it allowed the Soviet Union, seen as hostile, to complete its encirclement of Indochinese territory. Vietnam's military intervention in Cambodia in December 1978 was again to constrain Laos to take a position in a regional conflict which was beyond its control.

The third Indochinese conflict 1979–1989: Lao neutrality again at a dead end

Relations between Vietnam and the Kampuchean People's Republic soured from 1977. Conflict arose on the frontiers. The Khmer government spurned diplomatic negotiation proposed by Hanoi. The Khmer Rouge no longer shared Indochinese socialist solidarity and followed a policy of confrontation. The Pol Pot regime, supported by Beijing, developed an ultra-nationalist policy which was viscerally anti-Vietnamese. Faced with diplomatic impasse—Kampuchea broke off relations with Vietnam on December 31, 1977—and confronted with bloody Khmer Rouge incursions inside Vietnamese territory, Hanoi decided on a major military intervention in Cambodia. It wanted first of all to end the bellicose policies of Pol Pot's men, and also to deprive Beijing of an ally to its southeast. Vietnam wanted to avoid at all costs being caught between a hostile China to the north and a pro-Chinese Cambodia to the southwest.

On December 24, 1978, the Vietnamese army sent in twelve divisions, or 120,000 men, to invade Cambodia. They overcame the Khmer Rouge forces, which were only a shadow of the army which had successfully opposed American and South Vietnamese troops between 1970 and 1975, and occupied the whole country in five weeks. Hanoi then placed former defectors from the Khmer Rouge in charge of the country.

Unable to ignore such audacity, even though a Cambodian government under the umbrella of Hanoi did not constitute a direct threat to its national security, China decided to "punish" and "teach a lesson" to its insolent "vassal". In February 1979 it made a lightning military attack on north Vietnam. But the attack was a failure and showed deficiencies in the Chinese army. Beijing came out of the affair weakened internationally by its failed intervention.[11] Its intention of blocking Soviet influence in Southeast Asia led to the opposite result: the formation of a Soviet-Indochinese bloc.

The Lao leaders were aligned with Vietnam in the frontier conflict between Vietnam and Kampuchea. Laos was therefore the first country officially to recognize the new Phnom Penh regime under the patronage of Hanoi, in January 1979, scarcely two weeks after the Vietnamese invasion. From 1978, the Lao leaders had begun to denounce "efforts of imperialist discord and international reactionary forces" (the last term being reserved by the Vietnamese to indicate the Chinese) and so to affirm their determination to "crush" them alongside the Vietnamese people. In the same year Kaysone Phomvihane, then president of the Lao People's Democratic Republic, formulated a scarcely disguised attack on Beijing accusing the "imperialists and international reactionaries" of inciting "dissension among our people of various nationalities" and calling for a struggle against schemes "trying to incite the nationalities to carry out prolonged resistance against our revolution" (Evans and Rowley 1990, 72).

Apart from official declarations, Laos followed Vietnam with reservation. In the hope of halting the confrontation between Vietnam and the Khmer Rouge regime, the Lao leaders even tried to mediate in the dispute in December 1977. The Khmer leaders refused to meet them and accused them of authorizing the stationing of Vietnamese troops on their territory and launching attacks on Kampuchea.[12] The position of the Lao Communist Party in relation to China was not unanimous either. In 1978 before an assembly of party members gathered to celebrate the thirty-third anniversary of Lao independence, Souphanouvong warned those who were swayed by rumors and propaganda aimed at dividing the Lao and the Chinese (Evans and Rowley 1990, 73). This speech did not so much reflect criticism of the basically pro-Vietnamese policy of Kaysone as it did a neutralist attitude, the aim of which was to avoid a Chinese reaction to over-enthusiastic loyalty to Hanoi.

Foreign policy in Laos from 1975 until the middle of the 1980s was not just reduced to a simple schema of one puppet state subordinated to another. Once again, as during the Franco- and American-Vietnamese wars, the Lao leaders had to steel themselves to abandon the neutralist option. Given the deterioration of relations between their neighbors, "A neutral Laos", as Brown and Zasloff (1986, 251) stated, "would be quickly severed into sharply contending spheres of interest; the Chinese in the north, the Vietnamese in the east, and the Thai along the Mekong valley." The Lao rulers had a limited margin of maneuver with regards to Vietnam, the dominant partner in the alliance. They could not take decisions which went against the national interests of the "fraternal" nation, nor against their "special relationship"; neither of the two countries would benefit. Hanoi counted on the diplomatic and ideological support of Vientiane against Beijing, without which Laos would lose its only ally (along with the Soviet Union), in a region where the other states, led by China and Thailand, did not conceal their hostility to the Soviet-Indochinese alliance. Yet Laos paid dearly for its alignment with Vietnam in the regional conflict over which it had no influence. From 1979, the country found itself not only trapped in the vice of Sino-Vietnamese antagonism, but its support of Hanoi led it also into diplomatic isolation within the United Nations, when this body took up the Cambodian question in 1980. Its bilateral relations suffered also from this alliance, in particular with Thailand and the United States. Henceforth, these two countries would only see Laos through the prism of its alliance with Vietnam and the Cambodian conflict. In other words, the timid attempt towards a diversified foreign policy during the early years of the regime was fully blown to pieces.

In the course of the second half of the 1980s, Laos was to try to start a more autonomous foreign policy in relation to Vietnam. Contact with China improved with the exchange of visits of delegations of high level communist cadres after 1986. A Lao specialist went as far as saying at the end of the 1980s that Kaysone considered himself then as the only leader alive from the "thirty year revolutionary struggle" and that Laos was much less disposed to accept Vietnamese advice "given Vietnam's own political and economic problems" (Stuart-Fox 1989, 87). Without a doubt, too, the regional and international climate of détente at the end of the decade encouraged Laos to mark its distance from Vietnam. But, paradoxically, the 1990s and the beginning of the new century did not lead to a slackening of the links between the two states. In some respects, the "special relationship" was even strengthened, in a world and a region which had nevertheless become multipolar and more than ever interdependent.

Notes

1   In fact, Xieng Khouang, a buffer zone, recognized the suzerainty of both kingdoms, Lan Xang and Vietnam, from the fifteenth century.

2   Tran Ninh for the Vietnamese and Muang Phuan for the Lao. From 1834 to 1847, Siam conducted raids into the Lao territories on the east bank of the Mekong, as well as on the western and central parts of the Plain of Jars, in order to depopulate these regions. This led to the incorporation into the Vietnamese administration of the region of Hua Phan (Sam Neua) as far as Savannakhet, in the 1830s.

3   In fact he ruled over a split territory. The province of Phongsaly in the north was ruled both by the kingdom of Luang Prabang and the fifth military division reporting to the "résident supérieur" of Laos.

4   In the month following the French defeat at Dien Bien Phu, the American president Eisenhower predicted that the loss of Indochina would cause the fall of Southeast Asia, like the toppling of erect dominoes.

5   The attack on the American destroyer *Maddox* in August 1964 by three North Vietnamese patrol boats caused Congress to grant the American President Lyndon Johnson the right to take "all necessary measures".

6   We use the words of the well-known work of MacAlister Brown and Joseph J. Zasloff here, *Apprentice Revolutionaries: The Communist Movement in Laos*, 1930–1985, Hoover Institution Press. Stanford University, Stanford, California, 1986.

7   Laos has the unfortunate record of being the most heavily bombed country in the world per capita. See the Mennomite Central Committee (MCC), Mines Advisory Group (MAG) and Lao People's Democratic Government, *Summary Description: Unexploded Ordnance Project, Xieng Khouang, Lao People's Democratic Republic*, 1994.

8   A highland people with customs and culture very distinct from the Lao proper; they originated in China and lived in Laos from the nineteenth century.

9   According to Carlyle Thayer, this expression was used for the first time in 1976 by Kaysone Phomvihane and Le Duan during a visit to Hanoi of members of the Lao communist party. See Thayer 1982, 245–273.

10 See copies of the treaty in *Kao Pasason Lao* (KPL) July 19, 1977, and Vietnam
    News Bulletin No.27, August 3, 1977, published by the Embassy of the Socialist
    Republic of Vietnam in Canberra.

11 The four week war resulted in very heavy loss of lives: some 50,000 Chinese and
    Vietnamese, civilians and military, died.

12 The Lao authorities denied the second charge but not the first. See Stuart-Fox
    1998, 178.

2 A REGIONAL POSITIONING: INTEGRATION INTO ASEAN

A new international "order"

The Third Indochinese War concealed a much more complex reality than that of a local conflict between Vietnam and Cambodia. It involved, between 1978 and 1991, a considerable number of participants. In 1975 the communist victories overturned the international status quo in Asia. The withdrawal of the United States from the region gave China the opportunity to lay claims to becoming the new dominant power. But the regional ambitions of China were soon confronted by its other rival, the Soviet Union. From 1978 Sino-Soviet antagonism increased following the Soviet-Vietnamese strategic rapprochement. "The Cambodian conflict" then took on a global dimension. The political, strategic and economic influence of the USSR in the countries of ex-Indochina, through Vietnam, soon became intolerable to the Chinese People's Republic, and also to other states in the region, as well as to Europe and America. As a result, a broad front was formed, comprising ASEAN, China, the United States, Japan, and Europe, opposing the Soviet-Indochinese bloc over the Vietnamese military offensive in Cambodia.

It was only from the end of the 1980s that there was some détente in international relations in Southeast Asia. This easing of tension occurred as a result of a series of shifts in attitude at the global, regional, and local levels. This new international "order" opened the way to regional cooperation between the ASEAN countries and the three ex-Indochinese states. In 1988 Vietnam announced it would withdraw half of its troops from Cambodia at the end of the year. This proposed withdrawal was met with some skepticism by its opponents but was continued in 1989 and completed in 1990. Several factors can explain this action. Sino-Soviet relations improved during the Gorbachev era on both the economic and military fronts. The third Indochinese conflict represented the last obstacle to total normalization. The Soviet Union sought a rapid solution to the conflict which appeared to many intractable, and persuaded its Vietnamese ally to speed up its troop withdrawals, an essential condition for China modifying its position. Beijing then began to soften its foreign policy and abandoned its intransigent attitude towards Hanoi. From 1989, Chinese support for the Khmer Rouge seemed an anachronism.

The third Indochinese conflict had developed from Sino-Vietnamese confrontation, but also from the confrontation between ASEAN and Indochina, and more particularly, between Thailand and Vietnam. In reaction to the perceived threat to its frontiers by Thailand, the ASEAN countries supported the Thais, reinforced their military cooperation at the bilateral level, and gave diplomatic and military support to the Cambodian resistance, while at the same time applying an economic embargo on the former Indochinese countries. The resolution of the "Cambodian conflict" thus depended on an improvement in relations between these two traditionally rival countries. The change occurred in 1988 with the advent of General Chatichai Choonhavan to the post of prime minister in Thailand. During his first year in power, he gave what became a famous speech announcing his intention of "transforming the battlefields of Indochina into a marketplace". The rapprochement of Thailand and Vietnam, given the impetus of this predominantly economic orientation of Thai foreign policy, began in 1988 with the visit of the Vietnamese minister for foreign affairs to Bangkok, followed by that of his counterpart to Hanoi in January 1989. The complex conflict with Cambodia at its center was gradually to melt away and allow the signing of a peace agreement two years later (the Paris agreements of 23 October 1991).

The end of the third Indochinese conflict is also explained indirectly by internal changes which occurred in the Lao and Vietnamese regimes. In 1986, the sixth Vietnamese Communist Party Congress adopted a policy of *doi moi* (the policy of renewal).[1] The adoption of this new economic strategy was a strong signal of a change in Hanoi's priorities, which were to increase. The survival of the regime depended on an end to its diplomatic and economic isolation. In other words, the economic needs overrode the strategy of occupying Cambodia, which became all the more unjustifiable with the gradual removal of the Chinese military threat. Furthermore, the

Vietnamese presence in Cambodia represented an expense which was all the more impossible to continue as the massive economic and military aid from the USSR to the three Indochinese states began to be seriously reduced from 1989 and eventually ceased in 1991.

Lao also responded to this economic pragmatism. From 1979, four years after the imposition of a disastrous economic policy, the Lao Communist Party recognized that the construction of socialism would take time and required, at least temporarily, ideological flexibility. The programs of rural collectivization were abandoned in that year. The pragmatic camp triumphed again in 1986 at the fourth Communist Party congress which officially adopted the new economic strategy. An open door policy for foreign investors was accompanied by the introduction of the market economy with privatization programs and the imposition of competitive criteria.

The integration of former Indochinese states into ASEAN

The resolution of the Cambodian conflict began a new era in international relations in Southeast Asia. The Cold War was dead and the evaporation of the hostile triangle of China, USSR and the United States was complete. This geopolitical reordering of the region in general, and of former Indochina in particular, freed Southeast Asia of its proxy struggles between global powers and antagonistic groupings. It also opened the way to regional integration of the former Indochinese countries and of Burma, for which ASEAN would be the framework and the means.

Laos and Vietnam signed a treaty of friendship and cooperation with ASEAN in July 1992 and became observers at the twenty-sixth ministerial meeting of members of the organization, held in Singapore in July 1993. Vietnam joined ASEAN on July 28, 1995. Cambodia, an observer to ministerial meetings in 1993 and 1994, signed the treaty in January 1995. Burma, a guest in 1995 and 1996, achieved observer status after signing the same agreement in 1996. Laos and Cambodia, and then Burma, sought their official integration in March and August 1996 respectively. These new members were integrated in 1997, on the occasion of the thirtieth anniversary of the creation of ASEAN. The accession of Laos and Burma took place on July 23, 1997, a day before the opening of the thirtieth ASEAN ministerial meeting. Cambodia had to wait two more years. It was admitted into the organization on April 30, 1999. The brutal struggle between the supporters of the second prime minister Hun Sen and those of the first prime minister Prince Ranariddh, on 5 and 6 July 1997, prevented the integration of the kingdom earlier.

An economic justification

The expansion of ASEAN with these four countries had immediate and profound results. In truth, the new membership structure had always been a possibility. From its creation in 1967, ASEAN expressed its desire in principle to become a regional and not a sub-regional organization. Its objective was therefore to include all the countries of Southeast Asia. Without this political and symbolic vision of the "Southeast Asian family", the integration of the three states of former Indochina and of Burma could not have been contemplated (Amer 1999, 1,041). All the same, this regionalist project formulated by the founding members had never clearly spelt out which countries should form part of "Southeast Asia". For example, ASEAN accepted the idea of including Sri Lanka (formerly Ceylon) upon its creation in 1967, only to reject it ten years later when Colombo reconsidered its initial refusal. Without doubt, the idea of the "Southeast Asian region" (and implicitly the definition of identity of its members) only really began to take shape in that decade (Kraft 2000, 453).

Beyond the political vision of its founder members, the expansion of ASEAN also—possibly above all—rested on an economic rationale. The economic reforms begun by Vietnam and Laos inevitably led to the end of their diplomatic and economic isolation which the Cambodian conflict had created. The need for development aid, investment, and foreign currency (from exports and tourism) required an adjustment in their foreign policy, to put an end to international ostracism, on the one hand, and to improve the political climate on the other, a necessary condition for the reestablishment of economic links with the states constituting ASEAN. In parallel, from the viewpoint of the "ASEAN Six" (Brunei, Indonesia, Malaysia, the Philippines, Singapore, and Thailand), the integration of these four countries offered the prospect of an enlarged market for intra-ASEAN trade, and this, more particularly, though the ASEAN Free Trade Area (AFTA). The membership of Vietnam, Laos, Cambodia and Burma meant that ASEAN would constitute a market of more than 500 million persons, with a gross domestic product of 650 thousand million dollars (based on 1995 prices), the equivalent of 90 per cent of the Chinese economy (Kraft 2000, 455). In addition, economic integration would allow the gap between the rich and poor countries to be closed and avoid a split between them, a potential factor for regional instability.

ASEAN: a community of peace, security, and prosperity?

The resolution of the Cambodian conflict, obtained in large part thanks to a normalization of relations between the great powers, was without any doubt the direct and essential factor in the change in the intra-regional relations in Southeast Asia. The period of confrontation and defiance was over. Even before signing the Paris agreements, the Thai prime minister, Anand Panyarachun, stated that ASEAN should seek to establish a new regional order comprising all the nations of Southeast Asia in "peace, progress and prosperity" (*Straits Times*, June 26, 1991). The Indonesian minister for foreign affairs, Ali Alatas, even allowed himself a certain lyricism on this theme:

> One quintessential dividend of peace in Cambodia to strive for would be the dawning of a new era in Southeast Asian history—an era in which for the first time Southeast Asia would be truly peaceful and truly free to deal with its problems in terms of its own aspirations rather than in terms of major power rivalry and contention; an era marking the beginning of a new Southeast Asia, capable of addressing itself to the outside world with commensurate authenticity and able to arrange its internal relationships on the basis of genuine independence, equality and peaceful cooperation. (Acharya 2000, 195)

ASEAN was founded on the reconciliation of the regional players and the establishment of common objectives of stability and development. With this dual purpose, each state became a factor for peace for its neighbor; this was the essential key to integration. Some, however, thought that it was less the ambition to create a military and economic bloc, than the desire to create a regional security community which inspired the founders of ASEAN; their aim was to overcome the divisions resulting from colonization (Acharya 2000, 195).

From that time on, ASEAN had to confront a new challenge: how to enlarge the community with the former French Indochinese states and Burma. The project of a Southeast Asia that was a model of peace, security and prosperity became one of the primary forces in the process of opening up the association. This expansion, in the eyes of ASEAN leaders, offered the organization its best chances for confronting the new global stakes in an uncertain international environment. More prosaically, the search for stability and prosperity led necessarily to a strengthening of the regional autonomy of ASEAN in relation to the great powers, and in particular a China which rediscovered its ambitions in the region with the retreat of the former USSR and the partial withdrawal of the United States. Indeed, some explained the enlargement of the organization above all by fear of the hegemonistic ambitions of China (Rütland 2000, 421–451). It is true that the Chinese claims of sovereignty over the South China Sea (the Spratly islands, also claimed by Vietnam, Taiwan, the Philippines, Malaysia and Brunei) accompanied by an increased naval presence in the area, reinforcements of its position on some of the Spratly outcrops and the modernization of its armed forces, worry the ASEAN countries, in particular Vietnam.

The "Chinese factor"

By joining ASEAN, Vietnam showed its desire for "balanced relations" with the great powers, and above all, a regional political and military stability which would remove the threat of Chinese domination. From the beginning of the 1990s, after deciding on the improbability of a new world war, China reoriented its defense strategy towards one based on the possibility of regional territorial disputes as a principal source of conflict in the post-Cold War period. For some years, Beijing had increased its presence in Burma (the Chinese authorities provided the junta with increasing logistical support), Laos and Cambodia with a view to extending its political, economic and military influence. In short, the expansion of ASEAN appeared as a Southeast Asian attempt to provide its vast neighbor with a credible counterweight.

The enlargement of ASEAN can also be seen as the result of internal strategies, the aim of which was the desire to adjust the political and economic influence of the member countries. Thus the admission of Vietnam in 1995 was motivated by the desire, in particular expressed by Indonesia, to thwart the regional ambitions of a Thailand inspired by its vision of a "golden peninsula" (*Suwannaphum*). On the other hand, Bangkok sought to encourage the rapid incorporation of Laos, Cambodia and Burma with the aim of balancing the profile of ASEAN, avoiding a preponderance of the Indonesia-Vietnam axis. These hypotheses are bold given the fact that there is no bloc, not even in an embryonic state, grouping

Thailand, Laos, Cambodia and Burma on the one hand and Indonesia and Vietnam on the other. The groupings within ASEAN are much more flexible and complex.

If one considers as the principal motive for Southeast Asian cooperation the need to provide a counterbalance to China, the realistic argument (cooperation of one state with another or several others order to protect oneself against the threat from a third) has to be modified. The thesis of the "Chinese threat" has contradictions, arising from the increased participation of China in multilateral discussions and diplomatic initiatives. Furthermore, ASEAN, even with ten members, cannot hope to rival China. Its members have every interest in maintaining close relations with its huge northern neighbor. Some countries in ASEAN (Singapore, Vietnam, Malaysia) even see in China an ally to resist Western pressure and "American hegemony". China is considered the only power capable of standing up to the United States and constituting an alternative region of growth in the twenty-first century. The agreement to serve as a code of conduct in the Spratlys signed between ASEAN and China during its eighth summit at Phnom Penh in November 2002 illustrates the goodwill of the powerful neighbor which balked for a long time about bringing this territorial question into multilateral negotiations. Although this agreement has no coercive clause and is restricted to a political declaration (the object of which is to avoid recourse to force between the different disputants), its existence is already in itself a remarkable culmination after many years of tension which sometimes came close to military confrontation.

Laos' reasons for joining ASEAN

Although the initiative of enlargement came from the "ASEAN Six", it is worthwhile questioning the reasons which motivated Laos to join the organization. The inclusion of Laos, along with Vietnam, Cambodia and Burma, rested on political vision and economic rationalization at the same time as it was motivated by factors of regional security. The three former French Indochinese countries and Burma, freed from the ideological constraints of the Cold War, had no reason to refuse integration which promised to support their own economic development and guaranteed them both internal and international political stability. The reasons for Lao membership could in consequence be reduced to the mere fact that the country had no real motive for remaining isolated. But to be satisfied with this summary explanation would be to ignore the position of Laos in the new regional schema.

The political economist Nguyen Vu Teng (2002, 106–20), in a pertinent article, went beyond mere contingent explanations (the end of the Cold War, both the cause and consequence of the normalization of the international relations in Southeast Asia) to try and examine the fundamental reasons which brought Vietnam to modify rather radically its foreign policy. Hanoi now favored cooperation to a strategy which rested almost exclusively on an alliance with a great power, the USSR. The author examined the three major theories most often maintained concerning Asian international relations with the aim of proposing a conceptual framework for relations between Vietnam and ASEAN. Using this framework to examine the case of Laos can offer us the means of reassessing its place in the post-Cold War regional configuration.

The neo-institutionalist approach: cooperation rather than competition[2]

At first sight, states like Laos or Cambodia with limited political influence and weak economic and military capacity draw evident benefits, without a quid pro quo, by joining a regional organization like ASEAN. This accords them greater visibility on the international scene and, while ending their diplomatic isolation, it also allows them access to international forums, like, for example, the enlarged post-ministerial ASEAN conferences at which the most powerful states in the world are present.[3] Above all, ASEAN grants them the status of an equal partner in relation to neighboring states, even if they are more powerful. This advantage allows them to protect their interests within multilateral institutions where their lack of influence is compensated by coordination and collective decisions.[4] The neo-institutionalist approach seems to be very relevant in explaining the actions of a country like Laos; in other words, to understand the reasons that lead a state to prefer cooperation to competition.

This is the justification which the Lao authorities regularly advance for their joining ASEAN, and more so in relation to their southern neighbor, Thailand.[5]

The reorientation of Bangkok's foreign policy at the end of the 1980s was not without consequences. The country's natural resource requirements and economic opportunities were transformed into the parameters of its foreign policy. But Thai entrepreneurs soon acquired the reputation of being less than scrupulous businessmen. Their conduct was so reprehensible that the prime minister Chatichai Choonhavan himself had to intervene to forestall "unilateral exploitation" and request that they came to "bilateral" arrangements which could serve the interests of all parties. The Lao authorities indicated their displeasure in the bias of a radio program which had Cold War overtones: "Having failed to destroy our country through their military might, the enemy has now employed a new strategy in attacking us through the so-called attempt to turn the Indochinese battlefield into a marketplace...because their armed provocations were ineffective," (Evans and Rowley 1990, 271). Thai companies were also accused of causing environmental degradation in Burma, Malaysia, and Vietnam. To these contentious issues one has to add border incidents between Thailand on the one hand, and Laos, Cambodia and Burma on the other. The problems of illegal immigration, drug and arms trafficking, and prostitution were also raised (Snitwongse 2001, 194).

In a general fashion, the structures necessary for establishing institutionalized cooperation between the member countries of ASEAN in the economic, political or military spheres remain limited by financial, institutional, and technical constraints. A few months before the effective membership of Laos, its rulers did not conceal their concern about these questions which, though technical, were basic, like the ability of its cadres to communicate in English, the official language used in formal and informal ASEAN meetings.[6] The lack of personnel and technical proficiency prevented the four new members from participating fully in the many annual meetings of ASEAN. Although these meetings have been significantly reduced in number (from 200 a year to half that), they still represent an expense for these countries with very limited resources. This inability to take part in ASEAN's activities to the same degree as other members undoubtedly reduce the influence these countries might have in regional politics, in particular in the field of economics, where the lack of qualified personnel is particularly detrimental.

Unlike the European Union, for example, ASEAN is characterized by a limited capacity to legislate, indeed by an aversion to institutionally enacting terms and legal limitations. Rules and obligations are minimal. Codes of conduct and principles are favored over agreements, and conflicts are always massaged, if not resolved, internally. This very consensual approach and ASEAN's very informal methods, which work in a period of economic growth and between countries which have learned to appreciate each other over three decades of interaction, meetings, and joint activities, are not necessarily adapted to an enlarged ASEAN with four new members, totally unused to the ways and customs of the organization. From this fact, the ASEAN tradition of being "able to agree to disagree without being disagreeable," remain difficult for the new members to appreciate, little versed in the subtleties practiced in the numerous committees and sub-committees. In addition, the "lowest common denominator" approach run the risk of greatly weakening the substance of decisions (Boisseau du Rocher 1998, 296).

A realistic hypothesis: security and national interests

In theory, the neo-institutional approach makes the Lao attitude comprehensible. As an extremely circumscribed state, it was to profit greatly from a system based on cooperation. But it had to obey precise common rules and culminate in concrete results. ASEAN, a victim of its consensual reflexes and its (excessive?) flexibility, balked at taking a more institutional path where texts and rules would be of greater importance. On the other hand, the neo-institutionalist motives did not prevent, on the contrary, a realistic strategy.[7] In other words, the participation in multilateral institutions also served the particular interests of nations. In particular, economic development was always considered a powerful and reassuring factor in the eyes of the ASEAN members. Was it not economic requirements linked to internal politics which explained, in part, the smooth accession of Vietnam and Laos? Some even claim that the norms forming the basis of the collective identity of the organization have only produced up to now "a thin layer of institutionalism, cast over essentially realist behavior" (Rütland 2000, 443). This author even adds "For ASEAN the early twenty-first century will still be the period of realism" so long as ASEAN does not introduce fundamental reforms which will lead to a thorough process of integration.

The end of the Cold War should have marked the decline of realistic analyses in Southeast Asia. These rested chiefly on the triangular relationship between the United States, the USSR and China, and the relations these had with their allies in the region. But the normalization of the relations between the great powers and the end of tension between the former French Indochinese states and the nations in ASEAN did not really lead to international stability, in spite of the process of regional integration. The Asian financial crisis of 1997 and its consequences in the region, the "threat" posed by China and the risk of armed conflict in the South China Sea, were factors which fed the realist theses. Chinese activism was considered one of the reasons for the integration of Vietnam. To a lesser degree, this can also explain why Laos joined, for it cannot be excluded that Vientiane was equally preoccupied by the rediscovered ambitions of its huge neighbor (Leifer 1993, 273).

But the two neighbors of former Indochina did not share the same perspective of external threats. If the Vietnamese leaders thought that China had to be closely watched, the Lao government was more concerned about Thailand. Somsavat Lengsavad, the Lao Foreign Minister, explained that the country's membership of ASEAN would facilitate the solution of bilateral points of contention, notably those relating to the demarcation of the frontiers (*Far Eastern Economic Review*, January 23, 1997). The finalizing of Lao-Thai frontiers, which is still not complete in spite of significant progress in the last few years, remains a thorny subject and a source of tension between the two countries. Above all, a brief but bloody armed confrontation from May 1987 to February 1988 remains marked in the memory, especially that of the Lao leadership. "Now that Laos is a member of ASEAN, Thailand should think twice before resorting to force. It is not like 1988", Sayakane Sisouvong, Director-General of the ASEAN Department in the Ministry of Foreign Affairs, said in an interview[8]; "Now things have changed; we are equal partners with the same rights. Thailand can no longer consider itself the 'big brother'. We now have to exercise mutual respect." These words indicate fairly clearly one of the reasons why Laos became a member of ASEAN. This is in the neo-institutionalist and realist compass: the search for a cooperative structure to palliate inherent weakness, and the search for a national security strategy to offset historic disputes. Michael Leifer (1989, 146), one of the most fervent partisans of the realist current in Southeast Asia, made the point, in relation to ASEAN, that it is probable that some partners in the course of reconciliation will remain potential enemies.

However, the risks of a fresh armed conflict as violent as that of the late 1980s between the Lao and Thai armies in the border region seems much less likely now. Even if occasional tensions remain, relations between the two nations have evolved and are no longer poisoned by the ideological confrontation of the Cold War. The possibility of recourse to force to settle disagreements has receded. The foreign policy of Thailand in relation to the ex-French Indochina states in general, and to Laos in particular, has since been realigned: priority is given to economic growth, and exchanges like investments fit ill with war. The democratization of the Thai political system in the last ten years or so has also influenced indirectly its external relations in favor of greater dialogue.[9]

A calmer international climate, rather than Laos' membership of ASEAN, logically contributed to dialogue between the two countries. A joint commission to delineate the frontiers was set up in 1996 (Laos only joined ASEAN the following year). Today 76 per cent of the Lao-Thailand frontier, some 735 km long, has been officially accepted by both countries. But contentious areas remain, and work on agreeing on the 1,100 km of river frontiers, which is more difficult, has hardly begun.[10] The way ahead for Laos and Thailand legally to agree on their common frontier remains long.

The constructivist perspective: ASEAN as an emerging security community?[11]

If military confrontation with Thailand is hardly likely any longer, it is a possibility which remains etched in the minds of the Lao leaders. It is less a likelihood of the threat which causes their wariness than the memories of centuries of conflict. The subjective aspect in international relations is not taken into account either in neo-institutionalist theories (although they imply it; simplifying, cooperation leads to confidence), nor, of course in the realistic approaches where the state is a "cold monster".

From the end of the 1980s, the concept of "security community" gained popularity in defining the purpose and essence of ASEAN. Elaborated towards the end of the 1950s by Karl Deutsch, the concept is founded on the idea that a community is built on the "belief of the part of individuals in a group that they have come to agreement on at least this one point: that common social problems must and can be resolved by processes of 'peaceful change'" (Deutsch 1969, 5). Transposed to international relations, the concept of "community of security" groups states which, thanks to a tradition of exchanges, interaction and social mechanisms, are able to eliminate the use of force as a means of settling conflicts among members of the group (Acharya 2000, 1). This concept therefore reverses realist and neo-realist theories which present international relations as intrinsically opportunist and war as a means of resolving conflicts between "egotistical" nations. In truth, ASEAN is indeed a community founded on an "ASEAN way", a system based on compromise and consensus, a certain flexibility and a rejection of constraining legal obligations. The organization can equally be defined by the principle of non-interference, abandoning recourse to force, regional political autonomy, and the absence of collective defense.

In periods of conflict and confrontation between more powerful nations, Laos has always been obliged to join one camp, or otherwise run the risk of losing its independence. Conversely, the rules and values of a security community would guarantee it autonomy in internal policies as in its foreign policy. The lines of Lao foreign policy were set out by the president, Khamtay Siphandone during the seventh Lao People's Revolutionary Party congress in March 2001, clearly reflecting this feeling:

> Foreign policy and international relations play a strategic role in the creation of a favorable environment for the task of renovation...and [are] the guarantee of the role of the Lao People's Democratic Republic on the international scene. Consequently we should seize and profit by the opportunities, raise the responsibilities in foreign policy and in international relations, by adhering constantly to a peaceful foreign policy, one of independence, friendship and cooperation based on mutual respect for liberty and sovereignty, non-interference in the affairs of others, equality, and reciprocal benefits. Our policy in the diplomatic domain should be to pursue this harmoniously and smoothly according to strategic and tactical principles. We support the resolution of differences and conflicts by peaceful means. We do not approve of recourse to armed force, nor to the threat of armed force. We are strongly opposed to using diverse pretexts to intervene in the internal affairs of or to attack other countries.[12]

Perhaps ASEAN represents the opportunity for Laos to be able, finally, to conduct a neutralist international policy. ASEAN and Laos are joined in a "security community" in that they share identical values, such as respect for non-interference, the rejection of recourse to force, and the desire for autonomous action within a community. The constructivist approach makes the desire and efforts of the country for fully integrating itself into ASEAN more comprehensible. Every theory has however its limits in describing a complex reality.

First of all, ASEAN is not really a security community; or, more exactly, according to Amitav Acharya (2000), it can only be a "nascent security community", because the norms and values it defends are not always applied. We shall return to this point.

Then, if Laos has good relations with ASEAN as a whole, its relations with some of its members—in particular Thailand—are marked by recurrent tensions. The "shared values" remain relative according to the history, culture and national policies of each member.

Lastly, a foreign policy of "peace, independence, friendship and cooperation" does not exclude a hierarchical and realistic viewpoint of international relations. In his speech of March 12, 2001, Khamtay Siphandone went on to arrange Laos' relations with its foreign partners in a clearly started order of priority:

- To reinforce and increase relations and cooperation with "strategic socialist friends", in particular "promoting the tradition of special solidarity and cooperation in all domains with the Socialist Republic of Vietnam" and developing a "cooperation in all domains with the People's Republic of China.

- To maintain "good relations and fruitful cooperation with neighboring countries" thanks to "active" participation in ASEAN.

- "To revive and expand relations with Russia and the states of the former Soviet Union."

- "To increase cooperation with industrialized developed countries in the economic, commercial, investment, cultural, scientific, technological and others spheres."

- "To pursue solidarity and cooperation with non-aligned and developing countries" with "appropriate" participation in the activities of the specialized agencies of the United Nations and the Francophone Agency, as well as other financial institutions and international organizations."

It can be seen that the strategic partners, with Vietnam at the top and followed by China, still occupy a preponderant position in Lao foreign policy. But the only true innovation is that neighboring countries and ASEAN have supplanted Russia, formerly a central participant in Southeast Asia. Furthermore, a more pragmatic view of international relations seems to emerge: seeking the support of and cooperation with developed countries, mostly Western, before developing countries.

A problematic enlargement

A two-speed association

If the enlargement of ASEAN opened the way for new markets and diverse and abundant natural resources, and also offered the opportunity for new members to continue their economic liberalization, the expansion also strongly accentuated the socio-economic disparities in the association. Following the admission of the former French countries of Indochina and Burma, the difference between the richest and poorest economies in ASEAN was multiplied by five (Rütland 2000, 436). The size of the socio-economic inequalities created a de facto two-speed association. The four new members received special treatment. A delay was granted to them before joining AFTA, the free-trade area. It was put off to 2006 for Vietnam, 2008 for Laos and Burma, and 2010 for Cambodia.

Declarations and initiatives for narrowing this difference in development followed each other from 1997, tending to show that the organization was aware that without a better socio-economic balance between the ten countries, the regional economic integration of ASEAN would quickly come to an end. The persistence of such inequalities could even lead to the disintegration of the organization, according to some observers.[13] The risk of a two-tiered organization prompted the adoption of the Hanoi Plan of Action (HPA) during the ASEAN summit in the Vietnamese capital in 2000, although the need to narrow the gap between the "ASEAN Six" and the CLMV (Cambodia-Laos-Myanmar-Vietnam) group was not officially recognized and prioritized until 2001 in the *Hanoi Declaration on Narrowing Development Gap for Closer ASEAN Integration*. The urgency of the task seemed indeed to rise to the surface in the concern expressed at the thirty-fourth interministerial meeting of ministers of foreign affairs held in Hanoi in July 2001 over the "negative effects of globalization" which, in the absence of "effective measures" would "increase the difference in development between nations and regions"; in consequence, according to the text of the joint declaration, "efforts and resources" would be agreed to "promote the development of the most recent members of ASEAN (Cambodia, Laos, Burma, and Vietnam), giving priority to infrastructure, human resource development and information and communication technology."[14]

These declarations of good intentions came up against serious obstacles. If the "ASEAN Six" was ready to give technical assistance and grant preferential import tariffs to its new partners, a more systematic strategy and greater financial investment were not (yet at least) the order of the day. The organization does not possess, for example, a mechanism for regional structural adjustment, on the model of European structural funds. The proposal made by the former secretary-general of ASEAN, Ajit Singh, towards the end of his term of office, to create a special development fund to assist the new member states appears to have been lost in the upheaval of the financial and economic crisis of 1997. This made even more elusive the project of coordinating national economic policies, an essential condition for the successful regional economic integration of the "ASEAN Ten".

At the conclusion of the 10th ASEAN summit, held in Vientiane in 2004, the leaders of the four countries signed the *Vientiane Declaration on Enhancing Cooperation and Integration among Cambodia, Laos, Myanmar and Vietnam*. The Vientiane Action Programme (VAP) succeeds the Action Plan and will run until 2010. The most significant measure announced in the VAP is arguably the creation of a common pool of financial resources, an ASEAN Development Fund, to be made up from contributions of member countries. This fund will have a restricted funding mission, however: it will only fully support "small scale projects of a confidential or strategic nature", and for "complex projects of relatively large scale", it will limit the funding to "initial activities...leading towards obtaining major funding to implement the full project, from a dialogue partner or donor institution."[15] In other words, external funding (from dialogue partners, donor institutions and private sector) will remain an essential funding source for ASEAN projects (Pholsena 2005, 181).

It is therefore probably premature to speak of a free trade area and of the "ASEAN Ten" as a collective economic front. If AFTA increasingly appears like a tangible reality for inter-ASEAN trade between the six founder members (with import duties, today at 5 per cent, which will be lifted on most manufactured goods), the exceptions to the minimal tariff and other protectionist measures still appear in the economic agenda of these governments.[16] Furthermore, given the slow progress, some member countries prefer to conduct bilateral negotiations to the detriment of multilateralism, which naturally reduces the credibility of the regional organization in the international economic arena. In 2002, discussions between ASEAN and China, Japan, and India, which ended with trade and investment agreements between ASEAN and China and Japan, seem nevertheless to show that the organization remains, in spite of its economic weakness and its political feverishness, a credible economic partner.[17]

"Indochinese" summits

In this context, the initiative of the three former French controlled states in 1999 is not so surprising. The famous "development triangle" discussed by the Vietnamese prime minister Phan Van Kai, during the first tripartite meeting between Cambodia, Laos, and Vietnam in October 1999 at Vientiane, would thus serve as an economic motor for the three countries in order to permit them to catch up on their economic and technological backwardness in relation to the founders of ASEAN.[18] These three newcomers did not conceal their impatience over their slow economic integration within ASEAN.[19] But when the Cambodian, Lao, and Vietnamese prime ministers met in Vientiane for the first time in more than nine years after their last tripartite meeting, some questioned the purpose of this informal summit organized barely a month after the ASEAN meeting in Manila. The suspicion arose among ASEAN officials about the formation of an "Indochinese bloc" within the regional organization.

Almost ten years after the withdrawal of Vietnamese troops from Cambodia, Cold War reflexes remain. But if the fears of seeing the specter of an Indochinese bloc appear exaggerated, given the increasing socio-economic interdependence between the states and repeated affirmations of those in power, particularly the Lao and Cambodians, of their regional commitments,[20] it remains true that the leaders of these three countries share a similar vision of the stakes involved and the risks of a closer integration in a broader regional sphere.[21]

The democratic challenge for ASEAN

In fact, given the weakness of their respective economies, it is less economic cooperation than political and strategic factors which explain the resumption of the "Indochinese summits". It was therefore no great surprise when, in 2002, during the second informal summit, the prime ministers insisted on the "importance and necessity of reinforcing the traditional friendship and solidarity between the peoples of the three nations, [because they are] important factors for maintaining stability and promoting development in each country."[22]

This verbal demonstration of solidarity was not in all probability unconnected to the threats of interference in the internal affairs of ASEAN member countries, a sacrosanct principle of the organization questioned in 1998 by Thailand. Its minister for foreign affairs, Surin Pitsuwan, proposed that the members of ASEAN be authorized to discuss in public the internal affairs of each and every country if they had a bearing outside their national frontiers. Only the Philippines supported this initiative, put forward during the thirty-first interministerial ASEAN meeting in Manila, and which was later qualified as "flexible engagement". The proposal was rejected. Nevertheless, the mere fact that a criticism of the principle of non-interference was debated at the summit of the organization appeared a remarkable event.

Surin Pitsuwan's proposal reflected a desire for reform which would doubtless have given a fresh dynamism to the organization, whose credibility had been severely shaken by the economic crisis of 1997. But this initiative was not only the consequence of circumstantial events; it also demonstrated a political desire: the search for a common identity, beyond the minimal and non-compelling economic values and diversity so characteristic of Southeast Asia.[23] A new "generational" line seemed to seek to suggest a less narrow interpretation of the "Asian way" of doing things.[24] In parallel, for several years, suggestions had been made in non-governmental organizations and think tanks, principally based in three of the ASEAN member countries, Thailand, the Philippines, and Indonesia,[25] seeking a less elitist approach by the organization, a broader opening to civil society and taking greater heed of the needs of the people. In short, ASEAN faced an increasing desire for democratization in some countries, but this probably was not to be addressed in a significant way in the medium and long term at the regional level. In spite of everything, among the leaders of the "old boys club", the idea seemed to progress, if slowly; the outgoing secretary of ASEAN, Rodolfo Severino, in one of his last interviews, called on ASEAN leaders to encourage greater participation of the people because, in his words, "without that you don't get support in the common fight for common purposes".[26] But for the time being, the "community of caring societies" and the "increased civil society" (to which "ASEAN Vision 2020", adopted in Kuala Lumpur in December 1997, referred) still needed to be translated into daily reality in the majority of member countries.

China the unavoidable

The end of the Cold War and the dismantling of the Soviet Union overturned the global and regional geopolitical chessboard. The need for modernization and economic development both strengthened the conviction of the Chinese leaders that their foreign policy had to be oriented toward a more conciliatory line. A dramatic event encouraged China to normalize its relations with its neighbors. The criticisms of Western nations following the massacre at Tiananmen Square in 1989 led China to develop the argument which consisted in opposing "Western ideological domination" with "Asian identity and values". The 1990s would see China follow a "policy of good neighborliness" characterized by more accommodating and restrained conduct in relation to countries in the region. The increasing interest and influence of China in relation to its neighbors in the south—Vietnam, Laos, Cambodia and Burma—not only have to be understood in this new geopolitical context but also in terms of more local factors.

Vietnam, Laos, and Burma share a common frontier 4,060 km long with the Chinese province of Yunnan, in southwest China. It is difficult to reach from the center of China and was for a long time neglected by the authorities, being one of the poorest in the country. But bilateral trade and investment rapidly increased in the frontier regions of the four countries. This was facilitated in some cases by common ethnic and cultural origins, and opened a cooperative front between the new ASEAN members and their large northern neighbor.[27]

Directly linked to this geographic configuration, the stability of national frontiers is also extremely important in Chinese eyes. A peaceful environment without enemies on its southern flank avoids costly military expense and diplomatic tensions which are hardly propitious for economic exchange. However, China and its four southern neighbors also had to face up to transnational phenomena with the potential for increased destabilization (drug trafficking and other forms of smuggling, prostitution and illegal immigration) which ignore frontiers and state authority.

Even if Cambodia, Vietnam and Laos feed on the fear of Chinese domination, they cannot ignore the country, all the more so as, given an unpredictable international economic environment, Chinese aid is never lacking.[28] In addition to economic and strategic considerations, the political and ideological factor also appears to be crucial. Laos,

Cambodia and Vietnam (as well as Burma) have found in China a solid ally with which to confront increasing Western criticism of their political regimes in general and their leaders in particular. Vietnam and Laos, in particular, are opposed to international pressure on the questions of human rights and religious liberty.[29] In addition, Vientiane and Hanoi not only share with Beijing the same need for political survival but also closely follow the Chinese model of development, that is, economic liberalization under the control of the communist party.

China serves as a kind of screen from Western countries and non-governmental organizations which seek progress in the area of human rights and the democratization of their political system. This support is mutual: Vietnam, Laos and Cambodia defend the "one China policy" so important to their huge neighbor, and regularly demonstrate their support when China finds itself attacked by the West for its lack of democratic values. This strengthens in all of them the feeling of solidarity and systematic and ideological security which disappeared with the disintegration of the Soviet Union (Muni 2002, 127). ASEAN though is incapable of offering them better guarantees of stability and political security. To give one example, in January 2003, violent anti-Thai demonstrations took place in Phnom Penh, involving the destruction of several businesses and the Thai embassy, causing the evacuation of all Thai nationals, thus illustrating the lack of reactive capacity of ASEAN when confronted with unforeseen and politically sensitive events, even (or perhaps especially) when these occur in a member country. The principle of non-interference was followed to the letter and the organization was notable for its silence and inaction. Only China intervened by calling for calm and a return to dialogue.[30] A regional economic integration which fails to give concrete results, differing positions at the political level (the famous "flexible engagement" or discussions about ASEAN intervention in East Timor) and pressure for civil society in some countries, cause the new members to remain on the alert while profiting the regional and international opening up which the organization offers.

A multilateral policy linked to bilateral diplomacy

At the beginning of the twenty-first century, Laos still conducts a multilateral foreign policy, with industrialized countries (led by Japan, Sweden, France, and Australia), multilateral international institutions (the Asian Development Bank, the International Monetary Fund, the

World Bank), or ASEAN countries, which is not bad for a "small" state which, though surrounded by larger neighbors, has already survived a thirty-year war. The broad objective of Lao foreign policy, announced at the seventh Lao People's Revolutionary Party congress in March 2001, reaffirmed the desire of the leaders to have a diversified approach and a policy of international "friendship", by following a "peaceful and independent foreign policy of friendship and cooperation based on mutual respect for liberty and sovereignty, non-interference in the affairs of others, equality and mutual benefit."[31] In addition, the success of the 10th ASEAN Summit held in Vientiane in November 2004 showed Laos' commitment to regional affairs. It was the first ASEAN summit and the largest regional event ever hosted by the country. Over 3,000 delegates, including 800 foreign journalists, were invited. It was no small achievement for a country that joined the organization less than 10 years ago after decades of war followed by several years of diplomatic and economic ostracism from the international community.

It can be seen that Laos is anxious to retain its prerogatives. The governments of the three former French territories have a keen sense of what is good for the survival of their regimes. It is strictly in this context that one has to understand the resumption of these famous tripartite summits, and not as an improbable resurrection of the Indochina project. It is moreover useful to recall here that the idea of these meetings was at first proposed by Hun Sen as early as 1995. An association, even if it is more symbolic than substantial, between partners sharing the same political agenda, serves to consolidate a network of alliances in a foreign environment perceived as unpredictable and discordant; the more so as the three states, especially Laos and Cambodia, remain very dependent on international aid. In short, at the turn of the century, the political and strategic vision of former Indochinese states, subsequently dominated by the Soviet Union and then Vietnam, is no longer appropriate to define the relations between Vietnam, Laos and Cambodia. Each follows a multilateral foreign policy associated with bilateral diplomacy, the priorities of which are more than ever continuing economic development and maintaining the political status quo, especially for Vietnam and Laos. Henceforth, the continuation of the "special relationship" between the two countries has to be interpreted differently.

Notes

1   See Dovert and Tréglodé 2004.

2   When states agree to abandon justifications in terms of absolute gains (obtained by force) and favor obtaining relative gains (obtained through negotiation), cooperation is judged more desirable, maintained thanks to the support of networks, institutions (international organizations) or others (informal networks). In other words, negotiation reduces the perspective of important individual gains, but increases the possibility of benefiting from an equitable share in collective gains obtained though negotiation.

3   According to Grant Evans (2003), anthropologist and long-time Lao expert, the Lao leaders, thanks to their participation in the organization, are also able to learn the sophisticated language of international diplomacy which allows them to better reply to Western critics about sensitive subjects such as democratization or human rights.

4   The Lao government demonstrated its ability to organize international meetings when it held the ASEAN-European Union summit in 2000 in Vientiane.

5   Sayakane Sisouvong, Director, ASEAN Department, Lao Ministry of Foreign Affairs, Vientiane, March 2002; interview with Vatthana Pholsena.

6   Somsavat Lengsavad, the Lao Minister for Foreign Affairs, calculated that his country in the forthcoming three years would need more than 300 persons proficient in English. See *Far Eastern Economic Review*, January 23, 1997.

7   According to the realist tradition, interest is the chief referential for international action and its sole justification. The right of recourse to force should therefore be included as a necessity for states (which are central participants in international relations whose role is precisely to oppose anarchy) to ensure their survival. All the same, if international politics is above all a power struggle, peace can be maintained by a balance among powers. The system of a "balance of power" is therefore considered by the realists as above all a regulatory mechanism for international peace and stability.

8   In Vientiane, March 28, 2002, interview with Vatthana Pholsena.

9   The advent of Chatichai Choonhavan's ascension to power in 1988, the first elected member of parliament to become prime minister, affirmed the position of parties and civilians in the Thai political landscape in a transition all the more surprising as it was smooth. General Prem Tinsulanonda, who led the country from 1980, decided not to extend his term of office, in spite of pressing requests to do so from the military as well as civilians. This change was highly symbolic: Chatichai Choonhavan became prime minister without the support of the army. Similarly, constitutional mechanisms for transferring power following elections worked very well.

10 According to Mongkhol Sasorith, legal advisor, Department of Treaties and Juridical Affairs, Lao Ministry of Foreign Affairs, Vientiane, April 4, 2002; interview with Vatthana Pholsena.

11 Constructivism differs from other theories of international relations by the fact that it takes into account the importance of culture, ideas, doctrines, and history. States, or rather their leaders, remain central actors in international politics. But

the norms, values, historically constructed identities and perceptions, can equally define and influence their politics.

12 Political report presented by Comrade Khamtay Siphandone, president to the Central Committee of the Laos People's Revolutionary Party, to the seventh congress of the party, Vientiane, March 12, 2001, translated by the *Vientiane Times*, p. 22.

13 An ASEAN diplomat observed, following the thirty-fourth interministerial meeting of ministers of foreign affairs, that "apparently ASEAN, for the first time, recognized that it was on the verge of disintegration if this great disparity between its members persisted." *The Nation*, July 23, 2001.

   See also "ASEAN's prosperity depends on change", *The Nation*, 24 July 2001; "Doubtless, one of the major causes for concern is the growing economic disparity between rich and poor ASEAN members...The [recent] Hanoi meeting has shown that with growing differences between the members, there is no leader to take the wheel and steer ASEAN through its most turbulent time."

14 Vietnam News Agency, July 23, 2001, in *BBC Worldwide Asia Pacific Political*, July 24, 2001.

15 *Vientiane Action Programme (VAP), 2004–2010*, p. 23, htpp://www.aseansec.org; quoted from Pholsena (2005, 180).

16 To protect its car industry, Malaysia maintained high tariff barriers up till 2006. Likewise, the Philippines recently refused to lower its tariffs on petrochemical products. See "Every Man for Himself", in *The Economist*, 2 November 2002.

17 Amitav Acharya, "An opportunity not to be squandered", in the *Straits Times*, 12 November 2002. The author gives three reasons why ASEAN remains a credible partner for the regional powers (China, Japan, and India): common economic interests, the credibility (though much weakened) of ASEAN as a regional player, and the dangers of international terrorism, which is driving all the countries in the region, including India, towards organizing a collective security front.

18 This "triangular development" (the term used in the press communiqué issued at the end of the second informal summit in 2001) would allow the three countries to move towards the "ideal" status" of "three nations with a common position" ("Voice of Vietnam", January 26, 2002, in *BBC Monitoring International Reports*, January 29, 2002).

19 Margot Cohen, "Reality bites. ASEAN says its more developed members must help the others. A low-cost, basic approach is best", in *Far Eastern Economic Review*, August 16, 2001, p. 28.

20 The Lao and Cambodian ministers for foreign affairs, Somsavat Lengsavad and Hor Nam Hiong, hastened to reassure their colleagues by insisting on the point that during this meeting, the discussions covered "purely local" matters and had no connection with the regional organization proper; these informal summits only had the purpose of forming a pressure group within ASEAN (Kyodo News Service, October 20, 1999).

21 A foreign diplomat based in Laos for many years recently confided to us that at first the Lao leaders were not in too a great a hurry to join the organization. But once Laos was in ASEAN, it soon realized that if the country did not speed up its process of economic integration, it ran the risk of lagging behind the other members.

22   "Voice of Vietnam", January 26, 2002, in *BBC Monitoring International Reports*, January 29, 2002.

23   Surin Pitsuwan, interview with Vatthana Pholsena, Bangkok, April 1, 2002.

24   "Does ASEAN really care about its people's pain?", *Jakarta Post*, September 6, 2002.

25   Organizations like the Institute of Strategic and International Studies in Manila or the Center for International and Strategic Studies in Jakarta.

26   "More popular involvement needed for ASEAN", *Jakarta Post*, August 31, 2002.

27   The proposed construction of a highway to be completed in 2006 linking South China and the north of Thailand, going through two northwest provinces in Laos, is an example of this policy of economic integration.

28   In 1999, Cambodia received an interest-free Chinese loan of more than 220 million dollars.

29   Laos rejected the accusation in the annual report of the US Department of State accusing it of policies contrary to the fundamental principles of religious freedom and practice. See *Vientiane Times*, October 18, 2002. The Vietnamese People's Army daily, *The Quan Doi Nhan Dan*, in November 2002 launched a virulent attack on the United States, accusing "the American government of playing the human rights card to inflame, divide and fragment social stability", and added "All activities which take advantage of religious and ethnic matters to cause separatism, the fracturing of political stability, and sabotaging the great unity of the Vietnamese nation are obsolete and will certainly fail"; Agence France Presse, November 11, 2002.

30   See the *Straits Times*, January 31, February 4 and 5, 2003; *The Nation*, February 8, 2003.

31   "Political report presented by Comrade Khamtay Siphandone, President of the Central Committee of the Lao People's Revolutionary Party, to the Seventh Congress of the Party", Vientiane, March 12, 2001, translation in the *Vientiane Times*, p. 22.

3 BILATERAL RELATIONS WITH VIETNAM AND THAILAND

Laos and Vietnam: the origin and persistence of a "special relationship"

The emergence and development of the Lao revolutionary movement: the decisive role of the Vietnamese communists[1]

The Lao communist movement depended on Vietnamese support from the beginning. The formation of a new Lao resistance government (*Ladthabaan Lao to Taan*) and a new Lao communist movement, the Free Lao Front (*Neo Lao Issara*) was largely initiated and supported by the Democratic Republic of Vietnam through its political arm, the Viet Minh.[2] Our objective here is not to develop these complex relations in detail, involving the Vietnamese communists on one hand and Lao communist and non-communists on the other, but to show that the persistence of very close links between the two states has its origins in the common destiny of their leaders. The genesis of the Lao communist movement was inextricably tied to the combination of circumstances of the period, that is, Vietnamese political and military strategies and international events.

A curious revolution: the "uprisings" of August 1945

To understand the Vietnamese hold on the Lao communist organization, one has to go back to the months preceding the end of the Second World War and more precisely the "coup de force" of the Japanese of March 9, 1945 and the breakdown of French administration in Indochina. The collapse of the secret services and the French system of surveillance in Indochina and in Asia was to assist the Vietnamese revolutionary activities within Indochina and the region around, including the province of Yunnan in China and the northeast of Thailand. This allowed the Viet Minh to reactivate the *Viet Kieu*[3] networks on both sides of the Mekong, as well as Vietnamese communist cells outside the country, composed of Vietnamese communists who had fled Franco-Japanese repression in Vietnam and who had taken refuge in nearby countries to set up their bases. The internment of the French as well as the Japanese capitulation in August 1945 was to allow Ho Chi Minh's supporters to return to Vietnam, and to Laos as well, with the aim of preparing a simultaneous uprising along with the Vietnamese revolution of August 1945 in Hanoi.

Nationalist effervescence (at this period the Viet Minh still prudently extolled national unity and called for the liberation of Vietnam by "fighting against the French and expelling the Japanese") also affected the Vietnamese population in Laos. Highly concentrated in the urban centers, they numbered more than 30,000 persons in 1945. In truth, at this period, the communist networks in Laos were formed very largely, indeed almost exclusively, by militant Viet Kieu. These were therefore the true instigators of the famous Lao communist revolution in August 1945, so often invoked in Lao and Vietnamese nationalist historiography. It was therefore the Vietnamese in Laos who took over the towns of Vientiane, Savannakhet, and Thakhek between August 20 and 25, 1945.[4] In doing this they only followed the orders of the Indochinese Communist Party, dominated by Vietnamese communists who had issued the order some months earlier to its militants to begin an "Indochinese uprising" and to seize power in Vietnam, Laos, and Cambodia. As Goscha (2000, 76) notes,

> unlike most national revolutions, this uprising in Laos is exceptional precisely because it was largely, if not totally, Vietnamese and not 'Lao'. … It was, indeed, a curious Vietnamese revolution in Laos in 1945. The equivalent would have been a decision taken by the operatives of the Chinese communist party in Vietnam to launch a 'internationalist' revolutionary uprising drawing on the Huaquio[5] population in Hanoi, Haiphong and Saigon, and all that in the name of the Vietnamese people.

So in 1945 the Viet Minh exercised an essential role in the conduct of revolutionary activity in Laos. From the military point of view, already at this period Ho Chi Minh considered Laos as a buffer zone for the defense of North Vietnam. In the aftermath of the Second World War, as the French returned to Indochina, the determination of the Viet Minh to control Laos, or at least some of its territory, through its cadres sent from Vietnam and its Viet Kieu partisans, was equally motivated by ideological reasons as by strategic necessity. The French return to Laos in 1946 was to force the Viet Minh to reorient its networks to eastern Laos following the withdrawal of Vietnamese forces from their bases in northeast Thailand. It was important to protect the Democratic Republic of Vietnam from French attacks, hence the necessity of defending the western flank in the center and north of Vietnam, accessible by road from the towns in the center and the south of Laos (Napé, Thakhek, Sépone, and Savannakhet).

The founders of the Lao communist movement: I. Kaysone Phomvihane

Born on December 13, 1920 at Savannakhet, of a Vietnamese mother and a Lao father, Kaysone Phomvihane, the late leader of the Lao Communist Party and first president of the Lao People's Democratic Republic spoke and read fluently both Lao and Vietnamese, having been raised in both cultures. In addition, he had a Vietnamese name, Quoc. At the age of about ten, he left to study in Vietnam and was among the few Lao to study at the Indochinese University of Hanoi between 1941 and 1945. At the end of the 1930s he had begun to frequent Vietnamese political milieux, seeking the country's independence (according to his official biography he was active in the youth patriotic movements in Hanoi during the popular front, 1936–39, and in 1944 joined the Viet Minh). Returning to Savannakhet in 1945 he did not stay long and at the outbreak of the Indochinese war towards the end of the following year, he set off for Vietnam, where he met Ho Chi Minh. He then took part in propaganda activities in the Viet Minh in North Vietnam and northeast Laos.

Three years later, on January 6, 1949, Kaysone sought to become a member of the communist party and became a party official a few months later (on 28 July). He made a strong impression on his then superiors.[6] His dual Lao and Vietnamese identities undoubtedly contributed to his position (Grant Evans 2002, 87).

Among the country's future leaders, there were many with a Vietnamese connection, either because they had studied or worked in the country, or because they had married a Vietnamese (like Nouhak Phoumsavanh), or both, like Prince Souphanouvong, the half-brother of Prince Phetsarath. Born on July 13, 1909, he studied at the Lycée Albert Sarrault from 1921 to 1931, then at the National School of Public Works from 1934 to 1937, and entered the public works administration in Indochina in 1938. The young prince, through his work as an engineer, traveled widely through Indochina and in particular spent several years in colonial Vietnam. He got married in Vietnam in 1938 to a young lady from a very important family, Le Thi Ky Nam (Viengkham Souphanouvong) who was connected with the Viet Minh. So it was not surprising to see Souphanouvong appear from 1945 as one of the strongest supporters of a Lao-Vietnamese alliance and to play the part of intermediary between the Vietnamese government and Phetsarath with the aim of convincing the prince to create an "Indochinese bloc opposed to the return of colonialism". From 1945, the Vietnamese Democratic Republic counted on the support of the prince in the struggle for the emancipation of Vietnam, as well as on his Lao ambitions to promote Vietnamese interests in the internal affairs of Laos (Goscha 2000, 93). But reducing Souphanouvong to the role of legendary "red prince" is too simple. He was only admitted to the communist party in 1953, and people like Kaysone and Nouhak probably inspired more confidence in the Vietnamese communist leaders. They constituted the solid communist kernel in the war zones in Vietnam and were more integrated within the party.

The creation of a proto-Lao revolutionary state

In 1953, the attack in upper Laos and the province of Sam Neua (now Hua Phan) by Viet Minh troops confirmed the designs of the Vietnamese in Laos. The participation of Lao troops was minimal. Out of thousands of troops sent to Laos that year, there were only a few hundred native soldiers. The region of upper Laos took on a crucial strategic importance for the Vietnamese communist leaders. The arrival in 1950 of Mao Tse-tung's Chinese troops at the Sino-Vietnamese frontier allowed for the creation of a vast rear base and represented massive assistance on the north flank of Indochina. The control of upper Laos and in particular the province of Sam Neua offered a direct link between Sam Neua and the Viet Minh zones; in other words, it allowed Vietnamese troops to link the north with the center of Vietnam by going through northern Laos, and in doing so, circumventing the Tonkin delta where the French expeditionary corps was concentrated.

It could be said that the arrival of the Red Army in southern China on the Vietnamese frontier in 1950 constituted a major shift in the evolution of Vietnamese strategy and the consolidation of the Democratic Republic of Vietnam. Without Chinese aid, the Vietnamese army would never have been able to go so far to the northwest of Tonkin and be so effective in Laos. Likewise, the entry of Vietnamese troops in Laos marked the rise of Lao communism and its taking root in the two northern provinces of the country, Phongsaly and Sam Neua. But if a proto-revolutionary state was able to emerge in these provinces, it was certainly thanks to the Vietnamese army and not to any action by local communists. In spite of Vietnamese efforts, there were very few Lao communists.[7] Of the 2,991 communists attached to the Lao section of the Indochinese communist party at the beginning of 1951, there were only 81 Lao, or 2.7 per cent of the total. Even the troops attached to the Lao resistance government were dominated by Vietnamese volunteers, estimated at 6,500 soldiers, against 2,000 Lao (Goscha 2000, 196).[8]

The persistence of the "special relationship"

A multidimensional relationship

Economic and commercial relations between Vietnam and Laos today cannot compete with those between Laos and Thailand. In 2002, the Department for the Promotion and Management of Internal and External Investment listed 34 Vietnamese investment projects, a total of some 25 million dollars. But the number of projects effectively undertaken does not necessarily correspond to these lists in the statistics. The figures show that Vietnam is not only far behind Thailand but also behind China (in terms of investments; see chapter 4).[9]

The link between the two is therefore not really economic. The Lao and Vietnamese press zealously publish virtually every week news of bilateral socio-economic, military or cultural cooperation.[10] Probably the most visible sign of this sustained relationship is the frequency of official and informal visits (the latter not reported in the press). From 2000 to 2001, more than 200 visits took place between the two countries, including those of the leading Vietnamese and Lao dignitaries: on the Vietnamese side, the visits of the minister for foreign affairs Nguyen Dy Nien (February 2000), the prime minister

Phan Van Kai (May 2000), and the leading party official, the party secretary general Nong Duc Manh (July 2001), and on the Lao side the visits to Vietnam of the deputy prime minister for foreign affairs Somsavat Lengsavad (March 2000) and prime minister Bounyang Vorachit (July 2001).

The choice of Vietnam as the first destination of official journeys abroad by the president Khamtay Siphandone in May 2002 after his "reelection" as head of the country a month earlier is hardly surprising. During his visit, Khamtay was accompanied, as usual, by an impressive delegation of senior officials, among whom were the deputy prime minister and politburo member Thongloune Sisoulith, the principal private secretary of the Lao People's Revolutionary Party and permanent member of the politburo, Bouasone Bouphavanh, the minister for foreign affairs Somsavat Lengsavad, the minister for trade, Bouathong Vonglokham, and the deputy minister for national defense, Ai Soulingnaseng (*Le Rénovateur*, May 23, 2002). In short, almost all the most important persons in the government and the party took part in the trip. The welcome extended by the Vietnamese leaders was no less impressive; the red carpet was rolled out in front of the presidential palace and the guard of honor inspected by Khamtay, who was welcomed on his arrival in the country by the most important persons in the land, the party secretary general Nong Duc Manh and the president of the republic, Tran Duc Luong.

Socio-economic and cultural cooperation is less ostentatious but no less effective in consolidating these links. Lao and Vietnamese provinces are linked, like the "sister provinces" of Hua Phan and Thanh Hoa, Oudomxay and Nam Ninh, Khammouane and Quang Binh, or Savannakhet and Thua Thien-Hue, in addition to the twinning of the two capitals, Hanoi and Vientiane. This collaboration is fairly recent (though that of Oudomxay with the province of Nam Ninh dates back to the early 1980s). It particularly concentrated on socio-economic development, including financial assistance (provided by the Vietnamese side) and trade links with preferential tariffs. Savannakhet and its "sister province" in the center of Vietnam, Thua Thien-Hue, anticipated a reduction by half in the taxes levied on the goods they exchanged. Investments, particularly in agriculture, forestry, and construction, strategic sectors in the Lao economy, are favored.[11] This economic cooperation between the two countries by its nature leads to an increasing number of Vietnamese workers in Laos, estimated at around 10,000 in 1999 (Bourdet 2000, 169). The Vietnamese presence also extends to the banking sector with the creation of a joint-venture Lao-Vietnamese bank accompanied by the signing of a collaborative agreement between the two central banks in March 2000. From 2002 there was increased cooperation between the two national assemblies, though it is difficult to say now what legislative advice could be offered by the Vietnamese party. Education, another strategic sector in Laos, benefits from Vietnamese assistance with the signing of another bilateral agreement for five years in May 2001, which foresees the training of between 1,300 and 1, 450 Lao students in Vietnamese universities and professional institutions. Though not in the framework of this agreement, one should also mention the ideological formation of Lao cadres at the Ho Chi Minh National Institute of Political Science in Hanoi.

Not the least important aspect of the "special relationship" are the military links. In 2000, two delegations of senior Lao officers went to Vietnam, led the first time by the minister of defense General Chounmaly Saignason, and on the second occasion by the head of the political department of the Lao people's army, General Khampon Chanthapon. The first visit caused the Vietnamese prime minister Phan Van Khai to reaffirm the cooperation and support of Vietnam given to the Lao people's army in "times of peace". More precisely, he called upon "the armed forces of the two countries to closely coordinate the training of their personnel, to identify drug traffickers and counter-revolutionaries, and to contribute to building a Vietnamese-Lao frontier line both pacific and prosperous."[12] This declaration in the form of a warning was not accidental. On October 26, 1999 a small group of students had organized the first anti-government protest in front of the presidential palace, in the very center of Vientiane. The demonstrators were quickly arrested and imprisoned, but the Vietnamese and Lao leaders did take the warning very seriously (de Tréglodé 2000, 9–10).

In June 2000, the visit of the second delegation of Lao military personnel was probably not a coincidence either. From the end of March Vientiane had been shaken by a series of explosions in public places, which to this day has never been properly explained. According to a frequently quoted article, this series of outrages was orchestrated by certain members of the government with the aim of destabilizing the pro-Vietnam faction in power.[13] Some analysts see it rather as internal conflicts for power, as a struggle for a share of the spoils, and the outrage as "simply anarchic, perpetrated by people who had had enough of the system".[14] Whatever the case, the year 2000 saw troubles occur in the northeast, in the province of Xieng Khouang. Immediately, an official Lao delegation headed by the senior officials from the province went to Vietnam to meet the commission for external relations of the Vietnamese communist party.[15] Foreign newspapers talked of an uprising led by members of the Hmong minority and of an intervention of the Vietnamese army into Lao territory to provide help in putting down the rebellion.[16] This theory was firmly rejected both by the Lao and Vietnamese authorities and criticized by both of them as an external attempt to harm both regimes, and the "special relationship" between the two countries.[17] These events showed fairly clearly, whatever the truth of the matter, that the internal affairs of Laos were very closely followed by the highest echelons in power in Hanoi.

Mutual support

To perceive the reasons for the persistence of the "special relationship", remarkable for its longevity and apparent constancy, one has to take into consideration not only the Lao perspective. True, the uprising in northeast Laos in the spring of 2000 showed once again that the government was economically and operationally hard put to confront the situation alone, in particular in the military sphere. But also, the destabilization of the internal political environment in 1999 and 2000 consequent to a rather exceptional combination of events had certainly led the Lao authorities to seek to reinforce its links with the trusted ally, Vietnam. But this country did not come to assist its neighbor out of charity or merely in the name of "socialist solidarity", "the thirty year struggle", or even the "special relationship". One needs to look elsewhere for the reasons for this concern.

The threat of an uprising in the Lao provinces aroused in the Vietnamese leaders the very real specter of destabilization of their own regime through agitation by the ethnic groups, termed "minorities", living on both sides of the frontier. Hanoi may have seen, for example, in the famous protest movement against the regime in Vientiane in 1999—an act hatched by the Hmong community, itself influenced by American Protestant sects—organizations also present in Vietnam and whose influence was probably instrumental in the uprisings which occurred in the high plateaus in the south of the country a year later (see Guérin et al. 2003). One has to understand that Hanoi still perceived Laos and Cambodia as forming part of the Vietnamese security area. In other words, if the "counter-revolutionaries" were able to cross the "first line of defense" which these two neighbors to the west and south constituted, then, according to the logic of the

Vietnamese authorities, the regime itself would be in great danger. So, the opening of the country towards the end of the 1980s and the official adoption of a multilateral foreign policy in 1988 did not succeed totally in allaying the suspicions of outside plots which were aimed at overturning the regime. On the contrary, the confirmation in 1991 of a foreign policy of "diversification", scarcely a year after the disappearance of the Soviet Union, only reinforced the fears of those persons opposed to opening up and to the rapprochement of Vietnam with non-socialist countries. They adapted to suit the circumstances the threat of the "pacific evolution", a phrase used by Beijing at the end of the 1970s, taken up in its turn by Hanoi, to describe the strategy used by the "imperialists" with the intention of weakening socialism in the Soviet Union and eastern countries. Vietnam in its turn would be faced with the threat of this "peaceful evolution" and be "the next one on the list" according to the conservative ideologists of the regime (Thayer 1999, 15).

China: an increasing influence

Following the financial and economic crisis of 1997, Laos, in a "traditional" reflex, turned towards Vietnam and China, the two states it was closest to politically and ideologically. The turbulent period that Thailand was then passing through had severe repercussions on the Lao economy. The Vientiane authorities at once went to seek out other partners in order to diversify the country's economic relations. This reorientation of their international economic strategy was to favor China, which welcomed this rapprochement very positively.[18] The exchange of visits of the heads of state of Laos and China, respectively Khamtay Siphandone in July 2000 and Jiang Zemin in November the same year, confirmed the more important place these two countries mutually accorded each other and constituted the high point of a process of normalization of relations begun in the second half of the 1980s. The resolution of frontier disputes in 1992 without any doubt helped the two nations to reestablish a "normal" relationship, according to the Chinese ambassador in Laos. In 2001, the visit of the Lao prime minister, Bounyang Vorachit, on the invitation of the Chinese prime minister Zhu Rongzhi, strengthened the economic partnership between Laos and China. During this working visit, which required six months of preparation, China granted a loan of 35 million dollars on special terms to the Lao government, which supplemented an earlier loan of 12 million dollars granted in 1999 with the aim of financing investments in the two countries.

Outwardly, this visit appeared to emphasize the economy as the most important element of Sino-Lao relations. The great majority of Chinese goods into Lao are manufactured products, cheaper (but also often of lower quality) than those coming from Thailand. Thanks to their lower price, Chinese products very quickly invaded the market stalls of Laos. Motorcycles are perhaps the most visible symbol of this invasion. They are half the price of those built in Thailand and so are within the reach of a larger number of Lao people.

Thailand remains by far the most important economic and trading partner for Laos, but China now appears in second place in terms of investment, with 5.5 million dollars invested in 2001, chiefly in the cement, mining, and agricultural sectors.[19] However, all the Chinese projects are far from completion, and in 2002, of the 90 or so investment projects listed by the Department for the Promotion and Management of Domestic and Foreign Investments only about 60 are likely to be completed, the rest remaining on paper only.

In fact, the Lao leaders might consider China less as a potential replacement for Thailand in its economic relations and more as a protection against regional economic instability, as it represents an undeniable source of important investment, trade, and aid (some 5 million dollars a year, according to the Chinese embassy in Vientiane) which would allow them to spread their risks.[20] According to an official on the East Asia department in the Lao Ministry of Foreign Affairs, Laos has learnt the lessons of the 1997 crisis and does not wish to put "all its eggs in one basket".[21]

The obligations of China towards its "small" southern neighbors are effected logically to the detriment of Vietnamese influence over Laos and Cambodia. The rivalry between China and Vietnam over Laos is a recurrent theme in the country's political and geopolitical history. It has taken on in recent years a new dimension following the improvement in relations between Beijing and Vientiane. The bombings in Vientiane in 2000 which destabilized the country, without though raising any possibility of a change of direction, caused this rivalry to surface again.[22] At this point in time, it is difficult to maintain if there exists such a clear-cut dichotomy in the Lao leadership between the pro-Vietnamese faction and the pro-Chinese faction. It is however reasonable to think that Vietnam hardly appreciates the strategy of China to involve itself in a territory which Hanoi traditionally considers as belonging to its strategic security zone.

Laos and Thailand: a tense relationship

Past conflicts and present tensions

Thailand, to which we shall return, is the chief economic and trading partner for Laos. But the weight of past history remains a key factor between the two neighbors. Although one should be on one's guard against any over-determinist causality, the past can help explain certain attitudes. It is not by accident that, until now, Laos has constantly refused military training exchange programs with Thailand, whereas Cambodia received the idea favorably and Vietnam is ready to consider the matter. A high-ranking Thai officer declared in the course of a seminar on the military role in Southeast Asia in the post-Cold War period that "the political leaders in Vientiane have never trusted Thailand, because of an historical perspective which makes Thailand appear as an aggressor."[23] Without any doubt the strong support in Bangkok for the American army during the Vietnam War and the short but bloody frontier conflict of 1987–98 give cause for this reticence. Relations between the two countries have however clearly improved since the end of the Cold War, now freed of geopolitical and ideological hostility and the risk of armed confrontation (especially since Laos joined ASEAN in 1997).

Serenity and confidence?

A study published in 2002 by the Institute for Asian Studies at Chulalongkorn University in Bangkok tends to show that the Lao leaders in the capital, like those in the provinces, strongly doubted the sincerity of Thailand in its relations with Laos.[24] Of 39 senior nationals questioned, none placed any trust in the country.

The comments of Surin Pitsuwan, former Thai minister of foreign affairs (1997–2001) on relations between the two countries, does not contradict this: "Our policy is to maintain friendly relations with Laos and to stress cooperation. Prosperity and stability are our priorities. Laos needs a market for its agricultural products and Thai entrepreneurs are needed for the Lao economy. Likewise, Thailand needs a prosperous Laos, stable, and dependable... But the problem is the inferiority complex of the Lao authorities. They are afraid that Thailand will profit by Laos, and this attitude is difficult to overcome."[25] (Interview in Bangkok, April 2002, Vatthana Pholsena)

A "family" relationship in dispute

A great deal of the malaise between the two states probably arises from their inability (generally shared by other countries) to overcome a contentious past marked by disputes and conflicts which have barely healed and have been given different interpretations. But this powerlessness is perhaps paradoxically exacerbated by their very close geographic, cultural and linguistic proximity. The dominant race in Thailand and Laos have the same genealogical source. Recent linguistic, historical and anthropological studies tend to suggest that the original Tai[26] territory was located in an area going from the west of Guanxi and southeast Yunnan (in southern China) to the north of Vietnam and the northeast of Laos. The Tai military leaders formed tiny principalities, known as *muang*, which later were included in confederalist structures with shifting dimensions, such as the "twelve communes" (Sipsong Panna) or the "twelve Tai principalities" (Sipsong Chau Tai). Some Tai populations, pushed by the expansion of the Chinese empire, then began to migrate during the first millennium towards the northwest of mainland Southeast Asia.[27]

The descendants of the Tai are now dispersed across mainland Southeast Asia and especially on the southern borders of China, in north Vietnam and Burma, and in northeast India. They form the ethnic majority in Laos and Thailand. The most powerful of the warlords overturned the balance of the political systems by subjugating the weakest *muang*. This second stage of conquest began a process of political centralization which ended with the formation of states around the dominant *muang*, Chiang Mai for Lan Na, Luang Prabang (and later Vientiane) for the kingdom of Luang Prabang, and Ayutthaya for Siam (Condominas 1980, 270–271). Some of these Tai peoples remained outside a political structure and were transformed with the appearance of international frontiers into "minorities" within nation-states, whereas others, like the Lao and the Thai, established themselves over the earliest autochthonous inhabitants as the "majority".

The sharing of an historical, cultural, and common linguistic background and a genealogy between the dominant ethnic groups in Laos and Thailand largely explains the persistence of expressions of family relationship that indicate a viewpoint of relations between the two peoples as based on an ethnic rather than a national concept. *Ban phi muang nong* ("the home of the elder brother, the land of the younger brother") is a common expression employed in Thailand to define the links between the two nations. But one could also question, as did two Lao scholars, "Who is the elder brother and who the younger?" The Lao prefer to use a neutral formula, *ban kai heuang kieng* ("neighboring countries") to eliminate, as Mayoury and Pheuiphanh Ngaosyvathana (1994, 1) explained, the "connotation of paternalism in relation to Laos" in the Thai expression and to insist on "the need for the two countries sharing the same genealogy to live on equal footing and with mutual respect." The expression "elder brother/younger brother" nevertheless persists on the other side of the Mekong. It feeds on incessant quarrels between the two countries, putting the economic inequality in their relations on a verbal footing and distorting disputes between sovereign states into futile family quarrels.

A pan-Thai economic and cultural viewpoint

"The vision of the Thai leaders remains unchanged. It is based on a traditional concept, 'an imaginary community' whose frontiers go beyond those of the present territorial extent of the kingdom of

A premonitory reflection?

"The problem of Laos has to be considered and treated chiefly in relation to Siam, and, in some degree, in relation to Cambodia, two neighboring countries with which we have many links and not, as has been the custom up to now, just in relation to Vietnam, which has a far greater difference in temperament, civilization, customs and habits. Laos will always be politically and economically viable, not because it is tied to Vietnam, or placed on the same level as it, but when the Lao are allowed to enjoy more or less the same rights, the same freedoms, and the same standard of living as their brothers across the Mekong.

Indeed, on the two sides of the great river, the Laos (of the French Union) and the Siamese-Lao look at and observe each other every day. It is already sufficient to give these two people of the same family two different statues, two governments, two different political regimes. It would be wise not to make the situation worse through inequalities in standard of living nor in too obvious differences in treatment. Seesaw politics that would come of themselves, inevitably, would be dangerous even deadly for one or the other, or even both. The whole future of Laos lies there." (Katay Sasorith 1953, 92–93)

Thailand", a Thai university lecturer remarked.[28] The political and economic power of Siam lay in its gains in territory and population. Its expansionist ambitions were guided by an inclusive vision of an empire whose frontiers were continually changing in relation to conquests and in relation to which the peoples of neighboring principalities were seen as subjects whose incorporation was inevitable. Siamese expansionism at the expense of the Lao and Khmer principalities in the eighteenth and nineteenth centuries until the arrival of the colonial powers, Britain and France, undoubtedly propped up the nationalists' imagination in Bangkok. Many, for a long time, lamented the "lost territories" which were ceded to France.

This imperial past associated with a tradition of expanding outwards (see Dovert 2001, 177–239), ready to subjugate and to integrate, is perpetuated today in new forms. According to some, Thai expansion in relation to its neighbors is no longer military, but essentially economic and cultural. The foreign policy of the government of Chatichai Choonhavan (1989–91) has, it is true, helped to feed suspicion in this respect. In January 1989, the prime minister reaffirmed his desire to transform the battlefields of the former Indochinese states into marketplaces, and expanded his vision by presenting Bangkok as the business center not only of Thailand, but also of the former Indochina states, and Burma. Thai entrepreneurs were offered the role of transforming mainland Southeast Asia into a peaceful and prosperous region, a golden peninsula or *Suwannaphum*. To some observers, the Friendship Bridge, inaugurated in August 1994 and linking Vientiane with the town of Nongkhai in Thailand, has a dual function, operational and symbolic. It did not constitute simply an infrastructural project opening up new markets and exploiting natural resources (which Thailand does not have, or no longer has in sufficient quantity), but also, and especially, of building a zone of prosperity of a "Greater Thailand" (Reynolds 1996, 120). The development of the road network and telecommunications would progressively transform a traditionally "remote" and "hostile" country into a "land of opportunity" and of extensive wealth. In short, Laos would be henceforth included in a regional schema and transnational economic quadrilateral, in which Burma and Yunnan figured, under the leadership of Thailand.[29]

This imaginary community of a "Greater Thailand" is not only seen in terms of economic gains and market share; it is also present in the minds of all those in Thailand who seek an authentic Thai culture. The official concepts of Thai cultural identity (*ekkalak thai*)

—nation, monarchy, religion—still remain profoundly anchored in contemporary life and political culture. Nothing was left to chance in the previous century in the politics of constructing a national identity. For example, Craig Reynolds has shown how the different successive military regimes considered national identity as a factor directly linked to the country's security. From this flows institutionalized nationalism which culminates in a "cultural bureaucracy" including the National Identity Council within the Prime Minister's Office no less, having as its objective the development and popularization of the "intrinsic" nature of Thai national identity (Reynolds 2002).[30] But economic, cultural and technological globalization have overturned this homogeneous concept of national identity and culture, formulated by the central authorities and the elites, and propagated by modern state institutions (schools, the army, and the media). Like all multidimensional notions transforming daily life, globalization is a complex matter. It has its supporters and its opponents. The phenomenon may be neither "constructive" nor "destructive", though, but "productive" of new forms of knowledge and power. The debate causes anxiety among the people, though, and Thai society is concerned at the prospect of a progressive disappearance of its culture and identity.

The perception of the degradation or even the loss of Thai culture due to globalization gives rise among Bangkok intellectuals (and also Thai tourists) and all those connected to the policy of preservation or cultural production, to an increasing interest in the non-Thai Tai peoples. This is explained by Craig Reynolds (1998, 138):

> The Siamese Thai gaze to the north and the current fashion to study the Sinified Tai in southern China and the rest of northern Southeast Asia must be understood as a kind of ethnic nostalgia, a reclamation of identity that resides in the yet-to-be-globalized Tai minority peoples in the region.

This desire for authenticity, in particular in the middle and upper urban Thai classes, does not fail to include Laos. Thai tourists returning from their stays in Vientiane and Luang Prabang readily lament about the change in traditions and customs in Thailand, about the environmental degradation and their urban living conditions. "The Lao and the Thai have similar cultural traditions, but Laos still manages to preserve its own." This spontaneous remark, frequently repeated by Thai tourists, reflects their impression of belonging to a cultural family which extends beyond the borders of their country, but whose different members are arranged according to their level of development. Lao society seems, to Thai tourists, like Thailand used to be "before".[31] A visit to the country on the other side of the Mekong not only constitutes a shift in space, but also a journey into time past, guided by nostalgia for an idealized original form of culture.

But the Lao are not the only "younger brothers" clinging to traditional culture. In the eyes of the Thais, the Tai of southern China and northern Southeast Asia also belong to this "great ethnic family", and the "elder brothers" look on their "younger brothers" sometimes with envy, sometimes with condescension. This traditional perception of an ethnic area extending beyond the national frontiers of Thailand and which today guides economic expansionism and the narcissistic search for a Tai-Thai cultural identity hardly favors smooth relations between sovereign states. It does not assist either in a better understanding among peoples because the reality is there: "The Lao know everything about the Thais, but the Thais know nothing about the Lao." (Utamachant 2001, 202). The Thais consider the Lao without seeing them whereas the Lao observe and listen to the Thais through a reality partly constructed by the Thai media across the Mekong.

A battle of cultures and identity

Rather ironically, this idealized vision of a culture fixed in the past is also held and promoted by the Lao media and tourist professionals. The first lines of an article recently published in the *Vientiane Times*, the English-language daily, could easily have come from a tourist brochure. It said: "Vientiane's appealing mixture of cultures, French colonial history and Buddhist architecture make it an attractive place to visit…Visitors enjoy this landlocked country and its capital because it still preserves its culture, tradition, customs, and original nature."[32] Feeding on this image, the Lao authorities in recent years have expressed their concern about outside influences which they consider pernicious for Lao society.

The Lao government in particular expresses its increasing concern about the influence of the Thai media over Lao urban society. The Lao Women's Union criticized Thai television programs, reproaching them for encouraging dress codes and indecent habits at the expense of traditional dress, like the *pha sin* (the Lao sarong). Some Lao

> **"Party directive relating to cultural activities in the new era"**
>
> In parallel to achievements [in the construction and the development of national culture], many undesirable phenomena have appeared, such as: a way of life based on the quest for money, fashion, and false beliefs which are rapidly spread (in particular among our youth, who are unaware of our traditions and customs and the graceful national culture); behavior and practises contrary to the national culture, and which consider traditions only a means to make profit; activities deriving from a mercantile culture which only recognizes trade and material exchange without appreciating cultural values. [All these phenomena] trouble society, and the national legal system is unable to halt them. Furthermore, antique art objects are illegally leaving the country; alien cultural influences are penetrating the country and have a negative impact on the national cultural heritage. They modify the national cultural identity, and worse, gradually wipe it out.
>
> October 1994, following the Fifth Party Congress held in 1991.

authorities even accuse the Thai media of playing a predominant role in the increase of consumerism, even of criminal acts in Laos.[33] Even if it is difficult to verify the truth of these accusations, the reaction of the Lao authorities is hardly surprising, given the influence of the Thai media in Laos. They offer the local population access to news which gets around the systematic censorship of information put out by the Lao media. Their domination is evident in every sphere (television, radio, and press) and at all levels, including among the leaders themselves, even if they do not publicly admit it, but they are just as keen on the Thai radio and televised transmissions. More than three-quarters of the inhabitants of Laos are within range of watching or listening to the Thai media. Their quantity, diversity, and degree of sophistication marginalize the Lao media, whose budgets are derisory and whose margins of maneuver are very reduced. In other words, there is no competition: almost three-quarters of the Lao would prefer to watch Thai rather than Lao television (Utamachant 2001, 179).

A Lao journalist recently confided this disillusioned fact: "The differences between Thai and Lao identity are exacerbated in times of conflict and tension, which favor patriotic feelings. But in peacetime, the young Lao follow the Thais, because they lack role models in their country."[34] Yet, even if there is a genuine infatuation among Lao urban youth for Thai cultural products, the acculturation is not complete. In spite of the pessimism expressed in the Lao media, the identities remain distinct: the socio-economic indicators, as well as the political and social reality, are too far apart. They continually suggest to the inhabitants of the two banks of the river that they do not belong to the same society. Against several enthusiastic viewpoints expressed about Thailand in an investigation into young urban and semi-urban Lao, *Listening to the Voice of Young People* (1998), some girls expressed serious reservations. They were notably questioned about the reasons why they did not look for work in Thailand: "We are different [from the Thais]. We are afraid that they will tear us to pieces. They have a bad, lawless society and people do what they want." Or again "They would sell us as prostitutes and then the police would arrest us and we would go to prison where we are afraid we would be raped." In short, in spite of the cultural, linguistic, and geographic proximity and the strong polar attraction of poplar Thai culture, the Thais remain "different". Between enthusiasm and repulsion, their cultural domination produces ambiguous and contrasting results.

This strangeness, increased by a twisting of reality, is deliberately emphasized by the cultural policies of the Lao authorities. The defensive discourse in respect of a foreign and corrupting hegemony helps the government in its policy of affirming the country's national identity. Although today the Thai press and radio try harder to avoid tripping up over Laos, numerous contentious subjects remain and are transformed into subjects of nationalist dispute conducted energetically by the Lao authorities and media.[35]

The Lao authorities reacted more strongly in 2000 to contemptuous remarks about Lao women attributed to a Thai artist during a televised program. The extract below from an article published in a Lao language newspaper, *Vientiane Mai*, gives a feeling of the insult delivered to national pride, and also to the strategy of recovering from a statement (if indeed one had been made) which would probably have passed unnoticed without official protests from the Lao authorities.

> If Nicole [the Thai artist] lacked the necessary education to make a distinction between what is good and what is bad, the Lao people would overlook her naivety. But, quite the contrary, she received a good education, has a relatively high standard of living, and a certain fame. Therefore why should we pardon her for what she said? The only explanation is that she intentionally sought to affront the dignity

and reputation of Laos, which is unacceptable. Laos may be a small underdeveloped country, but the Lao people, on the contrary, are neither morally nor intellectually inferior to any nation.[36]

Relations between Thailand and Laos constitute distorting mirrors. Whereas the Thais see in Lao society a version of their social and cultural organization several decades back, the Lao authorities define their culture in opposition to the image given today to Thai society. This in turn serves as a kind of scarecrow to the Lao government in its policy of constructing a national identity.

Rather paradoxically, the Friendship Bridge illustrates this ambiguity where proximity distances people. It was hoped that this structure, inaugurated in 1994, would lead to a rapprochement between the two countries, and to exchanges between the two banks of the river. But it has become, in the eyes of some, the symbol of the link between Laos and consumerism and materialism. Some disapprove of the "unpatriotic" attitude of the Lao urban middle class of Vientiane who use the bridge at the weekends to go and wallow in the "corrupt charms" of Thai capitalism.[37]

A recent study of the impact of the Thai media on Laos, conducted by a researcher at Chulalongkorn University in Bangkok, showed how the Lao leaders and civil servants reacted to the images of Thai society and politics (Utamachant 2001). The result was hardly flattering to the "big" neighbor, but allows one to appreciate better the cultural gulf separating the political classes of the two countries. Thai political news confused and amused the Lao leaders: "Too much freedom, to the point where anything goes"; "It's total confusion, as if everyone went his own way", etc. The impression of muddle and political deadlock (because "there are too many political parties in Thailand") comforts them with the idea that "few rather than many parties" are best to obtain a consensus and to undertake reforms. The "social reality" of Thailand, projected by the Thai media, appears less amusing, indeed frightening. The Lao leaders consider it "dangerous" and "ferocious". They indicate their lack of comprehension when confronted with what they consider a lack of civic responsibility and social education in the presentation of different events on the Thai television channels, describing them uncompromisingly as a "disgusting spectacle" (ibid., 190–191).

Notes

1 For this section, we have chiefly based our comments on the remarkable doctoral thesis of Christopher Goscha, "Le contexte asiatique de la guerre franco-vietnamienne: réseaux, relations et économie (d'août 1945 à mai 1954)", 2000, as well as on the works of Brown and Zasloff 1986, Langer and Zasloff 1970, Stuart-Fox 1997, and Evans 2002.

2 The famous "congress of Lao people" in the province of Nghe An in August 1950 marked the official creation of a revolutionary resistance government, endowed with a political program copied on the Vietnamese model (it was in fact financed and formed by the North Vietnamese government).

3 Vietnamese living outside the present frontiers of Vietnam, in particular, here, in Thailand, Cambodia, and Laos.

4 The holding by Vietnamese civil servants of the most important positions (after those reserved for the French) in the administration of colonial Laos (in the offices of the "Résidences supérieures", the locally-recruited guard, as telegraph operators, postmen, and lorry drivers moving between Laos and Annam) no doubt greatly aided the Viet Kieu to bring about this uprising.

5 Chinese living in Indochina.

6 According to Vo Nguyen Giap's memoirs, Kaysone Phomvihane was first singled out in 1948, at a time when the Vietnamese general was seeking "young Lao in order to form cadres capable of organizing revolution in this friendly country". Giap was apparently very impressed by the young Vietnamese-Lao revolutionary since he spent three days introducing him to members of his general staff and his government, in particular the political-military cadres of Viet Bac responsible for north Laos (Vo Nguyen Giap, *Chien dau trong vong vay* [The struggle against encirclement], pp. 342–43), quoted in Goscha 2000, 165.

7 From 1947, military training schools in the province of Nghe An trained higher-ranking Lao officers. In October 1950 a Vietnamese telegram summarized the numbers attending a training course in north Laos, destined to strengthen an eventual Lao party; there were only 10 Lao for 117 Vietnamese (Goscha 2000, 192).

8 After his meeting with Giap, Kaysone and a group of Lao based in Vietnam went to the province of Sam Neua to run a propaganda unit. In January 1949 Kaysone announced the creation of the Lao liberation army. This date marks the birth of the Pathet Lao army in the official Lao and Vietnamese historiography.

9 But one also has to remember that even during the Cold War, the Soviet Union, and not Vietnam, provided the most aid to Laos.

10 *Vientiane Times, Sieng Pasason, Vientiane Mai, Kao Pasason Lao* (for the Lao side); "Voice of Vietnam", http://www.vov.com.vc (for the Vietnamese side).

11 In June 2002 a delegation comprising the leaders of Vietnamese provinces (among which were those from Kon Tum, Thai Nguyen, Nghe An, Quang Tri, Thua Thiuen-Hue, Ha Tinh, Khanh Hoa, and Danang) went to Laos and were received by the president of the national assembly and politburo member Samane Vignaket.

12 "Voice of Vietnam", February 24, 2000, in *BBC Summary of World Broadcasts*, part three, Far East, February 28, 2000.

13 Shawn Crispin and Bertil Lintner, "Behind the bombings", in *Far Eastern Economic Review*, July 17, 2000, pp. 26–27.

14 Grant Evans, "Demoralization but no revolt in Laos", in *The Nation*, August 16, 2000.

15 "Radio Australia, Melbourne", June 13, 2000, in *BBC Summary of World Broadcasts*, part three, Far East, June 15, 2000.

16 *Far Eastern Economic Review*, May 11, 2000.

17 "Voice of Vietnam", 19 June 2000 and *Kaosan Pasason Lao* (KPL), 8 June 2000.

18 Adisorn Semayaen, researcher at the Asian Studies Institute, Chulalongkorn University, March 2002; interview with Vatthana Pholsena.

19 According to Lao statistics, the total exchanges between China and Laos reached in 2000–2001 some 43 million dollars (of which 35 million dollars were Chinese exports to Laos), whereas for the same period the volume of trade between Thailand and Laos is estimated at 200 million dollars (much being due to the export of electricity from Laos to Thailand). Information provided by a foreign diplomat in Vientiane, April 2001; interview with Vatthana Pholsena.

20 Quote from a foreign diplomat who wishes to remain anonymous; interview with Vatthana Pholsena, Vientiane, March 2002.

21 Interview with Vatthana Pholsena, Vientiane, April 2002.

22 In July 2000, when there were sporadic explosions in Vientiane, one analysis held that "China and Vietnam support the opposing camps in the present struggle for power in the inner circle of the Lao leadership. In becomes a kind of war at second-hand over which of the two will have more influence over the country". Sunai Pasuk, in Shawn Crispin and Bertil Lintner, *Far Eastern Economic Review*, July 27, 2000, p. 26.

23 "Thailand: army chief details military relations with Southeast Asian neighbors", in *The Nation*, May 3, 2002.

24 "More than a river divides us", in *The Nation*, September 28, 2002; Khien Theeravit, Adisorn Semayaem and Thantavanh Manolom, 2002.

25 Frontier incidents during his term of office did not improve relations between the two governments. In July 2000, the attack on a frontier post in southwest Laos leading to the arrest of 28 men remains a matter of tension between the two governments In particular, the attempted extradition of 17 Lao nationals, in addition to the 28 detained in Thailand, irritates the Lao government which accuses its neighbor of deliberately delaying the resolution of the matter, which it denies.

26 *Tai* is used for the different ethno-linguistic groups which stretch from China to Assam and Malaysia speaking a *Tai* language belonging to the Sino-Tai group, and *Thai* is used to designate the language and cultural identity of the people of Siam, renamed Thailand in 1939. See Goudineau and Vienne 2001, 144.

27 The kingdom of Nan Chao which dominated the region from the first half of the eighth century to the invasion of the Mongols in the thirteenth century, had its capital and urban center near Lake Tali located in present-day Yunnan. Historians

now agree that the Tai speaking peoples were never in a dominant position in this political entity.

28 Kajit Jittasevi, Bangkok, March 2002; interview with Vatthana Pholsena.

29 International organizations like the Asian Development Bank (ADB) play an important part in this strategy of regional development by encouraging the participation of Southeast Asian countries. The ADB considers that the countries of the Greater Mekong sub-region (GMS), bringing together Vietnam, Laos, Cambodia, Thailand, Burma, and China (Yunnan province), will need 40 million dollars in the next 25 years to finance more than 100 projects, most of which concern transport, energy, and telecommunications (Bakker 1999, 224).

30 Katherine Bowie (1997) also analyses the very influential role of the "village scouts" movement, a paramilitary group closely linked to the army, the Ministry of the Interior and the monarchy, which, in the 1970s and 1980s, played a crucial part in the indoctrination of Thai villagers with the conservative values of Thai culture in the struggle against the communist insurrection.

31 Another common remark among Thai tourists who have been to Luang Prabang, the former capital of Lan Xang, is to compare it to Chiang Mai "twenty or thirty years ago."

32 "Vientiane, City of Ancient Culture", in *Vientiane Times*, January 23, 2003.

33 *The Nation*, January 28, 2001.

34 Somsanouk Mixai, interview with Vatthana Pholsena, March 2002, Vientiane.

35 "Between the Lao and Thai media, an agreement to disagree", on Radio France International (Lao language section) August 2, 2000. Vipha Utamachant notes with reason that "language is a weapon capable of wounding more seriously than the thrust of a knife. The Thais should not profit by their superiority in the media for aggressive attacks on Laos which then appears as the victim. We hope that the fruit of our research will allow the Thais to realize that whilst we are amused without thinking of the consequences, the Lao almost throughout the country are busy listening and watching us."

36 *Vientiane Mai*, April 25, 2000.

37 "Friendship Bridge in name only", in *The Nation*, January 19, 2002; a Lao journalist who wishes to remain anonymous; interview by Vatthana Pholsena, March 2002, Vientiane.

4 THE REALITIES OF A LESS DEVELOPED STATE

Key indicators of the Lao economy

Lao People's Democratic Republic is the only country in Southeast Asia without direct access to the sea. The country has borders with Cambodia (541 km) to the south, China (423 km) to the north, Burma (235 km) to the northwest, Thailand (1,754 km) to the west, and Vietnam (2,130 km) to the east. The demarcation of the frontiers with Cambodia and Vietnam is in the final phase of negotiation; while problems still remain with Thailand, as Thailand does not agree that Laos can claim boundaries based on geographic maps dating from the French colonial period.[1] The country has an area of 236,800 sq km, which is equivalent to that of Great Britain. It is endowed with abundant natural resources, with generous forests, and great hydroelectric potential. Its population was estimated at 5,777,180 inhabitants in July 2002, with a density of barely 23 inhabitants per sq km (the lowest in Southeast Asia). Laos is young, with 55 per cent of the population under the age of 20.[2] Demographic growth is the highest in Southeast Asia at 2.8 per cent. The GDP per capita is estimated at 370 dollars per person, increasing by 2.1 per cent per year.[3] This increase seems reasonable, but it is somewhat disappointing given the potential and assets of the Lao economy, such as its timber reserves or hydroelectricity potential.

In 2003, Laos was ranked 135th out of 175 countries by the United Nations Development Programme (UNDP) in terms of human development.[4] The country has many characteristics of poor economic development, with high demographic growth, indifferent sanitation facilities, and minimal economic and social structures. Although primary education is compulsory, adult literacy was only 65.6 per cent for the whole population in 2001, and only 54.4 per cent among women (UNDP 2003). In addition, inflation and the rapid devaluation of the national currency, the kip, in the last five years resulted in an increase in the cost of equipment, school materials and medicines, all of which affect health and education. Although education and basic health services are free, the needs of the population are far from being met. It is clear that the lack of government funds seriously limits development of schools, universities, and hospitals. The economic infrastructure is not sufficiently developed to allow an increase in the state revenues by means of a direct or indirect taxation system.

Belonging to the category of least developed countries (LDCs) like Burma and Cambodia in the region, Laos was not spared by the world slowdown caused by the economic and financial crisis which affected the region in 1997. Laos remains primarily agricultural. Agriculture, forestry and fishing provide more than half of its GDP. More than 85 per cent of the population live in rural areas. Industry occupies an increasing position, notably because of the emergence of the energy sector producing and exporting electricity to Thailand. In the long term, the secondary sector will occupy a more important position in the Lao economy, given the hydroelectric and mining potential in the country. The service sector, in particular activities connected with tourism and trade, today counts for a quarter of the GDP.

Figure 4.1: The composition of GDP

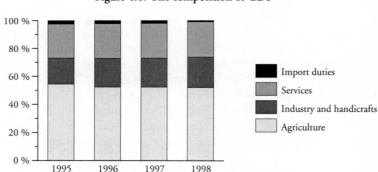

Source: World Bank. 2002. "Lao Logistics Development and Trade Facilitation in Lao People's Democratic Republic". Working paper. Washington, D.C.: World Bank, p. 1.

Laos is often designated as a "sponge" which absorbs large flows of international aid: more than 250 million dollars a year since 1990, or nearly 20 per cent of its GDP and about 50 US$ per inhabitant. This is the highest level in Southeast Asia. In addition, since it joined the Asian Development Bank (ADB) in 1966 and until the end of 2001, Laos received more than 950 million dollars in loans from the ADB.

Table 4.1: Projects financed by the ADB since 1966

Sectors	No. of Projects	US$m	%
Transport and Communications	11	304	31.9
Social Infrastructure	14	228.4	24
Energy	13	223.3	23.4
Agriculture and Natural Resources	11	126.8	13.3
Finances	2	50	5.3
Multi-Sector	1	20	2.1
TOTAL	52	952.5	100

Source: Asian Development Bank. 2003. *Annual Report* 2002. Manila: ADB, p. 14.

The share played by external commerce is relatively small, amounting to between 50–60 per cent of GDP, against 85 per cent in Thailand and more than 90 per cent in Vietnam.[5] However, trade figures do not include the substantial informal trade in wood products, rice vegetables and consumer goods. The internal market of Laos is also very small compared to its neighbors, especially China, Thailand and Vietnam. Most of the country's economic activity is limited to the corridor along the Mekong. One has to bear in mind, though, that there is illegal trading notably in the trade of vegetables, rice, timber and articles for consumption. In addition, part of household supplies, especially in the urban centers, is obtained from border towns in Thailand. These numbers are not included in Lao trade statistics. Lao and Thai cross-border trade usually avoid customs and other forms of taxation, so long as the activity is discreet and is not on an excessive scale. In 2002, the World Bank estimated that the informal sector represented half the GDP in Laos, and that the Lao economy was therefore much more open and permeable than it seemed. Illegal trade is not limited to products imported into Laos. Timber and garlic are smuggled into Thailand but there are also transit products coming from Thailand going to other countries in the region.

Some consider the distribution system of the informal sector very efficient, given that smuggling must satisfy customers' demands while controlling the cost of procurement of supplies. The system is so efficient that the Lao people can acquire Thai products at the same time as Thai consumers, even if they have to pay relatively more. This helps explain why legal distributors of consumer goods in Laos are unable to rapidly increase their turnover even though domestic demand increases. They are mostly powerless given the competition from parallel distribution networks.

Limited statistical means

The computer system of the National Statistics Bureau was installed in 1995 with funds from Sweden. It now has four servers and 52 client stations. One of the servers was supplied by the United Nations statistical division. The bureau only has four telephone lines and is not yet connected to the provinces nor to the Internet. It has a computer section with five technicians but they are not really trained in computers. The internet site is being developed thanks to ASEAN technical assistance, but the section lacks qualified personnel capable of developing, maintaining and overseeing it. In addition the National Statistical Bureau worries about its lack of means and the competence of its staff in relation to the confidentiality of the future Internet site and its statistical base.

Source: National Statistical Bureau, anonymous source, personal communication with Ruth Banomyong, Vientiane 2003.

The economic indicators presented in this chapter must be used with caution. The porous nature of the borders, as well as large-scale hydroelectric projects, conceals the true nature of imports and exports in the country. Moreover, the collection of statistics in Laos leaves much to be desired, in spite of the existence of a National Statistical Office within the Committee for Planning and Cooperation. Statistics between the different government departments are often contradictory and no one is sure how accurate they are. The system is not integrated and the government offices in Vientiane rely more on guesswork than real data. It is interesting to note that some sectors, like the Customs Department, have relatively accurate statistics but the information is still not centralised and remains uncompiled at each border post. Consequently, doubts remain concerning the reliability of the figures published by the Lao government and, for want of alternative sources, it is difficult, if not impossible, to find coherent statistics relating to Laos. It should be mentioned that reports by the United Nations, the World Bank, the IMF, and the ADB are usually based on figures provided by the government and then interpreted by experts in these organisations. Even if these statistics are used appropriately, they are based on faulty premises which make any coherent analysis difficult.

Figure 4.2: Growth in GDP components, 1992–98

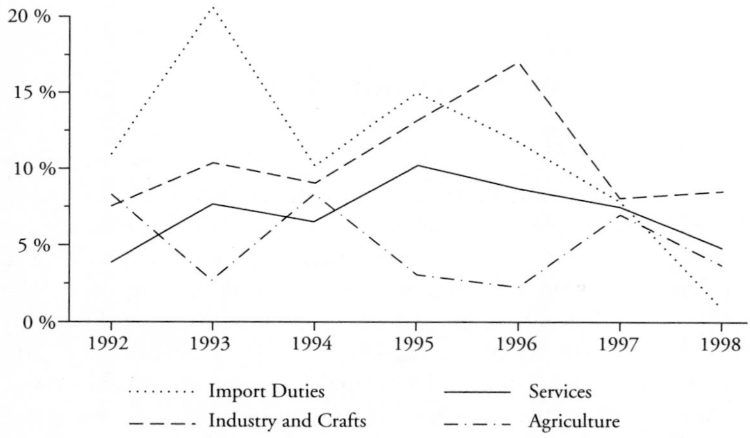

Source: World Bank. 2002. "Lao Logistics Development and Trade Facilitation in Lao People's Democratic Republic". Working paper. Washington DC: World Bank, p. 1.

Economic growth in 2001 climbed to 5.5 per cent, a slight reduction on 2000 (5.9 per cent), but an improvement on 1999 (5.2 per cent). Agricultural production rose and the macroeconomic environment became more stable since the Asian financial crisis of 1997. This primary sector, representing more than half of the GDP, varies strongly according to harvest outputs. These erratic figures are a reflection of the effect climatic variations on production and very basic agricultural technology. The financial crisis which erupted in Thailand in 1997 delayed the start of investment in several hydroelectric projects in Laos. In spite of everything, growth in industrial production, aided by the beginning of work in gold and copper mines in Savannakhet province in the south of Laos, continued to increase, helped by garment exports to the European Union. (In 1995, clothes exports from Laos lost their preferential access in Europe, however, this was restored at the end of 1997). When the hydroelectric project of Nam Theun II starts going ahead as planned (see below), construction activities will considerably increase until the dam is completed.

The services sector has increased by more than 6.4 per cent thanks to the tourism and furniture sectors and this in spite of very weak financial services. The share of the industrial and crafts sector also continues to increase despite the effects of the economic crisis of 1997.

A financially underdeveloped country

The banking system

An efficient financial system is important for expanding both industrial and agricultural activity. It is also a critical component in the provision of services to facilitate trade in goods and services, and providing instruments for trading, hedging and pooling risks. The formal financial system is limited to commercial banks and treasury bills. The ratio of M2 money supply to GDP is only 13 per cent, reflecting the shallowness of its formal financial system. However, this figure excludes the considerable amount of foreign currency that is not within the banking system. Nevertheless, this small ratio limits the power of the government to provide macroeconomic stability.

The economy has relatively little reliance on formal sources of finance. The credit provided to the economy is less than 15 per cent of GDP while the average for the ASEAN countries exceeds 100 per cent. Only about 11 per cent of all households carry debt and about 1 per cent has bank deposits. Eighty per cent of the small and medium rural enterprises do not take out loans; of those that borrow, most rely on family, friends and moneylenders. As for rural households, most lack access to short-term credit facilities for the working capital to finance inputs such as fertilizers and agrochemicals. There is a similar perception that the domestic savings rate is relatively low, but statistics are not reliable since they do not include savings in kind, such as precious stones.

The formal financial sector is limited to trade banks and treasury bonds. Apart from the Lao Central Bank, two state banks, two joint venture banks and seven branches of foreign banks, mostly Thai, complete the market. The Central Bank regulates interest levels for overdrafts and documentary letters of credit. Since 1995, interest levels for deposits and loans follow the mechanisms of the Lao financial market, except in periods of financial crisis, when the central bank regulates these levels.

The three state-owned commercial banks (Banque du commerce extérieur lao [BCEL], Lao Mai, and Lan Xang) were formed through the merger of seven banks that had originally been formed by splitting up the State Bank of Laos. These seven banks had inherited many of the bad loans from the period of the planned economy and were not provided with inadequate capital. They were recapitalized in 1994 by transferring US$25 million of non-performing loans to the Asset Management Division of the Ministry of Finance. This did not resolve the problem of non-performing loans, so they were merged into three banks in 1998. However, there was no recapitalization and these banks are now insolvent with about US$50 million of non-performing loans, which in 1999 constituted 60 per cent of loans. In addition, many of these loans exceeded 100 million dollars. Although the Lao Central Bank tries to conceal the fact, some 80 per cent of the public banks are today non-performing. This alarming figure is explained by the fact that a significant part of the loans were politically motivated rather than justified financially.

An agreement with the International Monetary Fund (IMF) required that the three public trading banks be audited and no further loans be granted to clients classified as "non-performing" debtors. A restructuring plan has been agreed, which included the fusion of the Lao Mai and Lan Xang banks, which became effective in April 2003.

Set up as a joint venture, BCEL is associated with the Vietnamese Industrial Development Bank. This Lao bank is fully owned by the Ministry of Finance. Its activities include trade finance, supplying services like letters of credit for imports and exports. Some 90 per cent of its capital is designated in foreign currency, mostly in American dollars. To open a letter of credit, BCEL requires a cash guarantee of 100 per cent of the total funds sought. It is therefore hardly surprising that exporters prefer to take advantage of the services of foreign banks. This regulation required by the BCEL indicates a certain lack of understanding of international practices. The Lao Central Bank is linked to private Thai investors and the foreign banks set up between 1992 and 1994 are, as noted, mostly Thai (six are Thai and one Malaysian). Thai banks concentrate on financing international trade and lending funds to support Thai investors and the Malaysian bank specializes in financing the clothing industry. The Standard Chartered Bank is also represented in Vientiane, and supplies offshore finance.

People have relatively little faith in financial institutions. The economy depends little—only 15 per cent in fact—on formal financing sources (such as a loan bank or a land bank), whereas in other ASEAN countries the figure is close to 100 per cent. Loans are spread more or less equally between the private and public sector. Though 11 per cent of households are indebted and about 1 per cent have bank deposits, most loans are effected through personal contact and/or pawnbrokers who demand very high interest rates. Most rural households have no access to short-term credit. Domestic savings levels are consequently relatively low, but the statistics do not include savings in kind, like gems or gold.

It is important that domestic banks increase their credibility among the people, and until then the reshaping of the banking sector is marking time. But fresh assistance from the World Bank, the ADB and the IMF could help change operational practices, provide credit policies and improve the supervision of banks by the central bank. This project has a good chance of being accepted by the Lao authorities, as the World Bank has stipulated this as one of its conditions to its guaranteeing the Nam Theun II hydroelectric dam.

The establishment of an efficient financial system is essential to support the country's industrial and agricultural activity. The policy of developing the textile industry and agriculture conforms to the government's aims of poverty reduction, which are linked to the requirements of the IMF. Vientiane has in truth very little room for maneuver in its fiscal and monetary policy, because of official and informal demands required by international financial institutions which tie their loans to clauses requiring the opening of the Lao economy. Financial aid is therefore not without ulterior motives. It is obvious that the big multilateral organizations are pushing for rapid freeing up of the Lao market without taking into account the adequacy of its measures given the country's economic and social reality.

Monetary and fiscal policies

The IMF imposed fiscal discipline and a prudent monetary policy on the government with the objective of sustained and lasting growth in the economy. IMF loans, like those of the World Bank, are conditional upon the application of macroeconomic measures approved by international financial institutions. The IMF publishes an annual assessment of Laos. A team from the IMF goes each year to the country, collects economic and financial information, and discusses the country's economic situation with Lao officials in charge of policy. On returning to its headquarters in Washington, the IMF team prepares a dossier which serves as the basis of discussion for the executive council, and the outcome is a summary by the director general, as president of the council, of the views of the different director generals. His report is then passed to the Lao authorities.

The Lao government, desiring to profit from financial aid provided by the IMF, seems like a model student today. It regularly quotes the World Bank and the ADB as partners in its policies of reducing poverty and increasing economic growth, hoping thereby to improve its standing. The Lao statistics for convertible foreign currency debts are surprising, at more than 73 per cent of GDP in 2000, but it is important to recall that the structure of this debt is subject to certain conditions, meaning that the granting of these loans is coupled with strict conditions relating to monetary and budgetary discipline. Some 83 per cent of its debt is with multilateral agencies, chiefly the ADB and the World Bank.

However, Laos still needs to show that all its fiscal and monetary objectives agree with those of international institutions, though no one is in a position to guarantee that this is so. Doubts over the trustworthiness of the figures supplied in Lao government reports intended for the IMF tend to increase these concerns.

The fiscal deficit has varied between 6 and 12 per cent of GDP over the last ten years. Between 1998 and 1999 fiscal deficits and the expansion of money in circulation led to a rapid depreciation in the exchange rate, contributing to an increase in the inflation rate. Yet from the second half of 1999 the government adopted serious measures to reduce its fiscal deficit and to limit the expansion of money in circulation. The annual inflation rate, measured by the consumer price index, has consequently been considerably reduced: from 128.4 per cent in 1999 to 23.2 per cent in 2000, and to 7.5 per cent at the end of 2001. Laos now aims to reduce the monetary supply by at least 20 per cent a year, after an increase of 120 per cent during the second half of 1999. It has regularly increased since, but is now more or less under control. The value of the kip was reduced by only 13 per cent during 2001.[6]

Since 2000, Laos has not recorded any serious slippage and its principal economic indicators are relatively constant.[7] But the instability of the national currency linked to high annual rates of inflation contributes to a reduction in real incomes. The increase in prices of basic products has led to a change in eating habits, while other consumption remained marginal. Civil servants have not seen their salaries increase to keep pace with the rate of inflation, which has obviously led to a reduction in their standard of living.

Economic dependency despite policy of sufficiency

The process of freeing the economy began in 1986 with the adoption of a new economic mechanism. The liberalization of the Lao economy subsequently increased in 1989 after the fourth Communist Party congress.

The ambitious aim of the government to move from an agricultural economy to an industrial economy so that the country could leave the category of least developed countries by the year 2020 ran up against many structural obstacles. The difficulties encountered included a very under-performing education system, a lack of qualified personnel, limited capability of local administration, underpaid civil servants, and so on. These handicaps placed Laos in economic dependency in relation to its neighbors and international organizations. Aid is not only tied to financial and technical conditions, it is also increasingly subject to social and political demands. Donors demand more efforts in favor of the protection of the environment and people affected by rural development policies, notably in their relocation. International aid represented 14 per cent of GDP in 2001, which further limits the country's autonomy.

The financial crisis of 1997

The financial crisis which overtook Thailand in 1997 seriously dampened Lao economic development and other ASEAN members were likewise affected. Thailand thought it could escape the crisis

Lao reform

From 1979 the catastrophic economic results of the four first years of the new regime in general, and the disastrous performance of the collectivization policy in the countryside in particular, forced the government to change its economic strategy. The seventh resolution of the Supreme People's Assembly adopted in December 1979 admitted that Laos had to "circumvent capitalism", that the construction of a socialist economy would take time, and necessitated, temporarily, an ideological change of direction. Consequently, the rural collectivization programs were abandoned, whilst some of the restrictions imposed on private production and the circulation of goods was abolished, as well as price controls of certain goods sold on the open market (Stuart-Fox 1986, 61). This shift to reform was confirmed by the Fourth Party Congress in 1986 with the adoption of a new economic mechanism, which marks a U-turn in the country's policies since it heralded the beginning of the transition from a planned economy to a market economy. Under the new system, the government encouraged the development of the private sector, abolished price and production controls, while granting financial autonomy and control to state enterprises. An open door policy was adopted for foreign investors and was accompanied by privatization programs and the imposition of competitive criteria. These reforms were to have, over time, an impact on local industry in Laos, and in particular on its capacity to export to world markets.

by turning to exports, but these were also affected by the economic slowdown. Thailand had "forgotten" that its economy was linked to the rest of the world. Considering itself as a newly industrialized country, it had above all overlooked a number of ominous signs which the government of General Chavalit should have taken into account.[8]

The agreement over the free trade area within ASEAN concluded in 1992 was immediately affected. As usual in a crisis, every nation tends to turn inwards in a protectionist reflex. Also the liberalization of regional trade raised fears of loss of national economic sovereignty.

Thailand logically shelved its regional projects, notably its investments in the infrastructure of Cambodia, Laos and Burma. It is interesting to note that trade between the member countries of ASEAN is not as important as might be thought. It is around 30 per cent, the majority of products of the member countries being exported

to Europe, North America and Japan.[9] The withdrawal of each
member country was all the easier and more rapid as the organization
prefers non-binding decisions to more exigent agreements. Most of
the agreements concluded within ASEAN do not indicate the means
of application; these are only negotiated after signing.

An abandoned training program

The setting up of an MBA course by Thammasat University for staff
in the central banks of Laos and Thailand had the objective of making
Lao and Thai civil servants study together and creating a banking
network. At the beginning, more than five intakes were envisaged.
For Thailand, the course was a way of sustaining the process of the
regional integration of Laos and developing its human resources.
Implicitly, the other objective was to build a network of class
comrades which would sustain, or at least facilitate, Thai interests in
Laos. However, the financial crisis halted the project after only one
intake and only 60 graduated, half of them officials from the Lao
Central Bank.

Clearly, the economic crisis of 1997 had a negative impact on
the regional process of economic integration in Southeast Asia,
and more particularly the least developed countries within ASEAN
(Cambodia, Laos, Burma, and Vietnam). Because of the crisis, all the
member countries of the association had first of all to reduce their
development programs and assistance to member countries. Before
the crisis, Thailand had an aid budget for Laos of more than 200
million baht a year. It offered numerous scholarships (in baht) for
studies in Thailand for Lao civil servants. After the crisis, the Thai
government considerably reduced its bilateral aid to Laos, preferring
to maintain its basic assistance through multilateral organizations.[10]

Economic dependence: the case of external Lao trade

The value of exports progressively increased in the last five years,
going from 308 million dollars in 1996 to more than 393 million
dollars in 2000.[11] It was considerably reduced in 2001, to stabilize
in 2002, because of a lowering of export prices, notably of timber-
derived products. Since 2003, the control of timber exports has
become stricter. But while the export of undressed timber is no

longer permitted, timber for construction represents an important part of the country's income.

The ready-to-wear clothing industry has also developed (exports rose to more than 77 million dollars in 2000), but the added value is relatively insignificant, with imports in this sector estimated at about 67 million dollars. The Lao clothing industry relies on the low cost of labor and quotas granted by the European Union. Without these the sector would not be viable, the more so as the cost of transport is very high given the distances covered and the fact that the garment workers are unskilled. The firms which profited from quotas are very largely foreign, and it should be noted that, according to World Trade Organization (WTO) agreements, quotas have been phased out since 2005, which signal an unpropitious future for the textile industry in Laos.

Table 4.2: Export destinations (US$m)

	1998	1999	2000	2001	2002
Vietnam	119.5	179.4	96.1	106.1	115.0
Thailand	28.9	51.6	68.9	81.0	85.0
France	23.3	18.2	27.1	33.7	33.4
Germany	21.4	27.0	20.8	25.5	24.1
Belgium	12.8	13.5	13.6	10.4	9.1

Source: ADB. 2003. *Key indicators of the Lao PDR*, www.adb.org/LaoPDR. Manila: ADB, p. 221.

Table 4.3: Major sources of Lao imports (US$m)

	1998	1999	2000	2001	2002
Thailand	411.3	452.0	419.1	451.7	444.0
Vietnam	80.7	181.8	77.7	85.8	93.1
Chiana	19.6	24.4	37.9	59.9	71.5
Singapore	22.1	37.0	32.9	28.9	29.1
Japan	21.0	24.9	23.6	13.0	17.4

Source: ADB. 2003. *Key indicators of the Lao PDR*, www.adb.org/LaoPDR. Manila: ADB, p. 221.

Figure 4.3: Value of industrial exports, 1994–98 (US$m)

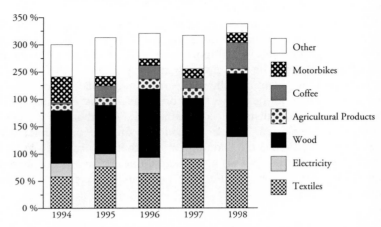

Source: http://www1.mot.gov.vn/Laowebsite/News.asp?kind=0, (accessed 20 December 2005)

Table 4.4: Lao Exports, 1998–2003 (US$m)

	Export items	Year 1 1998/99	Year 2 1999/2000	Year 3 2000/2001	Year 4 2001/2002	Year 5 2002/2003
1	Timber and wood products	62,271,712	71,270,000	80,193,611	77,799,706	69,950,205
2	Coffee beans	31,164,000	29,030,000	15,303,833	9,773,938	10,915,964
3	Gypsum, tin and gold ores	767,000	5,993,248	4,890,667	3,903,928	46,502,906
4	Non-timber forest products	2,548,709	4,163,165	6,617,544	8,223,654	5,722,816
5	Other agricultural products	11,234,100	5,092,457	5,706,247	7,661,796	11,123,119
6	Handicraft products	3,008,000	5,100,199	3,850,480	2,736,431	12,492,600
7	Garment products	80,500,000	94,370,000	100,139,447	99,937,863	87,115,268
8	Electricity	57,102,000	107,000,000	91,312,939	92,694,000	97,360,000
9	Other industrial products & miscellaneous	22,464,155	1,955,533	16,871,067	19,887,444	11,441,409
	TOTAL	271,059,676	323,974,602	324,885,835	322,618,759	352,624,287

Source: http://www1.mot.gov.vn/Laowebsite/News.asp?kind=0, (accessed 20 December 2005)

Laos, surrounded by other countries, is naturally oriented to its neighbors. Exports to the Greater Mekong Sub-region (GMS) represented about 65 per cent of its total exports. In 2002, two-thirds of Lao exports went to Vietnam and the rest to Thailand.

Imports have gradually reduced from 690 million dollars in 1996 to 591 million dollars in 2000. This reduction is in part due to a delay in buying equipment for the development of hydroelectricity, which represents a significant segment of the total of equipment imports between 1996 and 2000. In parallel, the share taken by petroleum in the value of imports has increased with the increase in price of petroleum products and the number of cars and motorbikes in the country. Most imports come from the GMS, more particularly from Thailand. The Thai petroleum company Por Tor Tor (PTT) has a virtual monopoly on petrol sales in Laos. Major consumers are dependent upon the Thai company which refuses to offer commercial credits to Lao retailers. One of its leading customers, DAFI (Development of Agriculture, Forestry and Industry Group of Companies), a public company partly owned by the army, has at present to follow a restructuring plan it agreed to in exchange for loans from the World Bank.

In 1997, in its annual report on Laos, the IMF recommended a diversification in the sources of revenue: fewer professional taxes and dues, compensated by an increase in indirect taxes, more particularly the basic tax on turnover, and increasing the base of income taxes. The government delayed implementing these measures in spite of repeated requests from international organizations. The state is in an impasse: on the one hand, it wants to obtain loans and welcome foreign investment, but on the other, it is difficult to change or restructure its state corporations.

The politics of hydropower—"blue gold"

The development of hydroelectric energy exports reveals the external constraints on the country's economic policies. Although the figures for hydroelectric potential in Laos vary enormously (Bakker 1999, 214), the country possesses, together with Yunnan, the greatest hydroelectric potential of the riparian states of the Mekong (including Thailand, Cambodia, Vietnam, and Burma). Laos currently has a capacity of about 600 MW, coming for the most part from five hydroelectric installations which are not used to full capacity: Nam Ngum (210 MW) to the north of Vientiane (the oldest dam, completed in 1971), Xeset (40 MW) to the south, in Saravane province, Nam Theun Hinboun (150 MW) in the center of Laos, Nam Leuk (60 MW) between Vientiane province and the special zone of Sayomboun, and Houay Ho (150 MW) in the south (between the provinces of Champassak and Attopeu). The first three went into production in 1998.

Since the end of the Cold War, the return of peace with the resolution of the Cambodian conflict, and the adoption of the market economy by socialist countries, the region has regained some dynamism. The Mekong appears to economic and political decision-makers, both local and foreign, as an "underused" river, a "virgin space" to be exploited to the benefit of the countries along its banks. Consequently, the policy of constructing hydroelectric dams has expanded in the 1990s, under governmental auspices, strongly encouraged and advised by private investors, foreign experts, and international lenders, who see in the exploitation of water—"blue gold"—the best development strategy for Laos. In their eyes it is the only possible route if the country wishes to attain prosperity and economic stability.[12] The ADB in its feasibility study said no less than this in 1996 when it declared "that the exploitation of hydroelectric resources represent for the Lao People's Democratic Republic the most direct route to increase exports and raise GDP growth."[13]

Table 4.5: Hydroelectricity production, 1995–2000

	Dams	Installed Capacity (MW)	Electricity Generated (GWh)					
			1995	1996	1997	1998	1999	2000
EDL*	Nam Ngum 1	150	966	1,043	1,054	844	979	1,117
	Selabam	5	20.8	21.1	23	20	24.7	24.3
	Xeset	45	96	177	136	78.7	161	168
	Nam Dong	1	2.4	5.5	4.1	4.8	4.5	5.7
	Nam Leuk	60						263.5
IPP**	Theun Hinboun	210				1,235.8	1,467.4	1,535.4
	Houay Ho	152.1					198	614.3
	TOTAL	623.1	1,085.2	1,246.6	1,217.7	2,183.3	2,834.6	3,728.2

Notes: * Électricité du Laos
          ** Independent Power Producers

Source: ASEAN Centre for Energy (ACE). www.asean.org/energy-sector/electricity/lao-pdr/ electricity generation.htm. Jakarta: ASEAN Secretariat.

Revenues coming from the sale of electricity do indeed play an increasing role in the growth of the country's exports. These have increased more than four times in just five years, from 24 million dollars in 1995 to 112 million dollars in 2000. Hydroelectricity even became the chief source of foreign exchange in 1999, exceeding receipts from exports of timber products and textiles, respectively 98 million and 100 million dollars in 2001 (ADB, www.adb.org/laopdr, May 2004). However, this evolution is on a fragile base, for 80 to 90 per cent of current production is exclusively exported to Thailand. Vietnam also buys electricity from Laos, but its requirements are comparatively modest.[14] The experts' opinions were straightforward: given the unprecedented economic boom enjoyed by Thailand from the beginning of the 1990s and its ever-increasing demand for electricity, Laos was assured of a market. But at the same time a very heavy dependence was created with a single monopolistic client whose power in negotiations was de facto considerable. The Electricity Generating Authority of Thailand (EGAT), the Thai public enterprise which regulates electricity supplies in the kingdom, is indeed in an unassailable position. It has several times managed to obtain very advantageous prices when signing contracts for buying electricity, to such a degree that the chief Lao negotiator in the discussions concerning the Nam Theun Hinboun dam declared his powerlessness: "We have no choice but to accept the conditions laid down by EGAT. Even if the agreements are unjust, we cannot waste our time and all the money invested."[15] The financial and economic crisis of 1997 provided additional proof of the fragility of the Lao position.

No doubt Laos has greater need to sell its electricity to Thailand than Thailand needs to obtain it from Lao, but one would deceive oneself if one thought that Thailand was dealing with Laos for humanitarian reasons, as some would have it.[16] In Thailand, the excessive exploitation of natural resources and, in some cases, the degradation of the environment, linked with the increase in resistance by rural communities against abuses (with the support of NGOs involved in the protection of the environment and policies of sustainable development), have led in the last ten years to a reorientation of Thailand's regional economic strategy. In other words, these different factors, ecological, socio-economic, and political have pushed Thailand to internationalize its economic strategy concerning environmental policies. Bangkok sought in its neighbors what Thai businesses could no longer supply, either because resources had been over-exploited, (Thailand has imported much of its fish since the 1960s), or because of local opposition—dam construction projects are frequently denounced for their negative impacts on the ecological and human environment (Hirsch 1995, 235–239).

Timber is undoubtedly the best example of the exploitation of natural resources beyond the frontiers. In Thailand, the ban on forest exploitation has been much discussed in the media since it was issued in January 1989. The trip of 80 high-ranking Thai military personnel to Burma, led by their commander-in-chief Chavalit Yongchaiyuth, in December 1988, and the first visit to Thailand of the Cambodian Prime Minister, Hun Sen, at the end of January 1989 took place with less media attention. Yet these two visits had a similar purpose: they revealed a new regional Thai agenda at the beginning of the 1990s, of developing, exploiting, and commercializing the natural resources of its neighbors (Hirsch 1995, 236). It is through this that Laos, like Cambodia, have become integral parts of the Southeast Asian economy, assuming the function of peripheral suppliers of resources for more economically developed nations which, though, have diminished natural resources.

The Thais are also involved in hydroelectric projects as investors. The long-term benefits will to be repatriated to Thailand. EGAT has created a subsidiary, the Electricity Generating Company (EGCO), one of the partners in the controversial hydroelectric dam of Nam Theun II in Khammouane province (see box). Before this subsidiary could become an investor in the project (at 30 per cent) EGAT and the Lao authorities had not been able to agree on the selling price. It was only in February 2002, some months after EGCO entered the project, that EGAT was able to finalize the pre-project selling price of electricity. The Lao partners here essentially filled the function of facilitating the necessary steps for foreign investors with central and provincial authorities.

The dependence of Laos is not limited to fluctuations in the Thai economy; its hydroelectric policy is based to a large extent on foreign support. Increasing the hydroelectric potential of the country requires that the Lao government seek financial assistance. The country also lacks technical experts. Consultants coming from countries well known for their expertise in this area, like the United States, Norway, France, and Sweden, rush to this new "market", all the more since dams are no longer popular subjects in national development, given their financial and human cost as well as their impact on the environment.[17]

The case of Nam Theun II

The dam, Nam Theun II, on the Nam Theun river (Nakai district, Khammouane province) in the center of Laos is the most ambitious hydroelectric project in the country. Not particularly large physically (being 50 meters high), the dam would produce 1,000 MW, mostly earmarked for export to Thailand. The financial implications are colossal: the cost of the project is estimated at around 1.2 billion dollars (in 1989 it was estimated to cost 800 million dollars), which accounts for more than half of the country's GDP. Returns on the investment have been downgraded. Whereas a feasibility project conducted in 1991 estimated that the dam would produce an annual revenue for the country of 176 million dollars, more recent reports (including those of the World Bank and an independent American consultancy, Louis Berger International) suggested a figure five times lower, that is between 33 and 38 million dollars. It is also to be noted that the statistical estimates were calculated on the basis of a unit price far higher than that finally agreed with EGAT, the Lao government, and foreign investors (4.129 cents as against an estimated 5.7 cents per kW/hour).

The project was initiated and conceived in the middle of the 1980s, and work on it only started at the end of 2005. It is not only remarkable for the money involved but also the controversy it aroused which went beyond the frontiers. The construction of the dam has raised serious concerns among foreign NGOs (working inside and outside the country), academics and development analysts. The consequences for the natural and human environment are known: the reservoir will flood 450 sq km of land, mostly on the Nakai plateau, which is home to rich and varied fauna and flora. It will cause the displacement of several thousand people, many of whom belong to ethnic minority groups. In addition, it is now estimated by the Nam Theun 2 Power Company—the project sponsor—that some 40,000 people who live along the Xe Bang Fai River will be affected by NT2.

Because of the economic cost of the dam, the scale of its ecological and social impact, and international protests, the World Bank, a key player in the project since the beginning of the 1980s, did not give its official support. But after several years of consultations, the World Bank finally granted financial and political risk guarantees in support of the project in March 2005.

Sources: Hirsch (2002, 147–171), International Rivers Network (1999, 68); "EGAT inks agreement", *The Nation*, February 6, 2002.

The dependence is therefore both technical and financial. It is not subject to market forces, but the government is not autonomous in its policy of constructing and operating the dams. Financed by the World Bank, the Nam Ngum dam has always belonged to the state, with Electricité du Laos managing it. But most of the other dams are (or will be) built on the "build-own-operate and transfer" (BOOT) system. According to this, a group of investors finances, constructs and operates the dam for a period of twenty to thirty years, after which the government reassumes its proprietary rights or the agreement is renegotiated. This concept naturally gives the government possibilities of financing and it does not take any investment risks. Some see in this a form of privatization of natural resources and, in this particular case, of the country's rivers. It raises other questions too, such as knowing if Laos would have the funds necessary to maintain the dams when they are twenty or more years old, and nothing guarantees or forces the private investors to maintain long-term, infrastructural renewal, especially if they do not wish to renew the agreement. The manager of EDL, Viraphone Viravong, summarizes the few alternatives remaining to Laos: "If we are allowed, we would have preferred a soft loan [from the World Bank and the ADB] to develop our own [hydropower] projects, like the way EGAT has developed its own hydropower projects. But both the World Bank and the ADB said they do not have money for large-scale projects in Laos. If you are poor, you don't have much of a say. That is the price to be poor" (Malee Traisawasdichai 1997, 18).

Lastly, the social and environmental impacts of the construction of dams are an integral part of these types of large-scale projects. They necessarily cause the flooding of large tracts of arable and forest land, forcing villagers, often consisting of ethnic minorities (as the dams are mostly built in peripheral areas) to abandon their traditional lands.

The damming of watercourses upstream modify the ecological environment downstream, cause a reduced flow in some parts (or too much in others), thus increasing salinity and disturbing the irrigation of rice fields, modes of transport, river biodiversity and fisheries. Rural communities suffer therefore from the construction of dams. In some ways these symbolize the appropriation by the state of local resources (water, forests, land) in the name of a developmental policy on a large scale. In other words, the hydroelectricity policy of Laos, like that of other countries in Southeast Asia (Vietnam, Thailand,

Cambodia) illustrates the priority given to national interests to the possible detriment of local concerns (Hirsch 1998, 55–70). Lastly, as in the case of Nam Theun II, Lao hydroelectricity policies are moving towards increased internationalization in which external participants (private investors, international organizations, like the World Bank, and foreign NGOs) progressively dominate the scene, to the detriment both of the country's economic sovereignty and also the local population, which, in the absence of a civil society and given the weakness of institutional mechanisms representing its interests, clearly suffers from insufficient participation in the discussions about the project (Hirsch 2002, 147–171). The project is now approved and construction has started after consultations conducted by the World Bank during the first half of 2005.

Hydroelectricity and development

In a study of villages displaced by the construction of the Nam Ngum dam, to the north of Vientiane, Kaneungnit, Khamla and Hirsch (1996, 265–277) showed that the policy of relocation created many problems, in particular over access to arable land (which would allow permanent and sedentary cultivation, whereas the displaced persons were not allowed to continue slash and burn cultivation. The number of persons needing settlement increased pressure on available natural resources, which caused local conflicts, sometimes exacerbated by ethnic differences. But it was less the dynamics of ethnicity than the increasing shortage of resources which determined the creation and increase of these tensions.

The local authorities, lacking personnel and means, were unable to arbitrate. The government has to face up to three distinct challenges in the development of hydroelectricity: encouraging national development, taking care of the living conditions of the people affected, and conducting a balanced policy in regard to natural resources (ibid.).

Dependence on international finance

Foreign direct investment and official development aid rose from 139 million dollars in 1999 to more than 250 million dollars in 2000. Bilateral and multilateral aid constituted some 80 per cent of overseas investments (or a quarter of total GDP). The ADB and the Japan International Development Agency (JICA), each provided substantial financial aid. Their annual contributions rose to 90 million, 75 million and 50 million dollars respectively (in round figures). Among the loans granted by the ADB, five concerned investment in the transport sector, four in agriculture, and one in the energy sector. A total of 27 projects financed by JICA alone were approved. Since 1977, JICA has set aside 576 million dollars for Laos; nearly 70 per cent of this budget has already been spent in various Japanese development projects. About a quarter of the current funds are earmarked for the transport sector, and a slightly lower proportion to rural development. Only 2 per cent is reserved for industry and 19 per cent for energy, which gives an indication of the delays occurring in giant hydroelectric projects.

After the financial crisis of 1997, relative stability in the economies of neighbouring countries returned, but did not allow for a boost in foreign direct investment.

Thailand accounted for about half of foreign direct investment in Laos and the United States roughly a quarter. Because of delays in the construction of dams, the spread of investment changed in recent years, shifting from the energy to the telecommunications and industrial sectors. However, given the scale of the hydroelectricity projects, this tendency will be reversed very soon.

The objectives of self-sufficiency

Food self-sufficiency

The country became self-sufficient in food in 2000. Very soon it is likely to produce regular surpluses. Agriculture remains the chief economic activity of the country and employs more than 80 per cent of the labor force. It constitutes half the GDP, but its share has tended to diminish in the last ten years because of increasing industrialization. Officially, rice production is the principal agricultural activity of the country; after that comes forestry. However, the share of forestry (5 per cent) is probably underestimated. This figure does not include the

Figure 4.4: Foreign direct investment, 1991–2000

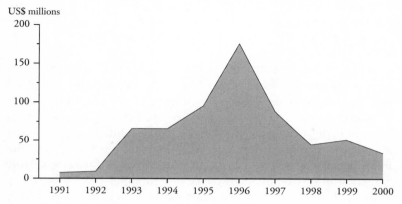

Source: World Bank. 2002. "Lao Logistics Development and Trade Facilitation in Lao People's Democratic Republic". Working paper. Washington, D.C.: World Bank, p. 3.

Table 4.6: Sources of investments, 1988–99

Country	%
Thailand	50.74
USA	25.79
South Korea	10.97
Malaysia	5.06
China	1.49
Other Countries	5.95

Source: World Bank. 2002. "Lao Logistics Development and Trade Facilitation in Lao People's Democratic Republic". Working paper. Washington, D.C.: World Bank, p. 4.

Table 4.7: Average investment by sector, 1988–99

Sectors	1988–1994	1995–1999
Wood	1.5 %	3.9 %
Energy	78.0 %	37.2 %
Industry	2.4 %	16.4 %
Mining	1.9 %	2.1 %
Telecommunications	1.5 %	23.0 %
Tourism	8.5 %	8.7 %
Other	6.2 %	8.7 %

Source: World Bank. 2002. "Lao Logistics Development and Trade Facilitation in Lao People's Democratic Republic". Working paper. Washington, D.C.: World Bank, p. 4.

huge quantity of timber cut illegally. The central government grants licenses but has neither the financial means nor the staff to control the forestry companies, which has allowed some license-holders to cut considerably greater quantities of timber than the quotas authorized.

Only 7.5 per cent of land in Laos is cultivated, while 86.5 per cent is classified as forest areas (this included, though, wasteland and degraded savannas relying on rainfall); 83 per cent of the rice is produced by flooded rice fields and dry rice fields. The rainy season lasts normally from May to October. Most rainfall occurs around the Vientiane municipality, west of Borikhamxay province, and the Bolovens plateau. Only 17 per cent of the fields are irrigated. Most irrigation infrastructures are concentrated along the banks of the Mekong. But the potential for irrigation is considerable throughout most of the country, in particular in the upper reaches of the Mekong.

Figure 4.5: Rice production, 2001

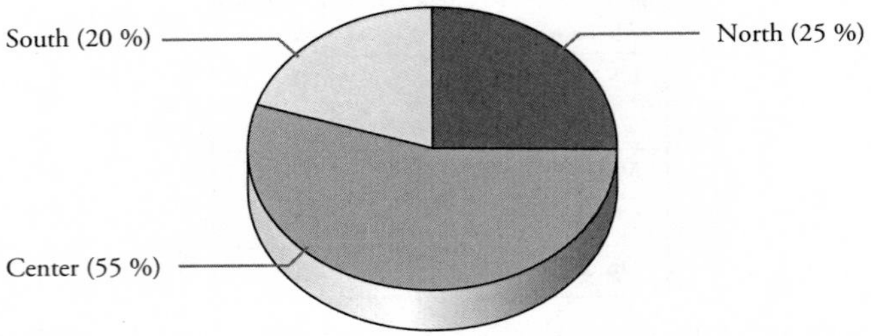

South (20 %) — North (25 %)

Center (55 %)

Source: World Bank. 2002. "Lao Logistics Development and Trade Facilitation in Lao People's Democratic Republic". Working paper. Washington, D.C.: World Bank, p. 7.

The chief rice-producing area is the central region, which supplies half of the national production. Rice is essentially grown for domestic consumption, the government desiring to keep its independence in food production. Some 90 per cent of the rice grown is of the sticky variety. Any surpluses are exported, chiefly to Thailand. The cost of production of rice is actually about half that of Thailand because of the lower labor costs and the relatively low use of fertilizer. The agricultural census of 1998–99 indicated that only 30 per cent of rural households used high-yielding varieties and chemical fertilizers.

Most farmers do not have the funds needed to buy these products. Rice production has nevertheless increased by about 9 per cent in the second half of the 1990s thanks to the development of new systems of irrigation which resulted in higher yields.

The average yield per hectare is estimated at between 2.5 and 4.2 tons. This reflects a system of agricultural production which is not very intensive. Only 7 per cent of rural households possess tractors. The lack of maintenance when they are not in use, and a lack of funds when they break down, means that one-fifth of the tractor owners hardly use them. There is no training program for servicing agricultural equipment. The spread of new technologies, in particular the use of fertilizer and high-yielding varieties, is hindered by the lack of access to credit. The peasants are relatively free of debt and want to stay that way. The erratic rice harvests are the result of climatic variations about which nothing can be done.

Self-sufficiency in food has been reached, but the rice market is not integrated, which explains the large difference in prices between the different regions. This results from many factors: a transport and communications network in poor condition, and also often marginal quantities of surplus rice produced by very many small-scale farmers. Production is fractured and it is difficult to centralize surpluses for sale. Difficulties of stocking and distribution add to the risk of producing shortages, and farmers do not have sufficient reserves to tide over several successive harvests. In spite of the success of the program for rice self-sufficiency by the Lao authorities, the country continues to seek international food aid to offset the structural deficiencies, whether they are technical, financial, economic, or logistical.

Other agricultural products

Apart from rice, agricultural production has increased by an average of more than 10 per cent since 1995. Production of coffee has increased from 10,000 tons in 1996 to 18,000 tons in 2002 and is the chief agricultural export by value. Coffee is grown on the Bolovens plateau in the south of the country. Experts estimate that the best coffee is produced in this area, which includes districts in the provinces of Sekong, Champassak, and Attopeu. The robusta type is chiefly produced (80 per cent), but arabica (15 per cent) is increasing, though the production of liberica remains marginal (5 per cent). As long as it offers the prospect of some profit, robusta will continue to be preferred by producers; the crop is gathered throughout the year, providing a more stable source of income to farmers.

Foreign investment in the coffee sector increased in parallel with the volume of exports to Europe. The Association of Lao Coffee Exporters was created by the Ministry of Trade and holds the monopoly on production. Coffee is bought by trading members of the association which also supplies loans to producers. One of the problems linked to the sale of Lao coffee is that some 50 per cent of production is bought by a single Thai trader in Bangkok. He therefore controls some of the pricing mechanisms. Lack of competence of quality control inspectors from the Ministry of Trade also has negative effects, because it slows down the control of coffee for export. Fairly frequently the beans are rejected by foreign wholesalers.

Coffee is considered by the Lao authorities as an agricultural product of high commercial potential. However, its development largely depends on overseas investors and buyers. The price received is subject to world demand, and Lao plays too small a role to have any influence over returns.

The Bolovens plateau in addition produces cabbages, potatoes, and ginger. Tea and pepper are also cultivated in the region. Thai traders supply seeds, fertilizers and pesticides; but production remains marginal. Laos continues to import much agricultural produce from neighboring countries.

Some pig, chicken and duck producers in the Vientiane area are considered to be important in the Lao context, but they are very small compared to the Thai agro-industries. The number of heads of cattle raised is declining, affected by sales to Thailand during periods of high inflation and the comparative advantage of Thai imports. Most cattle are raised on fodder, the supply of which is limited in the dry season, which affects the quality of the meat. The internal market for this sector remains negligible and dominated by a limited number of brokers authorized by state-run companies which buy cattle from the producers and transport it to authorized slaughterhouses (at least one in each province). The meat is then sold to wholesalers and then to retailers who supply the market.

Agriculture is for the most part in private hands, but the government continues to set price levels for rice and meat. Land remains the property of the government, but a legal framework authorizes its use by farmers. The allocation of land is based on the number of hours of full-time work each family spends in the fields which they claim the right to use.

No really significant cooperatives exist. Efforts to establish some in primary production, for the disposal of surplus or for trading, have had limited success. In the northern, central and southern regions, the agricultural markets are isolated because of the poor transport and communications network. The absence of markets, even at the inter-provincial level, results in considerable differences in sale prices between the different markets. The government does not supply direct subsidies for harvests nor guarantees prices. Most agricultural support comes from indirect subsidies for supplying agricultural credit through the intermediary of the Lao Bank for Agricultural Promotion. But, as the majority of farmers do not take advantage of these credits, their effects are insignificant.

Industrial independence and services

In Laos, the formal private sector is little developed, with less than a thousand private companies registered with a capital of more than 100,000 dollars, and less than a hundred with more than hundred employees. About half these companies are trading companies. In terms of value, five sectors account for more than three-quarters of national production: the transformation of food products, processing of timber, dressmaking, tobacco, and mining. Clothing factories are among the biggest, employing often more than 400 workers. Most of these factories belong to foreign investors. In the 560 small and medium-sized enterprises (SMEs) with more than ten employees, more than half are located in Vientiane and in the town of Savannakhet. The development of industry in Laos is hindered by four factors:

- the weakness of the internal market in terms of population and income;
- the disparity in the means of production and markets combined with topography which results in relatively high transport costs;
- insufficient public infrastructure allowing access to markets and ports in neighboring countries;
- industrial development essentially concentrated on exports derived from natural resources (hydroelectric dams) or cheap labor (the textile industry).

The chief constraints concerning exports are linked to transport costs and lack of information about markets. At a certain level, at least, finance is partially resolved by the Thai or other foreign banks in the country. As for exports to Thailand, the additional levies of Thai customs officers at the frontier constitute obstacles that are difficult to overcome.[18] In terms of regional agreements, the Thai customs tariffs have long remained high when compared to the other ASEAN countries (nearly three times more for agricultural produce coming from Laos). Nevertheless on January 1, 2003, a radical reduction of tariffs was introduced: from 20 per cent to less than 5 per cent, for goods accompanied by a certificate of origin. The Thai authorities, through this system of verification, seek less to encourage Lao exports than to assure themselves that these goods do not come from China or Vietnam.

In the Lao industrial sector, the garment industry appears the most dynamic, even if most of the 65 companies depend on foreign investment. Almost all their profits are repatriated. The foreign partners supervise the purchase of primary materials and sales. The Lao garment industry has largely developed as an alternative for nearby countries (especially Thailand) which cannot increase their production because of the existing quotas. This follows a typical model of delocalization where Laos offers a comparative advantage with its cheap labor costs, but this advantage tends to be blurred by computerized systems of design, cutting and sewing. In addition, growth in the clothing industry is limited by a lack of economies of scale, difficulties in importing raw materials and exporting finished products, as well as the limited availability of investment credits for equipment. Growth in exports will continue to be limited by the cost and difficulties of transport and transit, and by the end of the multifiber agreements in 2005.[19]

The country's growth in exports can be sustained in the medium term by improvements in the transport systems (road, rail or river), the availability of natural resources, and the low cost of labor, which has remained below that of the region. Improved access to the markets of the European Union and America, and the liberalization of tariffs and trading policies in the region, will continue to sustain the country's exports, but the chief difficulties lie in the selection of industries which can be considered as lasting, from the perspective of the country's development. The delay of the Lao government in formulating and implementing economic policies continues to hinder the growth of industrial activity. The risks are seen by entrepreneurs as considerable, deriving from the shifts in the legal environment, the poor coordination of strategies between the central and provincial authorities, the lengthy and complicated approval procedures for foreign direct investment, and generally, the vague bureaucratic procedures.

Notes

1   In August 1987, Laos and Thailand clashed in a short but bloody border conflict. The ceasefire was negotiated in February 1988 after five months of skirmishes, but without really solving the problem of demarcation. Difficulties arise at each new round of negotiation.

2   Lao National Statistical Bureau, *Lao Census*, Vientiane, October 2002.

3   According to a document issued by the Lao government during the ASEAN meeting at ESCAP (United Nations Economic and Social Commission for Asia and the Pacific) on October 18, 2002; Lao Ministry of Transport, Lao People's Democratic Republic, Vientiane, October 2002.

4   The human development indicators of UNPD include life expectancy at birth, adult literacy levels (as a percentage of the population above 15), the number of primary to tertiary students, and the GDP per inhabitant. See UNDP, *Rapport mondial sur le développement humain 2003*, Economica, Paris 2003.

5   World Bank, *Lao Logistics Development and Trade Facilitation in the Lao People's Democratic Republic*, Working Paper, Washington D.C., 2002.

6   There was a fresh slide in public finances from the end of the second quarter in 2002, which caused an inflationary surge (the peak was 18.2 per cent in May 2003), but the rate fell to stabilize at 12.0 per cent in April 2004.

7   At the time the kip was more or less stable in relation to the two principal currencies, the Thai baht and the American dollar, used in transactions, and the margin between the official rate of exchange and the parallel black market fell from more than 8.5 per cent in 1999 to 2.2 per cent in 2000. This exchange rate stability is crucial for the development of the country. With an increase in the inflation rate from May 2002 to March 2004, the kip still lost 21 per cent compared to the baht and 10 per cent to the dollar.

8   General Chavalit Yongchaiyuth was then prime minister.

9   ALMEC (a Japanese consultancy firm) ASEAN Maritime Transport Development Study, ASEAN Secretariat, Jakarta 2002.

10 Since 2001 the kingdom has launched a genuine regional policy. Henceforth it aims to aid Laos within the multilateral framework of the GMS, of ASEAN, or the UNDP. Thailand has also launched the Economic Cooperation Strategy in which is included, for example, the Neighbouring Countries Economic Development Cooperation Fund.

11 World Bank, 2002. It is interesting to note that the ADB indicates in its report the figure of 330 million dollars for exports in 2000. This clearly shows the difficulty

of obtaining reliable statistics for Laos. See ADB, *Key indicators of the Lao People's Democratic Republic*, ADB, Manila, 2003.

12   Interview with Jonathan Thwaites, Australian ambassador in Laos, by Vatthana Pholsena, Vientiane, April 2002.

13   ADB, *Etude de la stratégie opérationnelle du pays pour la République démocratique populaire Lao*, Manila, 1996, iii.

14   It is quite possible that this country may become a more important purchaser in the medium term. But this is not certain, because Vietnam's plan for developing electricity production (1996–2012), makes no mention of buying electricity from Laos.

15   "EGAT power play upset Vientiane", in *The Nation*, October 13, 1995.

16   The former vice-president of EGAT, Viroj Noppakhun, also explained, magnanimously, "We help the Lao. If we did not buy their electricity, they could not do business and could not develop their country!" (Malee Trasawasdichai, *Rivers for sale: a contemporary account of socialist Lao People's Democratic Republic in transition to the 'marketplace'*. Reuter Foundation paper 78, Green College, Oxford, 1997, 14.)

17   At the end of the twentieth century some 500 dams were demolished. See McCormack 2001, 6.

18   Customs officers frequently ask for "gifts" to facilitate crossing the frontiers. If these are not offered, goods are often stuck there.

19   These agreements, drawn up under the aegis of the WTO, controlled the export quotas of the clothing industry worldwide. Importing countries could control the import of textiles and clothes coming from developing countries. They could also favor some countries, such as Laos, but the ending of the multifiber agreements in 2005 has done away with these quotas.

5 LAOS–LOGISTICS PLATFORM FOR THE MEKONG REGION?

Regional integration from a Lao transport infrastructure perspective

Regional economic integration should theoretically proceed through the development of commercial exchanges between the member countries of a given geographic area. Laos currently takes part in two initiatives of this type (the GMS and ASEAN). The integration strategy is somewhat similar. It involves reducing administrative formalities, taxes, and other barriers to trade. Greater trade will stimulate the economies of member countries. As a consequence there will be separation of production sites and markets. Improving the logistics of exchanges between consumers and suppliers is a determining factor in regional competitiveness.

Production sites and transport systems affect the final cost of goods delivered. The choice of a production site does not only depend on the locality of an economic activity and the efficiency of the transport system. Investors also have to take into account the extent of the labor force, capital, and the institutional environment. Other specific factors, such as economies of scale and policies encouraging investment, can also influence the choice of site.

Even when regional integration conditions are adequate, the locality is not without consequence on the trade it is intended to foster. It generally creates new tariff barriers, sometimes very demanding, as well as quotas on goods coming from countries not party to the regional economic integration initiative. In the particular case of Laos, it is highly likely that the least competitive local producers would be adversely affected by the freeing of the internal market, and would encounter more difficulties to export to regional and OECD countries. Those risks are the reasons why the

Lao authorities have requested ASEAN that its market liberalization program be delayed.

In any case, addressing the problem of logistics is crucial. According to UN-ESCAP (2000), it is vital for an economically less developed country like Laos to develop transport and communication links with its foreign markets. Improvements in the efficiency of internal and cross-border movements can lead to a rapid increase in opportunities, thanks to Laos' comparative advantage in production costs. The transport system has, however, to overcome problems such as the country's low population density and rugged terrain. In particular, it is necessary to link effectively the economic centers of the country: Luang Prabang in the north, Vientiane in the center, and Savannakhet and Paksé in the south.

Roads

The road network in Laos is relatively limited. There are in all about 23,900 km of roads, of which 6,500 km of national highways and 7,200 km are designated provincial roads. In relation to the size of the population and the volume of traffic, though, the network seems almost extensive. The number of private vehicles is low: 150,000 motorcycles, 30,000 cars, and pick-ups, and 10,000 lorries and buses were registered in 2001, of which half were in the municipality of Vientiane. The volume of vehicles on the main highways is between 250 and 500 a day, while motorized traffic in rural areas is ten times less. In spite of real efforts to improve the infrastructure, some 40 per cent of the population still lives more than 6 km from the nearest road.

The two most important national highways are Route No. 13, partly financed by Sweden, linking the north-south axis of Luang Prabang, via Vientiane, to Savannakhet and Paksé before reaching the Cambodian frontier (in all some 1,500 km), and highway No. 9 from Savannakhet to Den Sawanh (209 km), going on to Danang in Vietnam. Highway No. 9 is considered an economic corridor for the ADB (of which more will be discussed later), which seeks to increase the role played by Laos in the transit of goods from northeast Thailand to Vietnam.

Mention should also be made of highway No. 3 which links southern China with the north of Thailand. Some 280 km long, it crosses northwest Laos. The construction of Highway No. 3 is funded by China, Thailand and the ADB (in the form of a loan to the

Lao government), each contributing to one-third of the costs. This highway is considered strategic for the development of the GMS (see next section). It will be completed by bridges. A small bridge—110-metres long—opened in October 2004 that already connects the province of Loei in northeastern Thailand to the province of Sayaboury in northwestern Laos. In addition, the Thai and Chinese governments will provide funding (amounting to 1.5 billion baht each) for the construction of another Lao-Thai bridge, linking Huay Xai (northwestern Laos) and Chiang Khong (northern Thailand). These infrastructural developments once completed are expected to reduce the traveling time between Kunming and Bangkok from five days to only one day. Currently, the Chinese authorities are very disappointed with the slow rate of completion on the Lao segment and have requested Thailand to partly finance the last section without consulting the Lao side.

The ADB, the Lao government and its neighboring states see Laos as a platform for the transit of goods in the region. But this desire to transform the country into an economic and logistic transit area remains hampered by difficulties, like those related to financing the construction and maintenance of these highways earmarked for transit. Having a network in good condition is certainly important for Laos' economic development, but if it is above all destined for transit, it runs the risk of causing problems for the Lao authorities. They do not know what kind of taxes they should levy on vehicles and goods which are merely passing through the country. The environment might suffer from a great increase in the passage of lorries between Thailand and China, just as it has in Thailand and Vietnam; some in Laos have doubts about the benefits of being a regional transit platform, given the damage already caused to the forests by the improved road infrastructure.

Between 1990 and 1995, more than half of public investment was used for the renewal and development of more than 2,000 km of highways. The investments were kept at a high level from 1995 to 2000, adding more than 1,000 km to the transport network. The funds mostly concerned national highways and urban roads, and most came from international grants or loans (Laos does not have the means to finance its road infrastructure). Foreign aid for transport rose to more than 500 million dollars between 1983 and 1996. This aid contributed to 65 to 80 per cent of investments for different road construction projects, whilst national financial sources continually decreased since the middle of the 1980s. Highway construction costs vary considerably according to terrain. In the mountains, hard surface all-weather dual carriageways cost about 265,000 dollars per kilometer. On flat land, it costs about a third less. It should be noted that Laos has no real budget allocated for maintenance after construction, preferring to use its funds to keep extending the network. A user-pays system of tolls would doubtless allow these strategic roads to be maintained, but there again the authorities have hardly moved beyond thinking about it.

While about a third of roads are classified as being in "acceptable condition", the classification and the definitions accompanying it remain subjective. For one thing, "acceptable" applies only to all-purpose vehicles. These classifications all the same serve as indicators to financial backers in the framework of their feasibility and economic development studies. The state of the roads differs significantly according to whether they are part of the national network or provincial and local networks. Some 70 per cent of the national network is open throughout the year; but only a quarter of the provincial and local network can be used in the rainy season. Only half the national network has all-weather surfaces. In spite of relatively low traffic, the roads deteriorate much more rapidly than the standards which determined their "economic life".

This can be put down to poor design, damage caused by overloaded lorries and a lack of maintenance budget devolved to provincial authorities. At present, the load limit for lorries in Laos is 8.2 tons per axle, against 9.1 tons in Thailand and Vietnam. But the difficulty in making sure these limits are obeyed comes from the fact that Thai lorries are often overloaded when they arrive in Lao territory, because of poor enforcement of limits in Thailand which, very often, are not respected. Some loads can reach as high as 12 or 13 tons per axle.

The transport network in Laos is maintained by relatively small private companies. The transport of goods in transit from or to Thailand is limited to authorized road haulage firms. Originally, this type of journey was restricted to the Express Transport Organization (ETO), a state-controlled Thai company, notorious for its poor service. The number of license holders was subsequently increased to include two transport firms, Ubonsahatham and TL, the only "Lao" agent (in fact it was a joint venture with Thai input), two multimodal companies, Regional Container Line, and the Thai railways.

In spite of an increase in competition between the service beneficiaries, the international freight rates remain comparatively

Table 5.1a: Average cost of transport from Thailand (Bangkok) to Laos (various cities)

Destinations in Laos	20 ft Containers (US$)	40 ft Containers (US$)
Thanaleng*	1,050	1,250
Vientiane*	1,100	1,300
Thakhek/Khammouane	1,200	1,400
Savannakhet	1,200	1,400
Chong Mek	1,150	1,350
Pakse	1,300	1,500
Borikhamxay	1,450	1,550
Champassak	1,450	1,550
Saravane	1,450	1,550
Sekong	1,500	1,600
Attopeu	1,700	1,800

Source: Lao forwarding agents (interviews with Ruth Banomyong, December 2002).

Table 5.1b: Some comparative transport costs

Journey	20 ft Containers (US$)	40 ft Containers (US$)
Marseilles ⇨ Singapore	650	800
Bangkok ⇨ Singapore	200	300

well under domestic freight charges. Exports from Laos to Thailand, often through Nong Khai (the twin city to Vientiane in northeast Thailand) can be undertaken by any vehicle registered in Laos. For transit freight, only five companies are allowed to proceed to the port of Bangkok. Their tariffs are relatively high, especially given the distance covered, between 700 and 1,000 km Bangkok–Laos.

In order to facilitate the transit of goods, documents such bills of lading and cargo manifests are required by the Thai and Lao authorities respectively. Not having the proper paperwork or following the procedures can cause delays of up to a week in delivering goods from Bangkok to Laos.

The main highways of Laos

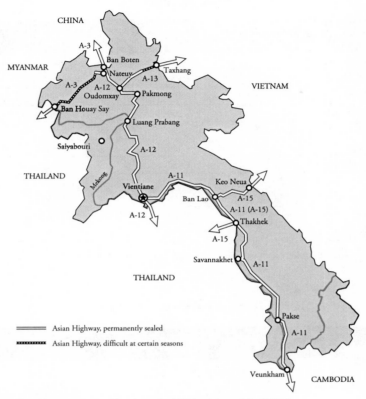

Source: http://www.unescap.org/tctc/maps/lao2002.jpg (accessed April 2004).

The costs of sending exports are more or less the same as for imports. But while the containers arrive full, they often leave empty. The cost of transport is not in itself prohibitive; the difficulties lie in crossing the borders, which increases the costs. The transport costs for sending a container from Bangkok to Nong Khai in Thailand is around 400 dollars, whereas crossing the border and delivering the goods to Vientiane increases this to 700 dollars for a distance of a mere 30 km further. Crossing the border does not justify this increase, but one has to remember that there is relatively light traffic on the route and few operators can provide transit services. Transport within Laos is relatively expensive because it is done on a piecemeal basis. There are plans for consolidation centers to be established in Luang Prabang (north), Vientiane (center), and Savannakhet or Paksé (south) but no decisions have been made as there may not be enough freight to justify such investment.

River transport

River transport chiefly follows the flow of the Mekong. The section of the river which passes Laos is 1,970 km long, of which 1,865 are currently navigable. Most traffic is concentrated between Vientiane and Saiyaboury in the northwest, a distance of 400 km. The main cargo are sand, stones for construction, and timber. Barges are also used to transport timber from the northern provinces to sawmills around Luang Prabang and Vientiane.

Laos has five main river ports: Vientiane, Savannakhet, Paksé, Paksan (in the center) and Tarket (in the north). These are used to load and unload locally consumed goods. They are also used in transport between Thailand and Laos. Most of the vessels are motorized barges with a draught of 1.3 meters. During the rainy season, the river forms an alternative to road transport all along the western frontier and in the north. Vessels weighing up to 400 tons can

---

Stay in Luang Prabang and navigating the Mekong, June 3–July 22 1984

Without the Mekong, there would be no Lao people. They are born navigators and the dugout canoe is their livelihood. At the high tide season, they leave their villages loaded with various goods, and come to camp beside the river, particularly at the estuaries of streams. There, at that time, important markets are set up, where the Lao obtain from the Khas in the mountains, in exchange for salt and textiles, all the rice they need; they are incapable of acquiring it otherwise, hating work in the fields.

The preferred places for the Lao for these exchanges are Ban-lat-Hane and Ban-lat-Hene, where during the high tide season, there is a market every week. Ban-lat-Hane is also, in the dry season, the point of arrival at the Mekong of Chinese caravans which come to trade at Luang Prabang. Ferries at this time of the year, working from both sides of the river, allow for its easy crossing.

Source: Pierre Lefèvre-Pontalis. *Mission Pavie en Indo-Chine 1879–1895* (1902, 88-89).

navigate throughout the year the northern section of the Mekong. Elsewhere, navigation is limited to barges of less than 200 tons. During the dry season, most of the river is only navigable by light boats, which limits the development of river transport. China has plans to blasts some rapids in order to make the Mekong navigable throughout the year. But these plans remain deeply controversial (see box).

Before the construction of the Friendship Bridge, financed by Australia, between Nong Khai and Vientiane in 1994, cargo in transit coming from or going to Thailand crossed the Mekong on barges.

Deep concern over Chinese plans for the Mekong

"In his 2002 report to the Mekong River Commission, Brian Finlayson of the University of Melbourne... described the Mekong River Navigation Improvement Project as aiming 'to improve the navigability of the Mekong River over a 331 km stretch between boundary marker 243 on the China-Burma border to Ban Houei Sai in Laos.' ...The first stage will remove '11 major rapids and 10 scattered reefs and shoals by dredging and blasting so that 150 ton ships can travel the Mekong...[and eventually] allow 4x500 tons Chinese barge trains on the Mekong.'

Downstream countries are increasingly alarmed by China's attempts to 'improve' the Mekong River, which flows through six countries from Tibet to Vietnam. Thailand is examining plans to protect its Mekong water reserves for its northeast territories. Vietnam's investments and projects in the Mekong delta will be affected by any reduction of the Mekong's waters. Cambodians worry that a lower Mekong level will kill the Tonle Sap, a huge inland lake, which depends on the Mekong's backflow during the flood season....

The plan to blast a Mekong channel for Chinese ships is part of an agreement which Burma, China, Laos and Thailand signed in April 2000....The Mekong River Commission paid for several independent reviews that found the Mekong blasting project proceeding too quickly, without adequate studies of the changes it could cause...The reality, however, is that protests and petition letters will probably have little effect on the Chinese hold on the politics and commerce of the Mekong region. The lower Mekong countries are unlikely to refuse Beijing the right of way through their sections of the Mekong River, for fear of economic retribution."

Adapted from Jaime Cabrera, "The Rape of a River", in *Bangkok Post*, January 5, 2003.

Most Lao exporters at the time had set up their factories along the river, and these barges could directly load or unload their goods. The share of internal river traffic has diminished significantly in the period following the construction of the bridge and still more since the improvement of Highway No.13. An additional decline is expected after the opening of the bridge being built between Savannakhet and Mukdahan (northeast Thailand). The Friendship Bridge led to an increase in exchanges between the two countries and has geographically shifted river transport operators to the south, to Thakek and Savannakhet. In its turn, the completion of the bridge between Savannakhet and Mukdahan will probably lead to a loss of customers for Lao river transporters in these provinces. In March 2004, the first Thai-Lao joint cabinet retreat took place in Paksé (southern Laos), led by the two countries' prime ministers, Thaksin Shinawatra and Bounyang Vorachit. Most significantly, the two-day meeting marked the official start of the construction of the second Lao-Thai Friendship Bridge between Savannakhet and Mukdahan. It is scheduled to be completed in 2006. In addition to the construction of the bridge, there are plans to expand Savannakhet airport into a regional hub, along the same concept as Geneva aiport which is a domestic airport for France but an international airport for Switzerland.

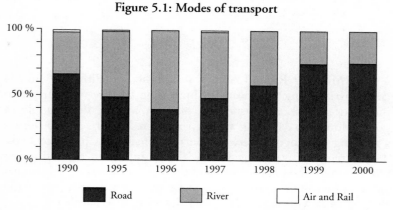

Figure 5.1: Modes of transport

Source: World Bank. 2002. "Lao Logistics Development and Trade Facilitation in Lao People's Democratic Republic". Working paper, Washington, D.C.: World Bank, p. 23.

French ambitions for the Mekong: from hope to delusion

In the nineteenth century, some people dreamed of and still believed in the Indochinese "Eldorado" and imagined in particular that the Mekong would be the highway to open all kinds of opportunities. Francis Garnier, an officer in the French navy, was one of the explorer-adventurers of the period.

"By May 1861 [Garnier] had already become fascinated by the Mekong River. This was the fascination he later called his *monomanie du Mékong*. Writing to his parents from Saigon, he recorded for the first time his belief that the Mekong could offer the key to the success of France's new colony in southern Vietnam. With more faith than knowledge, he assured his family that 'The Cambodia River (as the Mekong was still frequently described at this time) with its thousand branches which are navigable throughout, with its gigantic course up which one can travel for a hundred leagues from the sea, will carry to the heart of the new colony all the products of the interior.' Like many who were to come after him, Garnier appears to have been brought to this view by the great size of the Mekong as it flowed towards the sea through Cambodia and southern Vietnam. Neither he, nor others, paused to ask why there was no evidence of the trade along the river's course that would seem appropriate to its size. Despite their lack of detailed knowledge about the river's course, it seemed enough to know that somewhere to the north the Mekong flowed through China. With envious recognition that the British had already established a major commercial outpost at Hong Kong, men like Garnier thought that the Mekong could provide the French with their own access to the fabled riches of the Middle Kingdom."

Source: Milton Osborne. *The Mekong: Turbulent Past, Uncertain Future* (2000, 75)

The Mekong River Commission, based in Phnom Penh, is currently studying the means of increasing the use of the river in international goods transport. A plan for a more fluid supply of goods along the Mekong was approved on March 7, 2000 during a meeting in Rangoon between Burma, Thailand, China and Laos. The agreement was conceived with the intention of facilitating navigation on the upper reaches of the river. It foresaw navigational aids, improvements in river ports, and proposed ways to integrate the river network with the road network. Laos however hardly benefits at all from these plans, unlike China and Thailand. While the country tries to take advantage of the commercial possibilities offered by the Mekong, conceived as a "corridor of international trade", a very small part of goods transported is destined for the Lao market. It is also difficult to foresee exports by river for Laos, as the industrial center of the country is Vientiane, from where lorries take export goods to the port of Bangkok. For the present, the improvement in navigability of the Mekong would facilitate smuggling from China to the Thai market. The only advantage, in the medium term, which Laos can take from the agreement is in the promotion of tourist sites and cruises along the Mekong.

A strategy of improving transport in spite of transit difficulties

A certain number of agreements have already been signed with the aim of facilitating the movement of persons and goods between Laos and its neighbors. These agreements rest on solid bases, but their implementation remains difficult. Thailand is the country with which Laos has the most difficulties to resolve. The Thai authorities always have trouble in understanding the demands of their Lao partners in the matter of transit. The stumbling block in the discussions between the two sides is both technical and cultural. The Thai authorities consider that they treat Laos correctly, and that the Lao demands are unreasonable. Laos is a signatory to the Barcelona Convention of 1921 for the right of access to the sea by land-locked countries, but Thailand is not and does not consider itself obliged to accede to Lao demands. Here the "big brother-little brother" syndrome which marks Lao-Thai relations can be seen. The development in the countries through better economic integration would be to match demand with supply. Laos is rich in natural resources, whereas Thailand has a relative advantage in capital, technology, and human resources. The links between natural resources and capital movements, commercial exchange and economic migrations make economic sense.

The transit agreement reached in 1978 between the two countries cover procedures for exports in transit, and include measures against smuggling. The transit agreement conforms to the 1921 Barcelona Convention and the statutes on freedom of transit. As a signatory to the Barcelona Convention, Laos does not tax goods in transit if the necessary documents have been obtained from the ministries concerned. This is not the case with Thailand.

Bilateral commercial agreements between Thailand and Laos

- 1978: **Trade agreement.** Goods intended for international trade were identified as well as organizations which can conduct bilateral trade and the conditions relating to payment; state banks were selected to control the financial settlements between Thailand and Laos.

- 1978: **Transit agreement.** The text aims to facilitate exports and imports for goods in transit coming from or going to a third country; Thailand agrees to provide special conditions for goods which will satisfy the basic needs of the Lao people.

- 1979: **Settlement of authorizations, and trading permits** (amended in 1980, 1981, 1982, and 1985). Rules are set out for Thai traders dealing with Lao counterparts.

- 1990: **Agreement on the promotion and protection of investments.** Investors in the two countries see their investments protected.

- 1999 and 2001: **Agreements on road transport.** Agreement between the Lao and Thai governments concerning road transport and subsidiary agreements indicating the arrangements for road transport signed respectively on March 5, 1999 and August 17, 2001.

The agreement produced a legal framework allowing Thailand and Laos to draw up a list of companies eligible—five for each country—to transport goods in transit. This agreement is automatically renewed each year unless notification is given by either party three months in advance of the annual date of renewal, June 1. A new agreement was negotiated in 1999, and its enabling protocols two years later. The negotiations are generally very difficult, as Laos does not represent a priority to Thai officials in bilateral matters. The Lao negotiators often accuse them of a lack of sincerity in their proceedings.

The bilateral agreement of 1999 on road transport established transit conditions for goods and travelers. The text identified the border posts. It authorizes Lao goods to be brought directly onto boats anchored in Thai ports without having to stop at the transit depot of Klong Toey (Bangkok) and without additional customs authorizations from the two countries.

Table 5.2: Frontier posts in the 1999 Lao-Thai Agreement

Laos	Thailand
Ban Houay Say (Bokeo)	Chiang Khong (Chiang Rai)
Friendship Bridge (Vientiane)	Nong Khai (Nong Khai)
Thakhek (Khammouane)	Nakhon Phanom (Nakhon Phanom)
Savannakhet (Savannakhet)	Mukdahan (Mukdahan)
Vangtao (Champassak)	Chong Mek (Ubon Ratchathani)
Nam Ngeun (Saiyabouri)	Huai Kon (Nan)
Kenethao (Saiyabouri)	Nong Phur (Loei)
Paksan (Borikhamxay)	Bueng Kan (Nong Khai)
Paktaphane (Saravane)	Pak Seng (Ubon Ratchathani)
Ban Vang (Vientiane)	Khok Pai (Loei)

Source: Ruth Banomyong. 2003. *Transit Transport Issues in Landlocked and Transit Developing Countries*. New York: UN-ESCAP.

The agreement allows for seven transit itineraries in Laos, ten in Thailand, with agreement that the corridors can be modified if necessary. In Laos, these cover Highway No. 3 linking China with north Thailand, Highways 1, 8, 9, 12, and 18 between Thailand and Vietnam, and Highway No. 13 which is supposed to link Burma, Thailand, Cambodia, and Vietnam horizontally. In Thailand, these corridors stretch to the frontiers with Cambodia and Burma, but also Bangkok, the port of Laem Chabang, and the port of Maptaphut (both located on the Gulf of Thailand, the first to the north of Pattaya, the second north of Ranong).

For each transport transit operation all the documents are required with translations in English. The cargo is theoretically accompanied by a bill of lading, a packing list and a receipt. Even if English has become the language used in relations at frontiers between two states, the civil servants in charge of the inspection barely understand the language. A former Thai minister of foreign affairs in the Democrat government of Chuan Leekpai in 1999 conducted bilateral discussions in the framework of a treaty on Lao-Thai economic relations with his Lao counterpart in English, in spite of the close similarity of the languages of the two countries. The Lao authorities did not appreciate this stand.

The owner of the goods can select the transport operator from the official list. The status of these operators was clarified in a secondary agreement of August 17, 2001. However, the text requires that the operator be authorized to work in the contracting country which is not his country of origin. No explicit clarification about this has yet been given, as the negotiators have yet to agree on one. This is another expense increasing the overall transit costs: paying a Thai customs escort, even if no Thai customs officer currently provides such a service.

In practice, the rules are difficult to apply and become more complex as the number of participating countries increases. Vehicle inspections are carried out by each country and the certificates issued by the other countries have to be accepted according to an agreement signed by ASEAN member countries concerning the mutual recognition of official documents. The vehicle has to stop at designated rest stops and at places indicated in the transit agreement and that the transit vehicle has to leave the foreign country within the time stipulated, assuming that all the procedures went according to plan.

There is also an arrangement concerning the tariffs for warehousing and the price for transshipment, for the feedering of the lorries and for all the remaining services which should not be greater than the tariffs levied by national operators. While reference is made to rates fixed by governments, these are not those applied by the private sector. This kind of regulation runs the risk of paralyzing the movement of goods since market forces are not respected, and if the rate charged is too low, the operators could withdraw from the transit business which brings no returns. The agreements specify that goods can remain in transit for a period of 90 days. Beyond that, they are considered as unwanted items. This is an added risk for the owners of the goods.

Thailand is the chief partner for Laos in transit matters, but not the only one. In 1996 an agreement with road hauliers was signed between the governments of Laos and Vietnam. It identifies the permitted frontier posts. Lao exporters and importers can select any post in Vietnam, but most transit freight passes through the port of Danang, the rest though Cua Bas, Xuan Hai and Quy Nhon. These ports are inadequately equipped and cannot supply the necessary services for container transfers.

Table 5.3: Frontier posts in the 1996 Lao-Vietnam Agreement

Laos	Vietnam
Kao Cheo (Borikhamxay)	Keo Neua (Ha Thinh)
Dan Savanh (Savannakhet)	Lao Bao (Quang Tri)
Sop Hun (Phongsaly)	Dae Chang (Lai Chau)
Sop Bau (Hua Phan)	Pa Hang (Son La)
Ban Loi (Hua Phan)	Nam Meo (Thanh Hoa)
Namkan (Xieng Khouang)	Nam Can (Nghe An)
Tong Kham (Khammouane)	Cha Lo (Quang Binh)

Source: Ruth Banomyong. 2003. *Transit Transport Issues in Landlocked and Transit Developing Countries*. New York: UN-ESCAP.

In order to better exemplify the problems associated with transit shipments, an example will be given with regards to the textile trade. It shows the variants in cost and time which Lao exporters face in selecting Thailand or Vietnam. Two previous tables showed the transit costs (for a 20 or 40 ft container) to the port of Bangkok and the port of Danang. One has to bear in mind that the distances between the place of departure and the place of arrival are not the same. It is 700 km to the port of Bangkok, but more than 1,000 km to the port of Danang from Vientiane.

These two tables synthesize the costs the Lao exporters have to pay for access to the sea. It is interesting to note that even if Laos and Vietnam have a preferential agreement for goods in transit, Lao exporters continue to prefer to use the route through Thailand. The cost and length of time to reach Bangkok are more competitive, but Thailand also offers a much greater choice concerning destinations and more flexibility relating to the timetables of the shipping companies.

The following figure shows that crossing the frontier with Vietnam appears to be more efficient than that with Thailand. But these figures have to be used with caution because they are supplied by the customs officials of the respective countries.

Table 5.4: Textile exports by road to the port of Bangkok

Sector		Max. Duration	Min. Duration	Distance (km)	Cost (US$)
Vientiane–Thanaleng		1 h	30 mn	15	-
Thanaleng–Nong Khai		15 mn	10 mn	5	116
Customs Formalities		4 h	2 h	-	35
Crossing at Nong Khai		6 h	3 h	-	50
Transit Fees		-	-	-	20
Under-the-table payments	-Laos	-	-	-	13
	-Thailand	-	-	-	13
Nong Khai-Bangkok		20 h	12 h	650	406
Port Fees		-	-	-	60
Terminal Handling Charge		-	-	-	68
Expenses Related to the Bill of Lading		-	-	-	13
Thai Customs		-	-	-	6
TOTAL		31 h 15 mn	17 h 40 mn	670	**800**

Source: Ruth Banomyong. 2003. *Transit Transport Issues in Landlocked and Transit Developing Countries*. New York: UN-ESCAP, p. 65.

Table 5.5: Textile exports by road to the port of Danang

Sector	Duration	Distance (km)	Cost (US$)
Vientiane – Savannakhet	1 day	469	670
Savannakhet – Dan Savanh	1 day	263	370
Dan Savanh – Lao Bao *	1–3 hr.	1	100
Lao Bao – Danang	1 day	327	460
Port Fees (Danang)			53.2
TOTAL	3 days and 1–3 hr.	1,060	1,653.2

* Crossing the Frontier with Customs Clearance

Source: Ruth Banomyong. 2003. *Transit Transport Issues in Landlocked and Transit Developing Countries*. New York: UN-ESCAP, p. 69.

Figure 5.2: Comparison of average time spent at frontier crossings

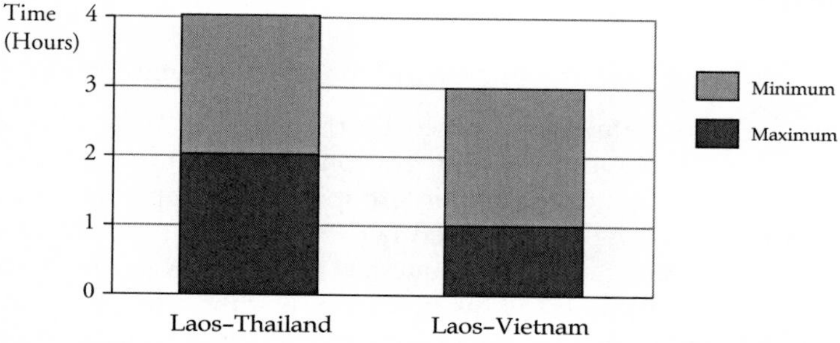

Source: Ruth Banomyong. 2003. *Transit Transport Issues in Landlocked and Transit Developing Countries*. New York: UN-ESCAP.

Commercial rivalry between Thailand and Vietnam: already a colonial dilemma

"One can understand the abandoning of the project to make the rapids navigable [to the south of Savannakhet and the north of Vientiane] if it were agreed to hasten the construction of a railway linking the middle Mekong to a port in Annam [the center of present-day Vietnam], as these rapids became a solid barrier which could not be overcome. But this is not the case; many more years were to pass before the products of the markets of Luang Prabang and Nong Khai could realistically reach the Annamese coast. On the other hand, if work on the navigability of the Mekong continues to be carried out with as much sloth as now, if we do not wish to take advantage of this 'moving highway', we will continue to play into the hands of the Siamese, and the Bangkok market, thanks to the railway going to Khorat, will receive all the produce of Laos which should know no other outlets than Saigon, Tourane, and Vinh."

Lucien de Reinach, *Le Laos* (1901, 78)

The Greater Mekong sub-region: a golden quadrilateral?

"A growth area", a "growth triangle", or an "economic corridor"?

The GMS program was initiated by the ADB in 1992 with the objective of promoting the integration of the countries in that region into a common economic grouping. The apparent success of the growth triangle established between Singapore, the state of Johor in Malaysia, and the Indonesian islands of Riau (especially Batam) stimulated others. Now grouping six states, the new cluster brought together at first four countries, including two northern Thai provinces, Chiang Mai and Chiang Rai, Keng Tung in Burma, Luang Namtha and Bokeo in Laos, and Xishuang Banna in Yunnan in southern China.[2] Two other countries in the lower Mekong basin, Vietnam and Cambodia, subsequently joined this growth area. The ADB was convinced that such cooperation is the natural result of market forces. In its eyes, increasing political liberalization formerly extolling self-sufficiency and centralization has allowed trade and other forms of economic cooperation to increase. The growing flow of goods and services would lead to greater specialization and more rational use of human and natural resources. This would enable the region to be more competitive in world markets, and encourage new activities, thanks to technological advances. Lastly, to complete this virtuous circle, there would be a rapid improvement in the regional economic integration, which would in turn attract a continued flow of investments from developed countries.

The concept and practice of economic cooperation between nations is not new. Their geometric form through a series of triangles and quadrangles appears to be more specifically Asian. Although the origin of this geographic-economic idea is difficult to determine, its popularity in certain academic and government circles is without doubt the result of the effort and desires of the ADB. The concept of a growth triangle, according to the ADB, should allow contiguous countries to exploit their complementarities in order to acquire competitive export advantages (ADB 1998). Growth triangles seemed like a novel solution to practical problems caused by regional integration of countries with different degrees of economic development, as well as different political and social systems. In addition, a growth triangle was seen by many Asian governments as an appropriate form of regional cooperation, given the limited political and economic stakes. Polygons are preferred to regional blocs because they are often strictly oriented to exports and because their non-exclusive nature does not lead to paranoia or retaliatory measures from other trading partner countries that do not participate in this form of regional cooperation.

The ADB put particular emphasis on restoring and developing regional infrastructures. The bank estimated that 40 thousand million dollars (half coming from the private sector) would be necessary in the next twenty-five years to finance about a hundred projects countries in the GMS countries, mostly in the transport, energy and telecommunications sectors (Bakker 1999, 224). The GMS transport program consists primarily of the building and development of three "Economic Corridors", namely the North-South, the East-West and the Southern corridors. The first two of these "corridors" will cross Laos. The North-South Economic Corridor (NSEC) will link northern Thailand, northwestern Laos and southwestern China; and the East-West Economic Corridor will connect central Vietnam in the east with Myanmar in the west, cutting across southern Laos and north and northeastern Thailand. These roads, composed of highways and feeder roads (the latter serving to link rural communities with the highways), are presented by the ADB and its partner countries with the goal of developing an efficient transport system, which will allow goods and people to move around the subregion without excessive cost or delay. In Laos, two highways are sections of those economic corridors: Road No. 3 that crosses northwestern Laos (from Houayxay to Boten) and will link Thailand to China, and Road No. 9 that crosses the southern province of Savannakhet from the provincial capital in the west to Lao Bao on the Lao-Vietnamese border. A report on the East-West Economic Corridor (EWEC),[3] a project integrating all economic sectors including transport, clearly announced the hopes of the ADB of creating a regional economic area, without frontiers or states, where the flow of goods and services, capital and human resources, would circulate without obstacles:

> The long-term development vision of the EWEC is to stimulate the growth of the participating areas and raise the incomes of their residents. This will be achieved by facilitating the efficient exploitation of underlying sub-regional complementarities, developing a range of competitive advantages that will enhance the overall competitiveness of the EWEC, and realizing the vision of the EWEC as a single, unified geographical and economic unit. But

it is important to recognize at the outset that the vision of EWEC
development must be a long-term one, given the far-reaching poverty
and under-development characterizing many sections of the Mekong
corridor."[4]

But the theoretical concepts of "growth triangles" and "economic
corridors" still have to prove their worth on the ground.

During a press conference on business opportunities in the
EWEC, the Lao deputy minister for communication, post, transport
and construction, expressed his optimism that the eastern part of the
corridor would turn the western provinces of Laos and northeastern
Thailand into a center for economic growth.[5] To this end, an
industrial base, the Savan-Seno Special Economic Zone (SASEZ),
was established in Savannakhet province in late 2003. Concretely,
special incentive policies have been devised to attract local and
foreign enterprises, including overseas Lao investors, such as periods
of tax exemption or special tax rates on imported products and custom
duties exemption on exported merchandise. The initiative though has
not yet attracted a significant number of private investors (Pholsena
2005, 176). On the other hand, the North-South Economic Corridor
(NSEC) has shown promising economic returns and commercial
activities on the Lao-Chinese and Lao-Thai borders as early as the
mid-1990s, even before the construction and upgrading of the roads
had begun (Walker 1999).

The economic rectangle of the upper Mekong: rhetoric and reality

The Australian anthropologist Andrew Walker examined the
transport and trade networks and their human participants (traders,
entrepreneurs, truck drivers, landing-stage supervisors, etc.) in
northwest Laos, in the frontier area of Laos and Thailand, to the
south of China and Burma. He shows that the vision of the economic
quadrilateral of the upper Mekong (linking north Thailand with
south China and going through Laos and Burma), anticipating a
relaxation of state control and deregulation, was faced with the reality,
not of "transformations", "cooperation" and "free trade", promised in
the brochures and reports, but of "continuity", "competition", and
"regulation". This is an irony of history: the change in economic
policies at the end of the 1980s had the result of re-establishing
and reinforcing age-old practices controlling the relations in the
northwest of Laos, north Thailand and south China. So, "As in the

late nineteenth century, and for most of this century, manufactured goods sold in the markets and shops of north-western Laos are imported predominantly from Thailand and China, and Chiang Khong has resumed its role as an important upper-Mekong trading centre" (Walker 1999, 73).

Behind the appearances of regional cooperation where the technical and economic parameters, supposedly neutral, in theory play a primordial role and where political rivalries have no place, it is the interventions and interests of local authorities which dominated the scene in the negotiations in the middle of the 1990s, when the promoters of the economic quadrilaterals were still discussing the best possible routes to link the north of Thailand with the south of China. Walker notes:

> Towns and provinces along the routes also have vested interests, with opportunities for infrastructural improvement, business expansion, tourist influx, local taxation and windfall profits on property speculation eagerly embraced by government officials and local entrepreneurs...increased mobility often generates intense, and uncertain rivalry between competing localities. Provincial administrations in Laos, despite efforts to centralize financial control, derive a large percentage of their revenue from trading taxes and are keen to maintain control of the key trading routes. In Thailand, provincial taxation is less important but provincial officials and businessmen are keen to secure both the direct benefits of trade and the secondary investment that tends to follow. It is not surprising that some of these local actors have been active participants in the marketing campaigns supporting alternative transit routes through Laos. (Walker 1999, 82–83)

The recent financial agreement for the construction of a highway which will link the northern part of Thailand, Chiang Rai, to Kunming in south China, passing through the Lao provinces of Namtha and Bokeo (see box) suggests that the political and economic players in Chiang Rai have won the toss. Likewise, on the other side of the frontier, local civil servants and entrepreneurs in Luang Nhamtha have succeeded in establishing the idea that northern Laos should constitute a central transport artery of this economic quadrilateral, convinced that the prosperity of their province depends on this road linking northern Thailand with southern China. But when confronted with the ideal of a golden quadrilateral forming a space without obstacles, the authorities, be they Lao, Thai, or Chinese, meet regularly to try and coordinate their actions against "bad influences" (drug traffickers and smugglers). Paradoxically, the rhetoric of economic liberalization is often accompanied with an increase in controls and political regulation.

Asian Highway No.3

On December 2, 2002, the Asian Development Bank approved a loan of 30 million dollars in order to improve a section of the highway linking China and Thailand through Laos. This section is part of the north-south corridor anticipated in the economic cooperation program of the GMS, and is known as Asian Highway No. 3. The Thai and Chinese governments co-financed the project thanks to a loan of 30 million dollars, each on a bilateral basis, with Laos. This country will take charge of certain local costs with the aid of loans from the ADB granted with flexible repayment terms. This is a unique example of two member countries of the GMS cooperating with the ADB to invest in a third country, with the aim of improving regional cooperation. This highway of 280 km, known as Highway No. 3 in the north of Laos, goes from Ban Houay Say (that is, the frontier with Thailand) to Boten on the Chinese frontier. For the present, trade is restricted to a narrow road without a hard surface, which cannot be used for four months of the year during the rainy season. The ADB will finance the work on improving a 74 km section and raising it to international norms (with two hard-surface tracks), but this may be insufficient if the highway is to carry the transit traffic between China and Thailand. China is getting more and more impatient as progress has been slow. Kunming has been earmarked as the main gateway for trade wih Southeast Asia by the year 2010 and Chinese trucks carrying over 50 tons of cargo per vehicle are now waiting at the Chinese border with Lao.

The north-south corridor constitutes one of the major projects of the member countries of the GMS. It is expected that Laos would underwrite some of the costs with the aid of the ADB. The loan it has been granted comes from its concessional Asian development funds; it is reimbursable over 32 years and includes a grace period of eight years. The interest rates are 1 per cent a year during the grace period and 1.5 per cent a year for the rest of the time. The question remains though whether Laos can afford to repay this debt after the end of the construction if no direct revenue accrues from the highway.

Opening up Laos

One of the ADB's priorities, in the framework of the GMS, is the opening up of Laos which it sees, like the Lao government, as an essential condition for the economic development of the country. The ADB has consequently urged the countries in the GMS to sign several agreements it has initiated.

An agreement for crossing the frontiers between Laos, Thailand and Vietnam to facilitate cross-border trade in goods and services was ratified at the end of 1999. China and Cambodia became associates to this, respectively in 2001 and 2002. The agreement's purpose is to harmonize legislation and facilitate transit rules between the signatories. In this respect, the agreement is similar to those developed by ASEAN. It allows agreed transport operators in any signatory country to provide transport in or through the signatory countries. Only cabotage is excluded.[6]

The protocols define the designated transit routes, the points of entry, and the types of vehicles which can be used. Fees for border transport services will be decided by market forces, but will also be controlled by a joint committee to avoid excessively low or high prices. This agreement takes into account the progressive adoption of simplified border crossings. This implies coordinating the hours of opening of border posts and the exchange of information about the cargo in transit. For agricultural and veterinary inspections, the agreement envisages the application of relevant international conventions.

Freight in transit is exempted from customs duties and other tariffs on goods. However, guarantees need to be provided to customs authorities for all types of transit goods. All invoiced expenses occurred by transit traffic are earmarked towards the maintenance cost of the transit corridors. Lao roads and bridges must conform to certain norms, and the country must ensure that the infrastructure is in good condition. Laos is currently in a difficult position because in wanting to become a logistics platform for the region the country must maintain and develop its road system. Laos does not have the financial resources and if the rates for using the communication highways are prohibitive, the regional hauliers will avoid the country.

The vehicles used for transit must observe the safety norms required in the country through which they transit. The country in which the vehicle is registered is responsible for the condition of the vehicle; the haulier must be in possession of a certificate of roadworthiness. The vehicles must also be properly insured for the countries in which they transit. The agreement aims to favor multimodal transport by presenting a special customs administration and developing a single authority for freight transport; but this at present is a pious hope.

Approval of the 1999 agreement required accepting the three protocols linked to the transit corridors and the points of entry and departure from the country. It also requires the acceptance of various annexes linked to customs systems. Recently, Burma expressed its desire to sign the agreement which was conceived with the intention of harmonizing bilateral agreements linking the member countries of the sub-region. But these agreements sometimes contradict others already in place. The customs formalities are negotiated under different rules. Medical examinations of drivers and insurance are not covered in the protocols. The annexes have yet to be negotiated, so that the agreement is at present only one of principle.

The proliferation of agreements hinders rather than helps Laos. The Lao government is drowning in bilateral, trilateral and multilateral agreements covering transit trade, which have different operational modalities according to their respective aims. Laos is also the signatory to numerous agreements which are not applied because of the difficulties arising from negotiations over annexes and protocols.

Opening up Laos: a colonial ambition too

The construction of a railway from Laos to Vietnam was a sort of *deus ex machina* for French colonial officials. All the economic problems of the country were expected to be solved by this single means, though some did recognize that this might take time. Despite the cost and numerous delays, it was an article of faith that the railway would be built, and would have the desired economic impact. Roland Mayer, writing in 1931, was convinced that 'the year 1936 will see the arrival of the locomotive on the bank of the Mekong, an event which will announce the economic awakening of Laos'. The Tan-Ap-Thakhek line continued to fascinate planners but after 1945 insecurity made construction impossible. The only railway ever built in Laos was 7 km long to enable transshipment of goods and people around the falls of Khone.

Martin Stuart-Fox, "The French in Laos, 1887–1945" (1995, 127–28)

ASEAN agreements

Laos' accession to ASEAN constituted an important step in the country's development policies. It permitted Laos to progressively integrate its economy in the regional and international context. But this did not occur without negative effects, from both the social and economic viewpoint. The fact that Laos joined ASEAN certainly enabled it to accelerate its economic development. But it is more than ever dependant on its regional partners, and more particularly Thailand, which supplies 60 per cent of its currently consumed goods, its equipment requirements and primary materials used in the garment sector.

In addition, trade with Thailand and Vietnam is subject to the rules of free trade established among ASEAN countries and the application of a common preferential tariff since 1994. This free trade area is supposed to bring a reduction on 85 per cent of tradable goods to less than 5 per cent of their value by 2005. At first, the agreement covered only finished products, including processed agricultural products; but it has spread to include non-processed agricultural products, while taking into account national policies protecting certain products. Non-processed agricultural products are divided into three categories: those which are subject to immediate inclusion, those for which a provisional exemption applies, and those considered sensitive goods. The fiscal levies on the first two categories were brought down to 5 per cent before the end of 2003.[7] All other products should be included in these measures by 2010.

The economic ministers of member countries signed three agreements in 1998 in Hanoi to accelerate economic integration in ASEAN. The framework agreement dealing with modalities of mutual recognition and the framework agreement facilitating the transit of goods are designed to make trade expand in the region. This last agreement has the greatest impact on the movement of goods to and from Laos. The objectives are very explicit:

- facilitating the transport of goods in transit;
- maintaining the ASEAN free trade agreement;
- integrating the regional economies;
- simplifying and harmonizing the customs regulations concerning transport and trade, in order to facilitate the transit of goods; and
- establishing an efficient system, integrated and harmonized, for transit within the member countries of ASEAN.

Table 5.6: Status of the ASEAN Protocols (as at Dec 2002)

Protocol	Status (December 2002)
Protocol 1 Designation of transit routes and rest areas	Held over since Oct 2001 because Malaysia and Singapore cannot agree.
Protocol 2 Designation of frontier posts	Held over: the member countries of ASEAN need to confirm the designated frontier posts (P 2) and the list of prohibited or controlled transit goods
Protocol 7 Customs agreement for goods in transit	
Protocol 3 Types and number of highway vehicles	The Philippines ratified P 3, signed 15 Sep 1999, and accepted by Laos, Burma and Vietnam.
Protocol 4 Technical classification of vehicles	
Protocol 5 Obligatory vehicle insurance	Cambodia and Vietnam ratified this 8 Apr 2001
Protocol 6 Services offered by customs posts	Held over: Singapore requires clarification of the protocol
Protocol 8 Sanitary regulations	Only Vietnam at present applies the protocol, although all member countries of ASEAN signed it on 27 Oct 2000
Protocol 9 Dangerous goods	Signed 20 Sep 2002 by all member countries

Source: Ruth Banomyong (2003)

But the agreement was still not implemented a year after being signed, because of difficulties arising over certain protocols.

It can be seen that signing the framework agreement by ASEAN member countries in Hanoi in 1998 did not fix everything. The negotiation of the protocols, which detail modalities of implementation, is very sensitive. Protocol 1, relating to the designation of dedicated routes for transit goods, has not yet been agreed upon. The difficulty lies in relations between Malaysia and Singapore. These countries cannot agree and a bilateral negotiation process has started, though without so far producing any concrete result. The problem reflects the lack of effectiveness of ASEAN as a supra-national authority. The designation of corridors and transit materials remains suspended. The problem seems to be so important that some member countries have asked for the exclusion of the two countries in conflict over discussions concerning transit corridors.

Protocol 2 about the designation of frontier posts could be quickly decided if Singapore and Malaysia first agreed to Protocol 1. Protocol 7 though will be difficult to agree as it depends on national customs services to establish transit customs regulations. It is therefore impossible to establish a goods transit agreement in ASEAN without involving all the customs services of member countries, as the negotiations were conducted by ministries of transport officials alone, which have no authority in customs matters.

Protocols 3 and 4, relating to trucks carrying goods in transit, are less contentious. The Philippines was the first country to agree to this, which is not surprising since the archipelago has no land border with other ASEAN member countries. Laos quickly signed these two protocols. The number of vehicles authorized to transport goods in transit was limited to 60 vehicles per country. This figure raises questions, because it is not known on what base it was proposed. The Lao negotiators may be happy with it, but for the private sector the restriction of the number of authorized vehicles is going to create serious problems, especially during periods when hydroelectric dams are being built (one Lao transport agent estimated that he needed at least 200 vehicles a day to keep the construction of a power station going).

Protocol 5 was signed by only two countries, Cambodia and Vietnam. Laos has not yet ratified it because the insurance business is very poorly developed (at present only one insurance company operates in the country). Protocol 6 concerning services provided by customs posts has been suspended by Singapore for reconsideration. The problem arises from the fact that Singapore's railway station belong to the Malaysian railways. There is no problem acceding to Protocols 8 and 9. However, only Vietnam applies Protocol 8, and no ASEAN member country really follows the rules for Protocol 9.

The fact that the most important protocols are still under negotiation shows fairly clearly that the agreement in principle for easing the passage of goods in transit is in practice worthless. The situation is particularly damaging for Laos which is not, for all that, more supportive of the process, still having hesitations about adopting multilateral norms.

Economic relations between ASEAN countries are more competitive than cordial. National interests continue to dominate over regional interests. In spite of the ASEAN Free Trade Area

ASEAN agreements concerning regional economic integration

Framework agreement on the liberalization of services

This document, signed by the economic ministers of ASEAN, should facilitate the activities of nationals of any member country of ASEAN in providing services in the countries of other members. The services included in the negotiations comprise air transport, maritime transport, telecommunications, and the tourism industry. Up till now, Laos has not signaled its agreement to the liberalization of the service sector.

Framework agreement on inter-state transport (September 2000)
The chief objectives are:
1. to facilitate the transport of goods from one state to another;
2. to sustain the realization of the free trade zone in ASEAN and the integration of the economies of the region;
3. to simplify and harmonize the customs regulations on the transport of goods in order to facilitate the transport of goods from one state to another;
4. to work together towards establishing an efficient regional system of transport, integrated and harmonized, covering all the aspects of transit and transport between one member country and another.

Most of the protocols are not yet in place. Because of this, the framework agreement is not applied. This agreement was signed in principle because an agreement of some kind had to be signed at the ASEAN meeting in Brunei in 2000.

Framework agreement on multimodal transport
This agreement established the principles on the minimal level of qualification for multimodal transport operators in ASEAN. The agreement should have been adopted at the end of 2003 but the process has been delayed by technical difficulties.

(AFTA), members can exclude goods and services for reasons of national security. In short, the political agenda of each member does not facilitate economic integration. The reality of all this is that Laos remains dependent on international aid and has not really succeeded in applying means to liberate itself economically. But for Laos, the most pressing problems concern the flow of goods, coming under inter-state rules which are not applied. It could be said that Laos does not speak from a position of force in the negotiations.

Notes

1   One could ask if the Thai authorities really knew the basic needs of the Lao people.

2   The region is also known as the "golden quadrilateral" (by analogy with the "golden triangle", famous for its opium production). In Thailand it is known as the "five Chiangs", namely, Chiang Rai, Chiang Mai, Chiang Tuing (the Thai name for Keng Tung), Chiang Roong (the Thai name for Jinghong, the capital of Sipsong Panna,) and Chiang Kam (the old name for Luang Prabang in Laos).

3   The EWEC consists of two segments: a western one goes from Phitsanuloke (Thailand) to Mawlamyine (Burma), including Sukhothai, Tak, Mae Sod, and Myawaddy, and an eastern segment going from Khon Khaen (Thailand) to Danang (Vietnam), embracing Kalasin, Mukdahan, Savannakhet, Quang Tri, and Thua Thein-Hue.

4   ADB, "Pre-investment study for the greater Mekong sub-region east-west corridor", Integrative Report, February 2001, pp. ii–iii; personal communication.

5   Jeerawat Na Thalang, "Help to upgrade Savannakhet airport", *The Nation*, July 27, 2004.

6   This is to stop vehicles not registered in a country from transporting goods coming from and being sent to the same country.

7   The decrease is now in place, but the arbitrary practices of certain governmental agencies continue to hinder the development of the ASEAN free trade area.

6 THE MYTH OF ISOLATION: OLD AND NEW CROSS-BORDER PHENOMENA

The pre-colonial "growth triangle"

The opening up of Laos, advocated by the government, international organizations and experts, has a perspective (a supranational vision), an ideology (the free circulation of goods and persons regulated by market forces), and a specific objective (economic growth). For the ADB, it is a question of linking the chief urban centers of the member countries of the GMS while offering Laos access to ports and markets for its exports. The projected road grid in the region, seeking greater liberalization in the movement of goods, services, capital, and persons across international boundaries, would have Laos placed at the center of a transport and exchange network. In short, that would have it abandon its geographic and economic "isolation", the chief cause in the eyes of political and economic decision-makers of its "structural vulnerability". It should be noted that the country is, at present, more an area of secondary transit than the chief artery controlling exchanges and resultant revenues. Moreover the discourse and plans for opening up reinforce, indirectly and implicitly, the traditional image of an isolated country, "marginalized", with an autarchic economic system, little adapted to the opening up of its frontiers and integration into a regional and world economic system.[1] Some historical perspective alters this vision, which is both dichotomic (the center pitted against the periphery) and unbalanced (unilateral control of the center over the periphery).

Commercial routes, both on land and water, linking China with Southeast Asia have a long and well-known history in Asia.[2] The existence of transport and trade networks in the cross-frontier area between Yunnan, Burma, Thailand and Laos from the first millennium of the Christian era reveal the strategic importance of this region long before the arrival of the Europeans. Over centuries, Yunnanese caravans followed trade routes to the east of Tibet, crossing Assam, Burma, Thailand, Laos and north Vietnam, going to the Chinese provinces of Sìchuan, Guizhou and Guangxi. Two main routes in particular linked the south of Yunnan with the north of Thailand: the Burmese route, to the west, from Keng Tung to the province of Chiang Rai, and the eastern route, which, from the province of Phongsaly (in the far north of Laos today), went westwards, passing Luang Prabang and the Mekong to reach Chiang Khong, near the present northern frontier of Thailand.[3]

Based on historical accounts and French and British colonial archives, Walker describes an intra-regional area at the beginning of the nineteenth century where exchange between the political center and the peoples of the plains and the mountains was not just in terms of tribute. A surplus of domestic production was not exclusively destined to the elites and politico-religious chiefs. The author suggests a system of exchange which is much more complex and diversified, where trade in consumables forged links between the mountain peoples, those of the plains, and the commercial and political-administrative centers (Walker 1999, 27–29). The pre-colonial states of Nan and Luang Prabang (today provinces in north Thailand and northwest Laos, respectively) flourished thanks to their strategic location on trade routes between Yunnan, northwest Laos and north Thailand.

The first French administrators noted as they traveled south that the Yunnanese muleteers transported silk, tea, salt, opium, furs, items in metal, etc, to sell in Siamese markets of the north (notably Chiang Mai) and in villages encountered along the way (Lefèvre-Pontalis 1902, 154). Raw cotton cultivated by the Khmu, the Lamet and the Yao, minorities in present-day Laos, on scattered plots in the mountains, constituted their chief trade goods on the return journey through Laos, and the Yunnanese acquired deer horns and bears' gall bladders, much in demand in traditional Chinese medicine (Walker 1999, 32).

From the 1830s, the state of Nan, thanks to its victorious military campaigns, had extended its influence beyond the present frontier of Thailand to occupy on the other bank of the Mekong the districts of Viengphoukha and Luang Namtha (now in northwest Laos) and much of Sipsong Panna in south China. With places on both sides of the river in its power, Nan could assert strategic control over regional trade. One of the chief caravan routes between Yunnan and the north of present-day Thailand passed through Luang Namtha and Viengphoukha, to cross the Mekong before reaching Chiang Khong, the second most important town of the state located at the river outpost. From the beginning of the nineteenth century, it developed into the chief trading center on the banks of the upper Mekong (ibid., 30, 32).

Many analyses of the social and political organization of the pre-colonial states of southeast Asia are based on the idea of fluctuating and poorly defined frontiers between the different political and religious entities. Walker demonstrates, on the contrary, a very rigorous spatial organization in the northwest of what later became Laos. The places for transit were well defined: Chiang Khong, through its ideal position on the caravan route, allowed the Nan authorities to control the traffic, both on land and river, and to profit from this regional trade by organizing toll points, collecting taxes on goods and extracting money from the traders in return for their 'protection' (ibid., 32–33). In short, Nan very early on applied the rules of modern international trade.

The pre-colonial state of Luang Prabang was rather different for a simple reason: having very limited space, its food supplies depended largely on its trade with the rice-producing villages close to the Mekong and its tributaries. Its food supply did not depend so much on the irrigated ricefields of the Lao in the plains, but on the dry rice produced by the Khmu and the Lamet. In other words, commercial relations with the mountain peoples constituted the central mark of this pre-colonial economy (ibid., 37). Whilst the mountain dwellers farmed, those in the plains occupied themselves with trade and crafts.

At that time, Luang Prabang was not only a trading center between the plains and the mountains. It also controlled some of the most important caravan routes and derived substantial profit from them, just like Nan, through the collection of transit taxes and other levies on goods. Oudomxay (now the chief town of the province of the same name, to the north of Luang Prabang) was also a meeting point for many caravans entering Laos from Sipsong Panna. There, produce as varied as minerals, cotton, salt, and cattle was exchanged (ibid., 40).

The arrival of the French in Laos at the end of the nineteenth century seems to mark a change in the transport and trade networks in this "triangle" which governments, international institutions and foreign experts so greatly desire to reproduce in our time, without always being aware of the fact that their project is nothing new. The

Occupational specialization at the beginning of the nineteenth century

Key lowland settlements, including Luang Prabang itself, were located at strategic transport junctions where trade with the upland communities could be regulated. Barter was the most common basis for exchange, with hill-dwellers trading primary produce for iron goods, fabric, ornaments and pottery produced in lowland Lao communities. The region around Luang Prabang is noted for its village handicrafts, and it is possible that this developed not only to support the royal court but also to encourage trade with uplanders... Salt from the salt-wells in the northern reaches of Luang Prabang's domain was also highly sought after by the hill-dwellers... Lowland traders and village shop-keepers also introduced European manufactured goods—cloth, thread, needles, dyes, condensed milk, matches, sugar, kerosene and mirrors—that were imported from trading centers in northern Siam... Cash transactions also occurred: Siamese *ticals*, Indian *rupees*, and locally smelted silver circulated widely in the region... (Walker 1999, 39)

ambition of the French authorities to create a unified geographical space on the political, economic and commercial levels explains their determination to conceive and proceed with the construction of roads between Laos and Vietnam, at the expense of trade with Siam.

The movement of goods and persons did not stop with the establishment of fixed and legal boundaries in modern times. However, if the cross-frontier movements are a permanent factor in human history, the differences between those of today and those in the pre-colonial period are both qualitative and quantitative. The considerable expansion since the end of 1980s in the regional and world economy has undoubtedly increased the movement of goods and capital, as well as human migration, and has even in some cases altered their character.

Stay in Luang Prabang and navigating the Mekong,
June 3–July 22, 1984 (Part 2)

With Ban-lat-Hane, Pak Beng is one of the principal transit points on
the left bank of the Mekong. Each year, when the caravans pass, the
king of Luang Prabang organizes a ferry service at Done Than, near
the confluence of the Nam-Beng, and the mandarins he delegates
receive a toll fee.

While on the right bank the common transit point is Done
Thuan, the places where the trails on the right bank end are many:
caravans arrive at Pak Ngim, Pak Sap, Pak Heu and Pak Kop serving
important centers like Muong-Luo, where Luang Yokhabat was
holding his assizes at the time we passed there, and Muong Ngin
where the Siamese energetically supported the territorial claims of
the rulers of Nan against the deliberately unacknowledged rights of
the king of Luang Prabang.

P. Lefèvre-Pontalis, *Mission Pavie Indo-Chine 1879–1895* (1902, 89)

A spectacular increase in tourism[4]

The spectacular development of tourism in Laos in the last ten
years or so, and more particularly in the second half of the 1990s,
undeniably confirms the opening up of the country. The number of
tourists rose from 37,613 in 1991 to 673,823 in 2001, or an increase
of 17 times, on a base, it is true, that was very low. In 2000, tourism
brought in 103.7 million dollars, or more than the profit from exports
of the clothing sector (100.1 million dollars), electricity (91.3 million
dollars), and timber and furniture (80.2 million dollars). From 1996
to 2000, tourism was the economic sector which expanded the most;
in only three years it rose from fourth place (43.6 million dollars)
to the first (79.9 million dollars). Regional tourism from Southeast
Asian countries produced the largest number of visitors, with 501,199
person in 2001, nearly 75 per cent of the total. Non-Asian tourism
was, though, more lucrative, since it brought in 67.4 million dollars
in 2001 (some 65 per cent of all revenue).

The inverse proportion between the number of tourists and the
revenue generated by international and regional tourism respectively
is explained in part by the length of stay. Whilst non-Southeast
Asian tourists stay an average of eight days in the country in 2001,
the tourists from nearby counties only spend on average between
one and four days. In addition, they spend less during their stay than

tourists who come from farther afield. For the majority of visitors from ASEAN (Thais at 55.9 per cent provided the most), it is frontier tourism, limited to the province of entry and for a very short stay. For the most part they do not venture into the interior.

In spite of the investments, the development of tourism is limited by insufficient infrastructure. Traveling from one place to another is difficult and accommodation limited. In 2001 the country only had 14,257 beds, 44 per cent in hotels and 56 per cent in guesthouses. This insufficiency could probably satisfy the government since it has decided to avoid the appearance of mass tourism like that developed in Thailand. It says it fears negative impacts on culture and society. Instead of mass tourism seen as "uncontrollable" and therefore "untoward", the authorities seek to promote ecological and cultural tourism, in their eyes more likely to respect and preserve the country's heritage. The economic realities, in particular the need for foreign exchange, run the risk of jettisoning these reservations, especially if demand continues to be strong. The increasing economic impact of tourism has however to be considered, since in 1995 (the most recent date for which figures are available),[5] in spite of its impressive progress, the sector generated little employment and only provided jobs for at most 3 per cent of non-agricultural labor, chiefly in Vientiane and Luang Prabang.

Migration

As can be imagined, the progressive opening up of Laos is not only seen by an increasing flow of tourists to the country. Business (12 per cent and 14 per cent of international and Thai visitors, respectively, in 2001 and 1997) or family visits (2 per cent and 5 per cent) also are the object of short visits. But there are few statistics on Lao nationals leaving the country. Those who go for shopping trips in the frontier towns, like Nong Khai or Udon in Thailand, mostly take the Friendship (Mitthaphap) Bridge across the Mekong (more than 80 per cent of cases in 2001), the vast majority (97.5 per cent) using a simple laissez-passer restricting their stay in Thailand to three days. For frontier provinces, business visits account for more than tourism, which is hardly surprising as internal and international Lao tourism remains embryonic. When the question of movements of Lao arises, one is chiefly considering economic migration. We shall return to the factors which explain this, but it can be stated right away that if Lao cross the frontier in search of work, it is above all to Thailand that they go.

Crossing the Mekong—just economic migration?

While regional migration is of course an age-old phenomenon that predates today's nation-states,[6] population movements have considerably increased in the last twenty years in Southeast Asia, to the point of occupying an important place in policymaking by governments which are more concerned than pleased by the phenomenon. Uneven economic growth across Asia, linked with a declining birthrate in some countries, have contributed to the emergence and development of regional migration to areas short of manpower. From the 1980s, the four "Asian tigers" (Hong Kong, South Korea, Singapore, and Taiwan) and Japan became the preferred destinations for migrant workers from the region. Likewise, Malaysia and Thailand appear today as lands of opportunity for people in nearby countries. In 1997 the estimated figures shows that the three countries with the highest immigration (Malaysia, Singapore, and Thailand) counted about 4.2 million foreign workers (ILO 1998, 28). To intra-regional migrations should be added the number of Asian workers going to the Middle East. While the flow has considerably slowed since then, it has been estimated that in the middle of the 1980s they numbered about 8 million persons. Generally, the Asian economic and financial crisis of 1997 did not lead to a net reduction in the total number of migrants, but possibly to an increase in the number of illegal workers in a depressed economic context, which favored a hardening of attitudes over immigration in recipient countries.

There seem to be no official figures in Laos about the total number of cross-frontier migrant workers. Little information is available to determine migration from Laos to Thailand. In October 2001, it was estimated there were 58,411 illegal Lao workers in Thailand.[7] The figures have to be treated with caution as most of those who cross the frontier do so illegally. The only official Lao information we came across were the figures drawn up in Savannakhet, the most populous province (about 707,000 inhabitants). The figures vary wildly even here, citing between 15,000 and 30,000 persons crossing the frontier between Laos and Thailand each year.[8] Furthermore, a recent assessment of illegal labor migration and trafficking in Laos shows the rapid rise in illegal labor migrants in its three target provinces in central and southern Laos. These provinces share borders with Thailand and are among the most populated in Laos—Khammouane, Savannakhet and Champassak—with an increase of nearly 40 per cent (from 32,789 to 45,215 people) over a period of less than one year (between December 1999 and September 2000). According to Thai immigration police reports, the majority of these illegal migrant workers were aged between 15 and 24 years, half of these under the age of 18.[9] The phenomenon is so widespread in some districts that it has been compared to an exodus with " a generation…missing from the community" (ILO 2003, 25).

It is difficult to be certain of all the motives which incite the Lao, and in particular Lao youth, to go to Thailand. The economic factors of this migration are familiar: on the one hand, Thailand's economy is in need of cheap labor in industries such as fishing, fruit-growing, livestock farming, food & beverage, entertainment, manufacturing and construction, while on the other, Laos offers few avenues for employment (other than subsistence farming) and scant opportunities for any kind of education or training beyond secondary school.

Migrant journeys

"Ms Khao, age 22, occupation now a rice farmer, completed primary school. She is married with one child. She had once gone to work in Thailand two years ago. At first there was a Lao agent who came to invite her to work in Bangkok. She sent her to another agent in Khemarat district, Ubol province, who took her to a place where she earned 2,000 baht per month sewing, with food and lodging provided free. The building was just like a house from the outside, but inside was a large garment factory. After work the employees would go to sleep upstairs and were not allowed to leave the building. Hours were from 7:30 am to 10:30 pm. Ms Khao worked there for 15 months. She was paid the first time after nine months and then only 600 baht, her first eight months salary was for the agent. After 15 months she was allowed to go outside. She met another Lao person who told her how to return home, which she did. She said the reason that the owner of the factory would not allow them outside was that he was afraid the police would see them and he would be arrested and fine.

Ms Nyay, age 25, completed lower secondary. Her parents are rice farmers and have a shop selling miscellanies. She has been going back and forth to work in Thailand over the past four years. She always goes to the same garment factory where she receives 2,500–3,000 baht depending on overtime. But from this she has to rent a place to stay and buy food. If she is thrifty she has money to bring back home. Nyuay says she likes to work in Thailand. The work is not difficult and she doesn't have to be out in the sun and rain. And sometimes she goes out to have a good time and enjoy life."

Ministry of Work and Social Affairs (2002, 24–26)

Some studies tend to suggest, however, that socio-economic conditions are not the only factor in deciding whether to seek work in Thailand, even if financial gain remains an essential motivation. Paradoxically, a rural sociological study conducted in 2002 showed that relatively well-off villages also supplied a number of migrants (Chazée 2002). Because these villages do not suffer from food shortages, and, indeed, on the contrary generate a surplus, they can free manpower for non-agricultural work, hence the possibility of migration. Departure is also motivated by the inactivity of young people in rural milieus; this situation largely arises from a structural problem of unequal access to land. The lack of arable land is an important factor in impoverishment descending through generations. Some 80 per cent of households have no rice fields since they have not inherited any from their parents, or because their parents quite simply had none themselves. Low income households are particularly likely to emigrate to Thailand.[10]

A smaller-scale study (eight villages in four frontier districts facing Thailand spread over two provinces, Saravane in the south and Saiyaboury in the northwest) also suggests the correlation between demographic growth and migration, without, excluding the economic situation as an aggravating factor. In Laos, large families, with six or more children, are fairly common, and agricultural work does not occupy all the offspring of a household. So after completing their studies, generally at the primary level, they are often unemployed.

What emerges clearly from these different studies is the structural nature of migration to Thailand, in particular among young people. Chazée (2002) noted that such movements are so common in the villages of Khong Sedone (Saravane province) and Pak Lai (Saiyaboury province) that it would be reasonable to define working in Thailand as an integral part of life in these villages. Some go further, maintaining that cross-frontier movements, which undeniably involve an element of risk and adventure, are rather like a rite of passage (ILO 2003, 26). Without going so far, it can be said that the desire for adventure and novelty certainly represents one of the motives fuelling the exodus of young Lao crossing the Mekong in search of work (Ministry of Labor and Social Affairs 2002, 18).

One study shows that 36.5 per cent of those questioned took the decision to leave with the agreement of their parents, but 50 per cent left without informing them. This tendency is more clearly evident among young people who entered Thailand in the region of the town of Mukdahan, where most people are ethnic Lao: they constituted respectively 27.6 and 62.1 per cent. In some ways, departure is also an act of emancipation. A study on the trafficking of children on the Thai-Burma and Thai-Lao frontiers shows that 96.6 per cent of young migrants say they left because others had done so before them (Wille 2000, 27–28). The report concludes that tackling the economic causes of migration will not solve the problem because young people also want "to see the world" or to get away from personal problems. The study noted in addition that the majority of young Lao migrants came from ethnic Lao villages, which are generally less impoverished than ethnic minority communities (ibid., 24).

Cultural proximity is reinforced by the extensive penetration of Thai mass media—television, newspapers and radio—into Laos. Many young Lao are fans of Thai pop bands and TV serials. They readily hum Thai tunes. A large proportion of young (and mostly ethnic) Lao, especially those in the towns, understand and speak Thai fluently, having been exposed since childhood to the language and popular culture of the neighboring country. It is perhaps not too farfetched to think that the spectacle of the consumer society "across the Mekong" incites some to cross the river to go and "see" and "have fun" or "earn some money", to be able to afford the goods which the Thai media extols.

According to migrant flow specialists, this type of endemic migration progressively takes on a life of its own, the motivation of individuals (financial gain, family survival strategy, desire for adventure) taking on a secondary importance. It is migration by networks, meaning it is based on a number of interpersonal links between migrants, former migrants, and non-migrants at the points of departure and destination. When the number of migrants reaches a critical figure, the expansion of the networks reduces the costs and risks of the journey, which logically leads to an increase in the number of migrants and perpetuates a cycle which feeds on and in its turn reinforces the networks. Most of those who left obtained information from people in their village, from friends or family. Those family members who had already worked in Thailand take on the nature of important intermediaries between the youth and the potential employer. Thus, a report notes that very few minors (9 cases out of 103 questioned), either Burmese or Lao, obtained information from people they did not know (ibid., 29). Other studies confirm the well-organized nature of cross-border migration networks, with some areas and communities in Laos even having long-established links with employers or industries in Thailand.[11]

The existence and use of networks in fact seem to limit cases of coercive trafficking thanks to a system that not only can match offer and demand, but also keeps the families of those who have migrated informed about the fate of their relatives (ILO 2003, 25). In a study conducted in districts in Saravanne and Saiyabury provinces, there were few indications of coercion and most departures were voluntary. Likewise the study on the trafficking of children across the Thai-Burmese and Thai-Lao frontiers concluded that migrant child labor was much more common among the Burmese.

Besides numerous enthusiastic views expressed in the study *Listening to the Voice of Young People*, some, girls especially, expressed much more nuanced views. Sometimes the perception of risk is exacerbated: "We do not want to go and look for work in Thailand. We are afraid that there they will tear us to pieces. Their society is lawless and bad. People do exactly what they want"; or "They will sell us as prostitutes, then the police will catch us and put us in prison, and we are afraid someone will rape us." However excessive these remarks may appear, they doubtless reflect the fact that the reality of many Lao workers in Thailand is not all pleasant as some youths would have it. Articles in newspapers appear more and more regularly in Laos, giving the accounts of young people misled by middlemen and who find themselves badly treated once in Thailand.[12]

Table 6.1: Motives for youth emigration

		"Because others have left"	"Because he did not want to work in the fields"	"Because he wanted to see the world"	"Because he wanted to own nice things"	Personal problems	Problems with parents
Ethnolinguistic Group	Lao	44.2 %	44.2 %	36.4 %	28.8 %	42.3 %	28.8 %
	Burmese	52.6 %	15.8 %	0 %	0 %	15.8 %	15.8 %
	Ethnic Minorities	15.6 %	15.6 %	15.6 %	19.4 %	21.9 %	15.6 %
Place of Interview	Mae Sai	60 %	26.7 %	6.6 %	6.6 %	16.7 %	13.3 %
	Mae Sot	33.3 %	0 %	14.3 %	19 %	21.7 %	17.4 %
	Mukdahan	96.6 %	72.4 %	37.9 %	37.9 %	41.4 %	34.5 %
	Nong Khai	43.5 %	8.7 %	30.4 %	17.4 %	47.6 %	23.8 %
Sex	Boy	86.5 %	40.5 %	18.9 %	10.8 %	24.3 %	18.9 %
	Girl	47 %	24.2 %	24.2 %	25.75 %	34.8 %	24.2 %

Source: Wille 2000, 23, 25.

A study conducted in 1997 estimated about 60,000 migrants working in the sex trade in Thailand, mostly from Burma (in particular from the southeast of Shan state), but also many Lao, Chinese (from Yunnan) and Cambodians. There were also girls from ethnic minorities living in Thailand without the right of abode and Thai citizenship.[13]

According to the United Nations, the number of women and children victims of trafficking in Southeast Asia is estimated at about 225,000 people a year, out of a global figure of more than 700,000. Research in Thailand about foreign workers indicated that 30 per cent of the 156,423 prostitutes of a nationality other than Thai in 1997 were under 18 years old, numbering about 4,900 persons. Figures are not available for the Lao among them, though it is known that the frontier town of Nong Khai has the largest number of foreign prostitutes (Wille 2000, 63).

Thailand and Laos have been collaborating for a few years now in an attempt to regulate the flow of illegal Lao migrants to Thailand and to meet the demands of Thailand's economic need for (cheap) labor.[14] The Lao and Thai authorities signed in October 2002 a memorandum to deal with clandestine labor and the trafficking of women and children between the two countries. According to this agreement, the Thai authorities will grant a work permit only to Lao workers who sought work through a job agency in Laos. If their application is accepted, these migrants are immediately given work permits for four years, renewable at the end of three years from the date at the end of the validity of their permit (*The Nation*, October 19, 2002). This agreement merely gives governmental recognition to the reality existing for a long time, but it is also true that the Lao authorities are unwilling to admit that the migration of young Lao into Thailand is a vital outlet for a national economy which is too little developed to absorb the increasing numbers of people of working age in Laos. Given the economic and demographic changes in Laos, it is reasonable to think that the phenomenon of migration, in particular from frontier regions, will continue to increase.

Migration and AIDS

The AIDS virus was first detected in Laos in 1990 and the first person suffering from the illness was detected in 1992. According to results obtained from investigations in 1990 to June 2002, there are 1,137 sero-positive persons, 377 who have the illness and 191 who

The fate of youths having sought work in Thailand, as related in Lao newspapers

Eighteen year old Noy Saybounkong escaped and survived after being forced into slavery on a local fishing boat in Pattani province, Thailand. Three of his friends disappeared and one died, according to a report from the Lao Embassy in Bangkok.

Noy ran away after he was allowed to go for a walk when the fishing boat reached the pier to sell some fish. Three of his friends disappeared after a few months, and he still doesn't know where they are, or if they are alive or dead. He says he saw one other friend die.

For about five months since stepping onto the boat, the boys were forced to work hard without payment and they fished for almost 24 hours per day. If they didn't or could not work they would be abused and beaten.

He said that they didn't have a chance to escape because the boat only came to shore once a month.

Noy and his friends were local boys from Ban Donetiu, Palansay district, Savannakhet province. Without education or local employment they talked with a broker about working in Thailand for a good income. They decided to go and meet two brokers, Mr Hane and Mr Leung, in Ban Thapo in the province in order to ask for jobs.

He said that the broker immediately accepted them and they were sent across the Khemmarat border checkpoint in Savannakhet province through a Thai broker, Mr Thavisak in Ubol Ratchathani province, Thailand. The Thai broker took them to the local fishing boat owner.

The five boys were some of many Lao people who cross illegally to work in Thailand. The trafficking of humans across the border is a serious form of human rights abuse.

"Slave boy survives terror boat", *Vientiane Times*, October 15, 2002.

have died from it since 1990 (*Vientiane Times*, October 29, 2002). Only 13 provinces out of 18 in all have the equipment to test for the virus. According to United Nations' statistics, the number of persons (children and adults) infected in 2001 would be about 1,400 (of whom 1,300 are adults aged between 15 and 49, including 350 women), or a rate of infection around 0.05 per cent and 0.025 per cent for women.[15] The rate is around 0.9 per cent in high risk categories, specifically prostitutes (called "hostesses", *sao bolikan* in official terminology).

Bounyang Vorachith against human trafficking

Prime Minister Bounyang Vorachith has called for a clampdown on the trafficking of young Lao abroad to work in Thailand. Speaking at a January 24 conference on labor and social welfare, the PM said that brokers who facilitate the trade in Lao labor abroad should be suppressed.

Bounyang spoke to 60 officials from provincial labor and social welfare services and suggested they pay greater attention to the management of local and foreign labor through strict law enforcement. While praising the sector for its general positive developments, the PM noted that the majority of Lao labor is below standard and unable to compete with foreign workers. "Both the state and private sectors do not pour efforts into wide-scale development of labor skills and employers are not satisfied with the loose discipline of local labor," he said. The PM also pointed to the unsatisfactory placement of graduates of upper secondary schools, prevalent unemployment, and the increasing number of young Lao people who work illegally in Thailand. These problems need to be remedied urgently. He urged authorities concerned to push harder and go to the grassroots to work in the real situation. He also called on local authorities not to allow a rise in social evils.

"PM speaks out against cross-border trade in Lao youth," *Kao Pasason Lao* (KLP), January 28, 2003,

In an interview with the *Vientiane Times* newspaper (October 29, 2002), the deputy minister for public health, Bounkouang Phichit, indicated that the country's leaders, international organizations and NGOs in Laos, considered the basic reason for the spread of AIDS in the country was mobility of persons. In future years, this will increase with "numerous road building projects due to start in 2003". The deputy minister mentioned two highways, symbols of the new Laos, the east-west corridor and the northern China-Laos-Thailand highway, and repeated that there would be an increase in population movements inside and outside the country, which would lead to a greater vulnerability to the virus. He called on ASEAN members to unite their efforts to combat the pandemic and assist migrant workers. David Feingold, an expert in transnational phenomena, summarized the subject more trenchantly: "These highways will transport drugs, girls, and the virus".[16]

When a country opens up, it exposes its people to all kinds of problems which did not previously affect it. But no one can really measure as yet the impact of the development of the road structure in Laos on the propagation of AIDS. A study on the mobility of peoples and vulnerability to AIDS in the northern provinces of Laos (Chamberlain 2000, 12) shows that many roads in that part of the country need repair, are being built, or can only be used in the dry season. This is the case of highway No. 3 from Ban Houay Sai (Saiyabouri) to Boten (on the Chinese frontier), which is considered "sensitive" in the matter of the spread of the epidemic. An informative study carried out by two anthropologists from Macquarie University in collaboration with the Lao government-affiliated Institute of Cultural Research shows some worrying trends with regard to HIV transmission associated with a newly-upgraded road (completed in 2000) in the northwesternmost corner of Laos near the Chinese border. Their study focuses on social change along Route 17B, which runs from the port of Xiengkok on the Mekong River (bordering Burma) to the border with southwest China. Albeit small in size, the road links the economic powerhouse of China's Yunnan Province with the Mekong River and Burma, and beyond, Thailand. Route 17B also traverses two districts, Long and Sing, in Luang Namtha Province, which have been the main loci of its impacts on local livelihoods, both in the lowlands and highlands. The authors point out two major catalysts of social change in these zones: in-migration of Lao and foreign (mainly Chinese) workers and traders, and local resettlement of ethnic minority groups to the lowlands to be near the road. The combination of these two movements of people, within a rapidly changing environment characterized by socio-economic development policies, trade opportunities and market enterprise, has increased both supply and demand in the sex industry and, in consequence, the risk of HIV transmission (Lyttleton et al. 2004, 89). The study argues that improved road access weakens the social and geographical boundaries that until now have kept the level of HIV infection low in most parts of Laos; Route 17B has effectively dismantled some elements of these boundaries in the districts of Sing and Long over the past few years (ibid., 73).

It is possible to draw up a hierarchy between different types of mobility: migrations beyond national frontiers over a long distance, cross-frontier movements, and internal migrations between towns and the countryside. These do not run the same risks of infection. For example, migrants who go a long way away are often persons possessing an above-average educational level; it is not always the poorest who are the most mobile. Ronald Skeldon notes that analyzing different types of migration separately leads one to wrongly divide the same reality. Trans-frontier studies suggest the existence of isolated "hot spots", whereas frontier towns establish links within larger systems of mobility at different levels (local, trans-frontier, regional). In other words, the "hot spots" have to be linked to broader human networks where the risk of propagation of the virus can be dramatic (Skeldon 2000, 12). Most importantly, social habits and the type of interaction represent a determining factor in the risk of infection. Skeldon (idem) notes: "The critical area now, however, lies in those more local, community-based situations in which rural and some urban people find themselves."

The twin provincial towns of Savannakhet in southern Laos and Mukdahan in northeast Thailand, for example, present this configuration where mobile populations and a local population live side by side in a familiar daily environment. Partial studies suggest that migration between Savannakkhet and Mukdahan is not solely motivated by economic reasons but stems more generally from the social history of the frontier provinces of the two countries, whose peoples are very close culturally, even if today their standards of living are unequal. People move daily between the two provincial capitals. They have the same ethnic and linguistic backgrounds and were part of the same political entity before Siam ceded the east bank of the Mekong to France in 1893. Their lives are marked by the same calendar and the same Buddhist festivals. Family and socio-economic links naturally arose over the years, helped by the river, which, far from being an obstacle, represents a huge navigation bridge between the inhabitants of the two banks and a powerful motor for socialization. People go back and forth between these two towns for various reasons related to daily urban life: business, work, trade, trips, family visits, or taking part in festivals. It is precisely this proximity which constitutes a favorable terrain for less vigilant sexual activity. Figures seem to show that the number of women engaged in commercial sex have increased in Savannakhet. In 1999 they numbered about 900 in the whole province, against 300 in the province of Mukdahan (Lyttleton and Amorntip 2002, 515).

Although they have a sense of their shared ethnic origins, it would not be accurate to describe the relations between the peoples of Savannakhet and Mukdahan as based on a common identity. The cultural, religious and family ties between the people of these cities do not erase stark economic inequalities and dissimilar social realities, nor does it obliterate people's sense of national belonging. Prostitution and AIDS are phenomena that best reveal the two faces of the links that tie the "sister cities". The economic opening of the frontiers and the development of trading between the two countries, coupled with increased educational and employment opportunities for Thai women over the same period, have favored the increase in the number of Lao prostitutes in Thailand. Lao women, it appears, are filling the gap left by their Thai counterparts in the sex industry.

Besides these socio-economic factors, there are also cultural and psychological causes. In the eyes of Thai men who frequent prostitutes in Laos, Lao women have two contradictory characteristics which make them unique objects of desire: they are both different, "exotic", and familiar. The oft-repeated description is that of "novelty". Yet, this difference is counterbalanced by the very cultural and linguistic proximity, which provides a sense of security and intimacy—hence, the illusion of a "safe" relationship—to these men in their relations with Lao prostitutes, which they cannot seem to find with the Thai sex workers with whom interactions are more openly commercial. In other words, these Lao women are the "other" erotically, but they do not represent an "other" as a threatening vector of virus transmission. One can trust them, they belong to the same family, the same community (Lyttleton and Amorntip 2002, 515). But it is precisely this kind of immediacy that forms the most favorable environment for less vigilant sexual intercourse, and constitutes one of the causes of the upsurge of HIV infections in these border areas.

Trade and smuggling: the example of timber

Bilateral trade agreements and projects of growth triangles in Southeast Asia are translated into simplified procedures at frontiers and the construction of the infrastructure (roads, immigration and customs centers). These new procedures have greatly stimulated the circulation of goods and persons, but also the volume of undesirable transfers: smuggling, drug trafficking, illegal export of precious stones, animals, etc. The legal and illegal trade in these products is synonymous with a loss of revenue, but also runs the risk of increased instability at frontiers (see box), and implicitly in the challenges and capacity of states to promote order and security. This is no doubt why, during the second informal summit between Laos, Vietnam, and

Cambodia in January 2002 at Ho Chi Minh City, priority was given to "reinforcing social order and the security of frontier regions" as well as the "development of coordination in the struggle against terrorist acts in the countries" and "cooperation for containing international criminals and illegal trade".[17] Outside economic priorities, political stability and national security constituted the other concerns of the Cambodian, Lao, and Vietnamese leaders.

Contraband

Hundreds of smugglers attacked one of the frontier crossing points between Vietnam and Laos, wounding six Vietnamese customs officers while a large band of smugglers crossed the frontier. This attack took place on Tuesday, February 16, 2002 at the control post of Keo Neua. Attacks on customs officers and state security services at this frontier have become routine and the smugglers have used ever more violent methods to shift their lucrative loads.

Adapted from *Bangkok Post*, April 19, 2002

International trade, both legal and above all illegal, of timber is one of the most lucrative in the region. From the Philippines to Vietnam, companies armed with concessions and/or traffickers transport tons of tree trunks on trucks across the frontiers. The undressed timber is sometimes re-exported by boat to East Asia (Taiwan and Japan). Three major sites are particularly affected by unlicensed felling: the Thai-Burmese frontier, the island of Borneo (shared between Malaysia and Indonesia) and Cambodia (Tagliacozzo 2001, 262–63). In this last country the return to peace opened the way for the logging companies of nearby countries (Thailand, Malaysia and Vietnam), whose forest cover had been reduced to almost nothing by excessive logging and bombing (in the case of Vietnam). The prognostics are already alarming: in May 1998, the World Bank estimated that at the same rate of logging for 1997–98, all the workable forest in Cambodia would have disappeared by 2003 (Guerin et al. 2003, 237, 234), and it does indeed seem that this forecast is not far off the mark.

In 1940 it was estimated that forest covered 70 per cent of the surface of Laos. Twenty years later this cover had diminished to about 64 per cent (Bouahong 1994). Without doubt, American bombardments of the eastern part of Laos during the Second Indochinese War seriously and adversely affected the environment. Since the 1980s, however, one has to find the causes for deforestation elsewhere. As in Vietnam, Cambodia and Thailand, the Lao authorities blamed swidden agriculture for being the chief cause of deforestation. That it was held to be mostly done by so-called "minority" people probably strengthens the conviction among some that these agricultural practices are "primitive" and "destructive" (the correlation is often, indeed, systematically made). The area given over to rice cultivated by shifting cultivation techniques has diminished, going from 245,877 hectares in 1990 to 115,800 in 1999, or a reduction of more than half (out of a total surface cultivated area of 4.7 million hectares). It should be noted too that the people blamed for this have shown themselves capable of living in harmony with nature over centuries.

Deforestation has also been blamed on felling for domestic use (2.5 cubic meters per person per year), on forest fires, on land clearing in order to increase perennial cultivation (chiefly by peasants on the plains) and, of course, on the activities of logging companies. The total of these factors brought about a level of deforestation varying between 0.3 and 2 per cent per year in Laos. In 1989, an investigation declared that the forest area was 47 per cent, which indicated an annual rate of deforestation of 0.8 per cent. It could be very much higher.[18] The Mekong River Commission estimated the level of deforestation at around 54,047 hectares a year between 1993 and 1997. At this rate, some experts predict that the country's forest cover will fall below 35 per cent between now and 2020 (idem). A more recent estimate indicated cover at 40 per cent in 1997 (idem). This figure aroused governmental ire and it forbade the distribution of the report.[19] If fact, it is not certain that the report revealed the true extent of the problem, in the sense that the criteria for defining "forests" need to be questioned, as some organizations consider that one should include mere savannas (Durant 1994).

Over the last few years a group of civil servants and foreign workers in Laos admitted, on condition of remaining anonymous, their concern when faced with what is really a "liquidation" of the country's forest resources:

A random day's observation of the border crossing at Thakhek in mid-1999 revealed 69 truck-loads of logs, sawn wood and plywood waiting to cross by the ferry to Thailand. Local residents reported that this was not unusual in early and mid-1999. Similar scenes were seen in mid-1999 at various crossing points with both Thailand and Vietnam, including Chong Mek in Champassak province, Lao Bao in Savannakhet province and Nam Phao in Bolikhamsay province. Further evidence of a sell-off of forestry resources comes from Savannakhet province, where the logging quotas averaged 15,000 cubic meters per year for the five-year period before 1998–99, but in that year [1999], the quota jumped to over 100,000 cubic meters (Anon., op. cit., 58).

Demographic pressure and the transition to a market economy require rigorous control of natural resources (especially concerning land use). However, with the arrival of new entrepreneurs in the exploitation of forestry, people living on high land confront interests beyond their ken. From the mid-1990s the causes of deforestation have become more complex. The beginning of work on infrastructure programs (roads and above all hydroelectric dams), rural development and programs converting forests into permanent farmland (a total of 3,035,000 cubic meters of forest land was redesignated between 1990 and 1999, equivalent to 57.5 per cent of all sawn timber over the same period, that is 2,078,000 cubic meters in the period 1995–99), necessarily involve felling. In any case, one needs to remember that logging is poorly controlled.[20] In this fresh destructive impulse (some twenty years ago, only 6,000 cubic meters of sawn timber was exported each year: Walker 1999, 166) one has the impression that those involved in clearing the land have become scapegoats.

The construction of hydroelectric dams, projects for which have multiplied since the mid-1990s, is particularly destructive. The collection of water for the future reservoir requires the "clearance" of the area, by cutting down the forest and expropriating land. In some cases, felling has been carried out even before the construction of the

Table 6.2: Source of sawn timber, 1990–99

Periods	Exploitable Forests		Forest conversion*		Total Timber Cut (millions of m3)
	Millions of m^3	% of total	Millions of m3	% of total	
1990-1994	1,030	51.8	957	48.2	1,987
1995-1999	1,213	36.9	2,078	63.1	3,291
TOTAL	2,243	42.5	3,035	57.5	5,278

* Conversion of forest cover into non-forest areas: infrastructure development (roads and dams), agriculture (permanent cultivation) and rural development.

Source: World Bank, SIDA, Finnish MFA, LPDR Production Forestry Policy, Status and Issues for Dialogue, 11 June 2001, vol.1, Main report, p .8.

project has been approved, as for the Nam Theun II dam. In 1990, 13 years before the contract for the dam was signed, the Bolisat Khet Phudoi (the Mountainous Region Company), an army-controlled company, had already begun selective felling, before increasing it on a larger scale from 1994 (Hirsch 2002, 155). Environmental impact studies for the future dam no longer had to worry about the risks to fauna and flora, as these had already disappeared. Experts found themselves confronted with a fait accompli and could not raise solid objections to the continuation of the project.

Table 6.3: Volume of timber felled, 1965–99

Period	Industrially Felled Timber (m cu)
1965–69	391,662
1970–74	518,416
1975–79	505,624
1980–84	786,839
1985–89	911,000
1990–94	1,987,000
1995–99	3,291,869

Source: World Bank, SIDA, Finnish MFA, *LPDR Production Forestry Policy, Status and Issues for Dialogue*, 11 June 2001, vol.1, Main report, p. 7.

Revenue from wood product exports rose to US$98 million in 2001, exceeding their 1995 level (US$88 million) after peaking in 1998, when sales brought in more than US$115 million, much more than the clothing sector (US$70 million) and electricity (US$67 million) (ADB 2003). In 2003, timber came third in revenue generated, after electricity (US$106 million) and clothing (US$100 million), and well before coffee (US$5 million).

Some have suggested that between 1994 and 1998, the government collected only part of this revenue from traded timber. It is true that its contribution to the state budget has continually declined since the mid-1990s, going from 20 per cent of the total fiscal receipts in 1994–95 to 12 per cent in 2002, due to an inefficient tax collection system added to a reduction in the price of wood (World Bank et al. 2001, 10).

Table 6.4: Percentage of state budget derived from logging revenue

Year	1994–1995	1995–1996	1996–1997	1997–1998
Estimated percentage of royalties paid	49 %	37 %	66 %	32 %

Source: Anonymous, "Aspects of Forestry Management in the Lao People's Democratic Republic", in *Watershed*, 5/3, MarchJune 2000, 57–64.

Thai and Malaysian investment count for much in the timber trade and industry (ibid., 10). This strong economic presence of two regional countries in Laos through joint ventures and franchises to some degree buttressed the argument, particularly widespread before the 1997 crisis, about a new regional geopolitical environment in which Laos would play the hardly satisfying part of a peripheral resource for the rapidly industrializing Thai economy (Hirsch 1995, 254). While the important role of overseas investors is clear, the strategies of nationals involved, who also benefited from this very lucrative trade, were often overlooked in the analyses. To counter the geopolitical thesis of Thai hegemonistic domination over regional natural resources, Andrew Walker recalled that the monopoly of felling and sale of wood to sawmills was granted to companies created by the Lao military after 1994. This is an illustration of what he terms the "power of the periphery" (still in the official sphere, though).[21]

The system of quotas constitutes another important lever which in theory allows the government to control the export of timber. The annual volumes of sawn timber are in principle determined and controlled by the Prime Minister's Office on the basis of proposals from the Ministry of Agriculture and Forests, the Ministry of Trade and Tourism, and the industry sector, which in turn base their reports on information received from provincial authorities. The timber quotas follow two different analyses, one based on the sources (forests which can be exploited, zones of infrastructure development, conversion into agricultural land or rural development) and the other on the objectives (development of national industries and exports). They depend on three parameters: the potential of exploitable forest area, the requirements in natural resources of the industry, and the financial needs of the government. However, the agricultural and forestry officials in the provinces and districts have complained of a lack of coordination (World Bank et al. 2001, 19). Some suggest that the calculation of the level of the quotas is chiefly based on the needs

Table 6.5: Annual quotas and real felling carried out, 1994–99

Period	1994–1995	1995–1996	1996–1997	1997–1998	1998–1999
Quota (Thousands of m³)	610	712	680	540	714
Share of Dam Sites	71 %	66 %	72 %	54 %	31 %

Source: World Bank, SIDA, Finnish MFA, *LPDR Production Forestry Policy, Status and Issues for Dialogue* 11 June 2001, vol.1, Main report, p. 20.

of the Ministry of Finance for royalties and the production capacity of state forestry companies and sawmills, virtually without consulting the Ministry of Agriculture and Forests.

The final figure, furthermore, varies during the year if budgetary needs or the national industry requires it. In 1989–99 the quota was increased by 60 per cent, from 450,000 cubic meters (in October 1998) to 714,000 cubic meters (in October 1999) (ibid., 20). The allocation of quotas is also curious since they only supply Lao sawmills with a minute fraction of the work. As sawmills have proliferated in recent years it can be imagined that the volume of sawn wood they supply considerably exceeds the quotas granted them (Anon. 2000, 59). Illegal deforestation could even represent six times the quantity of legally felled timber (ibid., 64).

It should be mentioned here that in Laos the distinction between legal and illegal felling is very fluid. No published report explicitly states the quantity of "unauthorized" felling, as the report by the World Bank, the Swedish International Development Agency, and the Finnish Ministry of Foreign Affairs (2001, 40) notes:

> in fact, every logging activity in Lao PDR has been authorized by someone who has, or believes themselves to have, or claims to be able to act with authority. Although there are clear stipulations prohibiting logging in NBCAs [National Biodiversity Conservation Areas], for example, provincial authorities continue with authorizations. In some strict sense, practically all logging in Laos is illegal due to the lack of management plans.

Some see timber as the chief means by which the government pays its "war debts" to China and above all Vietnam. An article in the *Vientiane Times* (July 30–August 2, 1999) mentioned the allocation of 90,000 cubic meters in the 1998–99 quota to cover "the reimbursement of [national] debts". However, no quota of this nature appears in official documents and it is difficult to obtain more information about the subject.[22] Timber used as a form of payment, in particular in some sectors like construction (highways and dams) and the purchase of equipment items (dominated by Chinese and Vietnamese companies)[23] has been officially forbidden since 1999, but still occurs. At the beginning of 2003, the Lao government decided to forbid the export of uncut timber. But it is again difficult to know to what degree the rule will effectively contribute to slowing this trade, in a context marked by insufficient controls and porous frontiers.

A symbolic seizure?

A special team from the agriculture and forestry department, Vientiane municipality, on January 18 seized 99 cubic meters of illegal timber while it was being transported in convoy.

According to KPL [the Lao information agency], the timber was cut in the Sinsay Forestry Conservation Area, Park Nguem district, and was identified as the work of the Vietnamese IMEXCO company and Bolikhamsay International Import-Export Enterprise (BIIEE). Some 17 cubic meters were discovered in a convoy of two trucks and the other 82 cubic meters in a separate convoy of 12 trucks.

According to the team, 12 trucks with 95 logs or 82 cubic meters belonged to the BIIEE. Vietnamese IMEXCO and BIIEE have a quota to exploit timber at Ban Xienglaina and Ban None, Park Nguem district, to open the way for electricity supplies to the villages.

Local people living in the area of the national Pou Khao Khua conservation park recently tipped off the authorities about the presence of the two companies conducting illegal logging.

According to inspectors, most of the logs were transported 800 meters from the national Phou Khao Khua conservation park. The inspectors also discovered various types of logs that were cut down on the Pou Khao Khua mountain range and some hidden in the bush for later transportation.

Officials say that if the national park continues to be pillaged by illegal loggers, it will be completely destroyed within 10 years and because it is a source of many of the nation's rivers, it will impact on the local ecosystem.

Source: Souphanphine Mixab, "Logging companies endanger future of conservation area", *Vientiane Times*, January 31, 2003

Notes

1   This tendency is found among universities: Jonathan Rigg and Randi Jerndal stated, in the mid-1990s that "Laos is no longer an isolated remote corner" (Rigg and Jerndal 1996, 145).

2   For a solid and condensed analysis of relations between China and Southeast Asia, see Stuart-Fox 2003.

3   For details on the caravan trade between south China and the northeast part of Southeast Asia, see the excellent article by Andrew Forbes (1987).

4   In this section, the statistics chiefly come from an unpublished report by the United States Embassy in Laos.

5   In spite of their attractions, Luang Prabang (the former royal capital) and Champassak (the temple of Vat Phou, the Khone falls, the Bolovens plateau, etc) only attract 5 per cent of tourists, and Xieng Khouang (with the Plain of Jars and Hmong villages) only 2 per cent. See Bounthavy and Taillard 2000, 126.

6   They even apparently constituted an important factor in the formation of states. See Dovert in Dovert and de Tréglodé 2004, 1–27 and 31–113.

7   The Committee for the Administration of Illegal Migrant Workers in Thailand, www.chula.ac.th/ARCM/registration2001. htm (26 October 2002).

8   UN Institutional Project on Human Trafficking in the sub-Mekong region, "Overview paper of human trafficking in the Mekong sub-region", Vientiane, February 25, 2002. According to the provincial authorities, more than 15,000 young people sought employment in Thailand in 1995 (Samrane 2000).

9   ILO/IPEC [International Programme on the Elimination of Child Labour]. 2003. "Lao PDR—Preliminary Assessment of Illegal Labour Migration and Trafficking in Children and Women for Labour Exploitation", Bangkok, ILO, p. 19.

10 A foreign consultant working in Laos for several years, interviewed by Vatthana Pholsena, Vientiane, May 23, 2002.

11 The report explains: "In the villages visited [in Kammuane Province, Central Laos], the communities reported that there was an organized cross-border trafficking network. Each village had two mobile phones provided by the traffickers in Thailand, for villagers to make appointments and arrangements with them. Anyone wanting to cross into Thailand could call the traffickers who would tell them where to cross the border so they can be picked up on the Thai side and sent directly to a destination pre-arranged by the traffickers." (ILO 2003, 25).

12 Even if the Lao authorities recognize there is the lack of work for young people, they are beginning to denounce illegal employment and the movement of labor to Thailand. See "Prime Minister speaks out against cross-border trade in Lao youth". *Kao Pasason Lao*, January 28, 2003.

13 Kritaya Archavanitkul and Pornsuk Gertsawong, "Migrant women from Thailand's neighbouring countries in Thailand's commercial sex trade", Institute of Population and Social Research, Mahidol University, Nakhon Pathom (Thailand), 1997 (in Thai), quoted in Stern, n.d., p. 30.

14 An example of such collaboration is the agreement signed in September 2005 between representatives of the Thai construction industry and the Thai Ministry

of Labour to import workers from Cambodia and Laos (10,000 workers) for Thailand's construction sector (*Financial Times*, Thai Press Reports, September 19, 2005).

15   UNAIDS, "Report on the Global HIV/AIDS epidemic 2002," in Table of country-specific HIV/AIDS estimates and data, end 2001, www.unaids.org, p. 1 (October 24, 2002).

16   "Can Laos keep Aids at bay?", BBC Asia Today, October 30, 2002, http://news.bbc.co.uk/1/hi/world/asia-pacific/2372307.stm (October 31, 2002).

17   "Voice of Vietnam", January 26, 2002, *BBC Monitoring International Reports*, January 29, 2002.

18   World Bank, Swedish International Development Agency (SIDA) and the Finnish Ministry of Foreign Affairs, June 11, 2001. *Lao People's Democratic Republic Production Forestry Policy: Status and Issues for Dialogue*, vol. 1, Main Report.

19   Anonymous. "Aspects of Forestry Management in the Lao People's Democratic Republic". *Watershed*, 5(3), March–June 2000.

20   For the first three factors, see World Bank et al. 2001, op. cit., p. 6.

21   This monopoly was granted to three state enterprises all under complete or partial control of the Lao army: the Bolisat Phattana Khet Phudoi, the company for the development of agriculture and integrated forests (better known under the name DAFI), and the company for general services and imports-exports for agricultural and forest development. For more details about these companies, see Walker 1999, 178–180.

22   A foreign diplomat, returning from a recent journey to the Lao-Vietnamese frontier in Khammouane province, reported the passage of an impressive number of trucks loaded with tree trunks going to the port of Danang. They could have been intended to export to Japan (Vientiane, April 2002, personal communication, Vatthana Pholsena).

23   The province of Phongsaly, the most northerly in Laos, shares a common frontier with China, and was granted a supplementary quota of 20,000 cubic meters for the fiscal year 1998–99, in the framework of an agreed deal with a Chinese company granted a road construction project. The total quota for the province of Phongsaly was barely 1,500 cubic meters the previous year. See Southavilay and Castren 1999, 26.

7 SOCIETY AND CULTURE: CONTINUITIES AND CHANGES

Moral, cultural and economic discipline

The "New Socialist Man"

From 1975, the regime undertook the construction of a new socialist state and to this end began a policy of transforming the masses, a fundamental and indispensable step in the vision of the new leaders. Recourse to the general population was logical, as, for want of economic, financial and technical advantages, the country had abundant if poorly qualified labor. In consequence, the human factor very early played a crucial role in the economic and social development strategies. In a country where the vast majority of the people lived in the countryside, the peasantry found themselves, whether they liked it or not, in the front line of the revolution. The objective was to achieve a social homogeneity which would transcend individual identities, which in the case of Laos meant ethnic and religious identities. The state was in a hurry to create a new class which would serve to facilitate the transitory period to socialism. In 1978 an accelerated program of agricultural collectivization was therefore launched. Badly conceived and poorly prepared, it had disastrous results, with a huge decline in production accompanied by strong resentment among the peasantry which, though, was not at first hostile to the new regime.

In the minds of the leaders, rural collectivization should bring everything one desired for in an underdeveloped country: economic and alimentary independence. The success of the program would also have constituted proof of the superiority of the socialist mode of production and, by this, reinforced the legitimacy of the regime. The collectivization program was not therefore just seen as a means to achieve economic security, but also as an instrument of political consolidation. Growth in production leading to better living conditions would have contributed to social assurance and reduced the risks of destabilization. Lastly, the leaders hoped that collectivization would give birth to the "New Socialist Man". In other words, the collective plan came from a desire to profoundly change a rural country.

From 1976 a campaign of ideological and cultural renewal was launched. It had high ambitions: the moral, spiritual and cultural life of the people was to be transformed in order to create "new individuals" with high revolutionary morality.[1] The new culture should be based on love of socialism and on patriotism. As Grant Evans observed, the idea of the "New Socialist Man" of the 1970s and the beginning of the 1980s reflected conservative values, inspired by the cultural standards of the ethnic Lao people (Evans 1996, 4).

Contemporary culture

Although the project of creating "New Socialist Men" progressively disappeared, the regime did not abandon the idea of "remodeling" people, a desire expressed in this reworked concept of "contemporary culture". A quarter of a century after the beginning of this campaign of moral, intellectual and cultural rectification, the conservative rhetoric aiming to discipline attitudes and behavior remains.

Notice from the Ministry of Information and Culture concerning activities in bars and discotheques

It is stipulated that playing and singing foreign songs is forbidden. Nevertheless, these activities are tolerated if they constitute no more than 20 per cent of all songs sung during any one evening. The dress worn is also subject to official rules. Men are absolutely forbidden to wear "eccentric" clothes, to have long hair or to wear earrings. Women are not allowed to wear trousers, skirts or any style of clothing contrary to Lao traditions. These amusement places must be sufficiently well lit for people to be seen because "a low level of lighting can lead to indecent acts."

Source: Adapted from Notice No. 848, October 14, 1999, in *Vientiane Mail*, March 21, 2000.

But moral and cultural conservatism would not have been enough, according to the government, to preserve Lao society from "untoward" outside influences and the propagation of "anti-social behavior". Economic discipline is also required. The burden of dependence is another evil which the authorities try to attenuate by multiplying injunctions to "self-sufficiency" and "autonomy", all the more so since the financial and economic crisis of 1997 considerably affected the country's economy. The "unbridled consumerism" and "considerable expenditure on [foreign] luxury products and services" were condemned in the press. Questions were raised about the purchasing power of some citizens who had acquired imported goods illegally (*Kaosan Pathet Lao*, April 24, 2002). Official discourse drew on the social conscience because "the Lao people must stand on their own two feet" and each citizen should "question the dress he wears, what he eats, drinks, and uses" (*Vientiane Times*, January 31, 2003). Economic liberalization and opening to the outside world since the end of the 1980s helped a renewal of political, moral and cultural control. And, confronted with the sometimes brutal changes, one can now see in the people and in the state, a certain renewal of traditions accompanying the desire for economic autarky and a resurgence in religion.

The crisis of modernity and the Buddhist renewal

In 1998 a curious article devoted to Buddhism was published by the Department of Religious Affairs of the Lao Front for National Construction (FLCN), the leading mass organization the country. The argument was fairly heterodox and differentiated quite clearly the official rhetoric concerning religion, since its authors had evidently no intention to emphasize the common points between Buddhism and socialist ideas, but rather to explain the spiritual force of religion in general and Buddhism in particular. The article evoked the role of Buddhism in various domains, such as education and art. Still more surprising, it explained the political role exerted in the past by Buddhist monks as advisors to the sovereign. It was also recalled that countries should be governed according to Buddhist principles and commandments. The conclusion maintained that progress in science and technology would never reduce the importance of religion:

In our time, some think that religion will disappear when men have reached a sufficient degree of understanding of science and technology. But the opposite is occurring. The more the sciences and technologies develop, the more men feel the need to achieve spiritual and moral happiness. In other words, their thirst for superior values in morality, justice, humanity, civilization and peace increases. In sum, as long as religion keeps its role as a moral refuge for humanity, we can be sure that religious principles and virtues will forever remain in men's hearts.[2]

This assertion openly contradicts the socialist project of the previous decades which dreamed of "industrial man" guided by dialectic materialism.

The resurgence of Buddhism in official ideology, parallel to a decline in secular nationalism in Southeast Asia, is the sign, according to some, of a "crisis of authority" and a "legitimacy deficit" for those in power (Keyes, Hardacre and Kendall 1994). Asian states adopted the European model without really criticizing it. In their search for modernization and desirous of building a "modern" nation-state in the twentieth century, the leaders sought to construct a lay identity in the heart of society henceforth guided by rational norms and principles, which were supposed to supplant traditional religious beliefs. But this imported modernity did not produce the desired community spirit. On the contrary it produced a social *anomie*. This "crisis of authority" would have led to a social and cultural void which would have replaced this religious renewal, this "spiritual essence" that the modern nation-state is incapable of producing.[3]

The fact is that the religion has returned to the political scene. To prevent this phenomenon eroding or threatening their authority, Thai, Burmese, Lao and Cambodian leaders linked themselves to spiritual renewal in order to better control its popular manifestations, but also and above all to profit by this source of legitimacy. In Laos, the Buddhist clergy, the *Sangha*, remains under the control of the authorities, while having regained its popularity, maintaining close links with the past (Stuart-Fox 1999, 168). Institutionalized Buddhism has seen its role evolve in recent years, but this is nothing compared to the infinitely more solid and ancient alliance between the state, the monarch and religion in Thailand.

In reality, besides ostentatious gestures, heavily promoted in the media, at popular Buddhist festivals, the Lao government also tries to present a secular image of Buddhism. An article in the French language newspaper *Le Rénovateur* (May 18, 2000), spent time explaining the relations between Buddhism and Marxism in Laos, maintaining that the religion and the ideology, far from opposing each other, complemented and reinforced each other. The only difference between Buddhism and Marxism is simply a question of degree: Marxism tries to build a happy and egalitarian society, while Buddhism seeks to aid individual well-being. The article notes, however, that neither the old regime nor the Lao communist movement correctly used Buddhism; the old regime was corrupt, and the present one does not understand it. But under the aegis of the party, Buddhism has removed its superstitious elements and at the same time the party has recognized its past errors. Thanks to this new purified and rehabilitated form, Buddhism has become more popular than ever.

The attempt to show the compatibility between Buddhism and Marxism is not new in Laos. Since 1975, after the communist victory, political seminars taught Buddhist monks that the two systems possessed identical principles, "essential equality between individuals", and followed the same fundamental aim—seeking well-being through the elimination of suffering (Stuart-Fox 1999, 161). The government also desired to convert the monks into teachers of the socialist program, in particular in the countryside. But the convergence of the two philosophies never culminated in the creation of a Buddhist socialist doctrine, as was the case in Burma. The party did not envisage the suppression of religion, but the authorities worked until the end of the 1980s to limit and control the *Sangha*, criticizing practices considered as wasteful (such as donations to temples) or forcing monks to attend political seminars. The objective was to submit the *Sangha* to the will of the state (Evans 1993, 135).

Today the That Luang festival, celebrated each year in November in Vientiane, certainly offers one of the most striking examples of the symbiosis between Buddhism and socialism. The religious monument built in the sixteenth century by King Setthathirat as a centrifugal symbol of the kingdom of Lan Xang has replaced the hammer and sickle as a national emblem. The Lao leaders are happy to be seen in front of the cameras making offerings throughout the That Luang festival, which has become over the years a showcase of national culture such as it is conceived and paraded by the regime, that is, a mixture of socialist discourse, Buddhist rituals, and demonstrations of "multi-ethnic" culture.[4]

A changing urban society

One of the rare sociological studies conducted in Laos was organized by the Australian anthropologist, Grant Evans, in collaboration with the cultural research institute attached to the Ministry of Information and Culture.

The program, called the Vientiane Social Survey Project, took a sample of 2,003 households scattered through six districts of Vientiane municipality. In its introduction, the report explained the origins of the project by the awareness of the Lao government of the emergence of "new social problems, especially among the youth" caused by the "economic opening of the country [and] Lao society to the outside world."

These same preoccupations troubling the authorities were at the origin of another report, *Listening to the Voice of Young People*, published in 1998 specifically targeting Lao youth.

In order to better understand Lao youth

Lao PDR is a country in economic transition and, as a result, is experiencing rapid social changes which present tremendous challenges to both policy makers and communities. The government is particularly aware that these changes are affecting young people both in the large towns and to a lesser (but increasing) extent in the villages. There is acknowledgement among both parents and decision-makers that values amongst the young are changing and that this might affect young people's sense of Lao identity.

Rapid economic change is bringing benefits to the country but is also affecting societal patterns. The effects of these changes can be seen in neighboring countries where rural-urban migration, juvenile crime and drug abuse are increasing. Young people with increased expectations have become disaffected and feel marginalized. Here in Lao PDR some of these problems are beginning to emerge and be noted in urban areas. The Lao People's Revolutionary Youth and the Lao Women's Union are particularly aware that there is an emerging problem with glue sniffing and increasing reports of young people being involved with delinquent behavior. There is also an awareness that little is known about the patterns of migrant labor and trafficking but a sense that this may be increasing. Identifying appropriate responses to meet these changing needs requires coordinated efforts and an understanding by adults and policy makers of what young people think, and feel about the changes that are occurring.

Source: *Listening to the Voice of Young People* (UNICEF 1998, 1)

A meeting was held in October 2002 at the Ministry of Information and Culture to discuss the means of "preserving social order, culture, and the country's traditions" endangered, it was said, by the anarchic development of amusement places in the urban areas (such as beer gardens and nightclubs) which encouraged gambling, alcohol abuse, drug taking, theft, prostitution, and violence.

"Cultural management" consequently became a priority for the Lao authorities who wanted to combat this "dangerous urban culture".[5]

Looking to the outside

The perception Lao youths might have of the outside world is interestingly analyzed in the report of the *Vientiane Social Survey Project*. The replies to questions give a simplified perspective of the image the Lao living in urban society have of "abroad", and also of their own country in relation to the rest of the world.

Persons were asked to name the country they would most like to visit if they had the chance (Table 7.1). The United States came out tops by far, with 32 per cent of replies, followed by Japan (14.4 per cent), and Thailand in third position (10 per cent). Thailand preceded the communist regimes of China (7.1 per cent), and Vietnam (5.9 per cent). Neither Russia nor France were mentioned.

However, when the questionnaire touched on the subject of a model for "modern" society, the replies were rather different (Table 7.2): more than one-third (37.2 per cent) replied Laos itself; Japan came in second place (26.3 per cent), followed by Singapore (19.9 per cent). The group of "modern developed countries" only received 5.7 per cent of the votes; the other countries named (including the United States) individually totaled less than 5 per cent of the replies. Thailand and Vietnam only achieved an extremely low score of 0.1 per cent. As for China, it did not appear in the list, unlike France (3.4 per cent).

Young Lao therefore seem to have a relatively positive image of their society since rather more than one-third of those questioned would like the country to remain as it is, even though the socio-economic indicators are very low. This result contradicts the currently aired view that ordinary Lao consider their country backward. If the Lao are concerned about the poverty of their country and its low level of economic and technological development, they are nonetheless proud of their culture and their way of life.

Table 7.1: "If you could visit another country,
which would you choose?"

Pays	%
United States	32.0
Japan	14.4
Anywhere	11.4
Thailand	10.0
Nowhere	9.2
China	7.1
Vietnam	5.9
Australia	3.4
Canada	1.4
England	1.3
Switzerland	1.3
Singapore	1.2
Germany	0.9
India	0.4
Hungary	0.1

Source: Cultural Research Institute, in collaboration with Grant Evans, *1997–98 Vientiane Social Survey Project*, Ministry of Information and Culture, Vientiane, 1998, question 42 (1,910 replies).

The good image of Japan and Singapore can doubtless be explained by analogy. They seem to be examples of economic success, but have neither sacrificed their values nor their culture. On this count, the capitalist system is not rejected, although the United States and France hardly appear. The socialist model seems to have lost its attraction (Vietnam hardly appears and China not at all). The lack of enthusiasm for Thailand is hardly surprising, given bilateral relations and inter-community difficulties.

While the Western model arouses little enthusiasm in Laos, it is hardly criticized. The country is therefore different from Malaysia, Indonesia or even Thailand, where the discussion about the bad effects of the West occurs regularly. Hardly 2.3 per cent of those questioned considered foreign influence on young people responsible for juvenile delinquency: 28 per cent blamed the lack of parental control (Cultural Research Institute 1998, questions 44 and 57B).

Table 7.2: "Which society would you most like to be taken
as a model for Laos?"

Country	%
Laos	37.2
Japan	26.3
Singapore	19.9
"A Developed Country"	5.7
United States	3.6
France	3.4
Russia	2.8
Hungary	0.7
Thailand	0.1
Cambodia	0.1
Vietnam	0.1

Source: Cultural Research Institute, in collaboration with Grant Evans, *1997–1998 Vientiane Social Survey Project*, Ministry of Information and Culture, Vientiane, 1998, question 43 (1,867 replies).

In the other study of youth, a quarter of informants considered—some without conviction—that foreigners in general brought "bad things" into the country. Those who expressed this opinion lived mostly in the capital and so were exposed to a foreign presence. Among the "bad things" they cited were glue sniffing, drug taking and cigarette smoking, as well as AIDS or Western culture. One often heard: "The foreigners come into our country for their own interests" and sometimes even "Not one of them is really good" (this was the view of a schoolboy in the age group 16–18). Most people questioned, however, considered the difficulties that Laos experiences were not caused by foreigners. They invoked even the "necessity to communicate with other countries", one of them adding, in order not "to remain backward" (another schoolboy of the same age group). Some also recognized that "foreigners brought useful things like factories which sustain the economy".[6]

Tourists in general also aroused ambivalent comments. While some noted they "are purveyors of bad Western culture, pornographic films, illnesses [especially AIDS] or they push Lao to take drugs", others considered that they "brought money into the country" and stimulated "investment, the supply of equipment and technical know-how" (ibid., 84).

But the foreigner is not the only acculturation factor covered in the *Vientiane Social Survey Project*. Political and social systems have notably contributed to disorient youth. Those born after 1976 (that is, more than half the population) have grown up in a period when, in addition to surveillance and political control were added the breakdown of society and loss of reference points. During the first fifteen years of the new regime, "the city [of Vientiane] and its inhabitants suffered from a social and cultural malaise" (idem 29). The Lao authorities only recently and progressively encouraged the return to cultural practices which constituted part of daily life under the old regime. The parents and grandparents of those now between 15 and 25 years old have not been able to teach the young people the traditions as their own parents formerly did, for fear that they were incompatible with the ideological line of those in power.

A two-speed society

The inability of socialism to generate social and economic progress has caused the growth of a feeling of frustration and disillusion which is increasing. For part of the population, cynicism and nihilism have replaced confidence and hope (Cultural Research Institute 1998, 29). To this disenchantment can be added a feeling of injustice when confronted with increasing inequality in Vientiane. Some people have material goods to show off (designer clothes and motorcycles among the young, cars and/or more and more luxurious houses for adults), which can only add to the dissatisfaction of the majority.

This resentment concerning a society seen as increasingly divided is reflected in the different viewpoints expressed in the Vientiane Social Survey Project: "an accident was caused by a drunken motorcyclist traveling at speed. However, he came out of it free and without a police report at the police station where he was taken, thanks to his connections with well-known and influential families." As many as 71.1 per cent of interviewees confirmed having heard similar stories. Moreover 76.6 per cent of interviewees considered that "there is corruption now in Vientiane". Nearly half of those questioned (44.2 per cent) considered that "egoism, covetousness, and greed" motivate this corruption; others think rather that some indulge in it in order to obtain a recognized social status (15.6 per cent) or to remedy economic difficulties and/or a low salary (12.6 per cent).

The feeling of a two-speed society is beginning to emerge and can also be seen in the question concerning young delinquents, whom 29

Table 7.3: "In your view, what is the reason for corruption?"

Reason	%
Egoism/covetousness/greed	44.2
Desire for social status	15.6
Economic problems/low salary	12.1
Some positions make corruption easy	9.9
It has always been like this/ anyone who can do it will do so	5.5
Absence of strict control or laws	5.5
No view expressed	4.0
Want causes corruption	3.2

Source: Cultural Research Institute, in collaboration with Grant Evans, *1997–98 Vientiane Social Survey Project*, Ministry of Information and Culture, Vientiane, 1998, question 65 (1,287 replies).

Table 7.4: "In your view, who do you think tends to have delinquent children in Laos?"

	%
All groups	53.5
Rich and powerful families	20.9
Poor people	5.8
Soldiers and policemen	4.2
Don't know	7.5

Source: Cultural Research Institute, in collaboration with Grant Evans, *1997–98 Vientiane Social Survey Project*, Ministry of Information and Culture, Vientiane, 1998, question 57A (1,968 replies).

per cent saw as coming from "rich and powerful families", 5.8 per cent considering that they came from the least fortunate levels of society. Although the creation of a socialist republic in December 1975 was meant to rid the country of the ancient regime, many attributes of the former society have survived. The political culture in Laos depends to a great extent on personal and family relationships and patronage. New families with access to the highest levels of power have emerged, while older clans have resurfaced, and clients of lower status search them out as patrons. Under the former regime, powerful clans were constituted by aristocratic families; today, powerful figures (usually LPRP members) fulfill the same role.[7]

Juvenile delinquency

The most serious social problems identified in this inquiry are: theft (cited by 22.1 per cent of fathers and 19.8 per cent of mothers), alcohol and fights among youths (30.8 per cent and 25.9 per cent), unemployment, economic problems and waste (20.1 per cent and 25.9 per cent).

In *Listening to the Voice of Young People*, delinquency was generally invoked and gave rise to widely divergent replies. Young people were asked to indicate the three most dangerous evils for their society (Table 7.6). Glue sniffing clearly came out tops; it was cited by 49.3 per cent of persons questioned (in first, second and third position). Theft came next with 38.8 per cent of replies, followed by fights, also very worrying (30.9 per cent). In the replies of the youths, there was no mention of unemployment, lack of respect for adults and traditions, foreign influence or even failing in one's studies. These were problems cited by their elders in the framework of the other inquiry.

It should be pointed out that in a preceding section of *Listening to the Voice of Young People*, glue sniffing, as well as betting and gambling could also be considered in a positive light, as mere "relaxing activities", particularly among young boys. Gambling, they said, allows one to "win money", and glue sniffing facilitates socialization and meeting friends; it is done rather like drinking alcohol.

The *Vientiane Social Survey Project* questionnaire was also concerned with the reasons which caused youths to turn into delinquents. The lack of parental control was the first reason given (28.8 per cent), followed by the desire of the youths themselves (22.2 per cent), socio-economic changes and the collapse of moral values (11.2 per cent). External influences came next (7.6 per sent) ahead of a poor education (6 per cent), unemployment (5.6 per cent) and the desire for money and a better social status (5.2 per cent). According to the inquiry, antisocial behavior is more linked to changes concerning family structure and social life than economic problems (lack of money, desire for money or status, unemployment).

In Laos, as in other countries experiencing rapid change, parents feel they are less and less able to transmit knowledge and practices which would allow their children to find their place in society. The children frequent other places for socializing, like school groups, groups of friends, workmates or the army, where they acquire as much, if not more, experience. The weakening of the parental role is

Table 7.5: "In your view, what are the most serious problems facing society?" (Parents' responses)

	Father %	Mother %
Theft	22.1	19.8
Alcohol/fights among youths	20.8	25.9
Unemployment, economic problems and waste	17.9	16.9
The poor condition of the roads	11.4	10.5
Prostitution	9.0	9.5
Glue sniffing/drug taking	7.2	7.4
Not respecting the rules of the road	3.9	3.7
The young people imitating foreign manners	2.4	2.1
Betting and gambling	2.1	1.8
Lack of respect for elders/hierarchy/tradition	1.7	1.3
Scholastic failure/education	0.9	0.7
Lying	0.5	0.3

Source: Cultural Research Institute, in collaboration with Grant Evans, 1997–98, Vientiane Social Survey Project, Ministry of Information and Culture, Vientiane, 1998, question 44 (1,650 replies from fathers, 1,190 replies from mothers).

Table 7.6: "According to you, what are the most serious problems facing society?" (Youth responses)

	TOTAL %	Girls %	Boys %
Glue sniffing	49.3	50.3	48.4
Theft	38.8	35.3	41.9
Fights	30.9	25.7	35.5
Housebreaking	22.9	22.8	23.1
Betting	22.1	19.2	24.7
Drug taking	18.1	16.2	19.9
Prostitution	17.8	22.2	14.0
Rape	17.3	27.5	8.1
Alcohol	14.4	19.8	9.7
Road Accidents	8.2	10.2	6.5

Source: UNICEF. 1998. Listening to the Voice of Young People. Vientiane: UNICEF, p. 69

therefore at the center of the problem. It is in any case seen as a latent source of social tensions and misunderstanding between generations (Culture Research Institute 1998, 32).

Losing Lao values and traditions?

On the adults' side, the concern revealed in the *Vientiane Social Survey Project* is not surprising: 60.5 per cent of parents considered that young people today did not respect traditions (Table 7.7). Their manner of dressing came first (46.9 per cent), followed by lack of respect for elders and the hierarchy (22 per cent), alcohol, fights, gambling, and outings (12 per cent); everything which indicated a loss of values. Not going to the temple or not respecting Buddhism came next (8.4 per cent) and foreign influence came way down, figuring in only 3.6 per cent of the replies.

Adults are therefore above all shocked by the way some young people dress. But the youth, questioned in *Listening to the Voice of the Young People*, expressed a more complex—sometimes even ambiguous—opinion about this question, in particular the silk skirt (*sin*), which undoubtedly remains one of the symbols of traditional Lao identity in general and of Lao women in particular. If the *sin* is one of the five "least liked items of clothing" (for more than a quarter of the girls), it is also considered one of the items of clothing

Table 7.7: "According to you, what are the most serious infractions of present-day youth?"

	%
Not following traditional dress codes	46.9
Not respecting elders or the hierarchy	22.0
Drinking alcohol/having fun/fighting/betting	12.0
Not going to the temple or not respecting Buddhism	8.4
Adhering to superstitions	3.8
Being influenced by the West	3.6
Having long hair	1.5
Speaking in a vulgar fashion	1.2
Stealing	0.6

Source: Culture Research Institute 1998, Question 41 (1,362 replies)

"the most liked" by not less than 95.8 per cent of the same persons. Some therefore strangely replied that they liked and did not like the *sin*, hence accounting for a percentage which goes well beyond 100. All the girls preferred trousers though, and almost all like the blouse (95.8 per cent). On the other hand, miniskirts, bell-bottom trousers and shorts are only moderately liked (respectively 56, 39.2 and 35 per cent of the girls said they did not like to wear them) (UNICEF 1998, 39).

The fact that the question concerns the basically trivial question of clothes entails some modification in the image of a disoriented society facing socio-economic and cultural change. The changes are undeniable, and particularly visible in the urban environment; but Lao society, or more exactly the Lao ethnic and cultural components seem a long way from being upset or fragmenting socially. The general population, including the younger generation, seems to preserve its cultural cohesion. In 1998, 78 per cent of families questioned in the Vientiane Social Survey Project observed at least some of the chief Lao traditions. Likewise, Buddhism remains largely adhered to, at least in the municipality of Vientiane where, for example, 84 per cent of married women questioned had made offerings to the Buddha the previous week, usually in a temple in their neighborhood. Lastly, the pollsters asked young people what being Lao meant. The long list which followed presents a picturesque and heterogenous image, probably influenced both by official propaganda and stereotypes of Lao identity. In any case, it appears that as in any other country, the youth have, in spite of everything, retained some cultural references, even if they are in evolution.

What does "being Lao" mean?

- To be Lao is to wear the *sin*, but also jeans; to wear jewels, but also the traditional scarf (*paa bieng*);

- To be Lao is to eat grilled fish, fermented fish sauce, grilled eggs, sticky rice, boiled chicken and papaya salad;

- To be Lao is to take part in giving alms to monks, in *baci* ceremonies, in the *bong fai* fireworks festival, in boat racing, in the That Luang festival, in the Lao new year, and the rice harvest festival, in the inauguration of new buildings, etc.

Source: UNICEF. 1998. *Listening to the Voice of Young People*. Vientiane: UNICEF, p. 50.

Youth and their future

According to the 1995 census, the number of people in the workforce (over 10 years old) was 69 per cent of the population (71.23 per cent female and 69.5 per cent male). For a essentially rural country like Laos, the agricultural sector counted most of the active persons, 84.7 per cent, services only 10.3 per cent, and industry just 3.3 per cent. An analysis of the unemployment level in the country probably better reflects market reality in the so-called modern sectors.

A Lao journalist's views on the future for youth in the country

These days finding a job with a good income can be difficult for Lao youth coming from the countryside. Without proper knowledge, many rural youth have to accept any job offered by brokers and never know what their lives will be like after accepting a job.

It can be noticed that a great deal of young girls from rural towns flock into the cities with hopes of finding a job with good money. Some girls come to work for garment factories. Some are still eagerly looking for a job. Many work as servants at wealthy people's houses and some beautiful girls are tricked into prostitution at entertainment facilities especially in Vientiane municipality, says Sinathone, writer for *Pathet Lao* daily.

More sadly, what is most depressing and embarrassing is that Lao girls have been lured to work across the Mekong river. Such a phenomenon should not occur in this era of globalization.

Finding jobs, says the writer, is a task of the Ministry of Labor and Social Welfare or the Lao Women's Union or the Lao Youth Union or Lao Trade Union. But in reality these organizations have not shown much of a performance in the public's eyes.

More than 20,000 students who finished their studies this year, as well as a number of primary students who have no chance to continue their studies at high school level and those who did not manage to finish primary school have to struggle for a job according to their destiny.

These people understandably don't want to do farming because of the low income and heat in a paddy field. They prefer to find work indoors in exchange for a salary or wage without having to stand in a farm and bear the heat. Some girls decide to become prostitutes or a minor wife of wealthy men, known locally as *mia noi*, because they don't have a job and they want to be able to feed themselves, not because they are starving for sex as some people think.

The writer believes that there are some ways out of this situation, if many sectors concerned as mentioned above join hands together especially in the task of finding jobs for young girls in order to prevent them from being lured to work across the Mekong River.

The writer declined to elaborate on how to deal with the problem in the near future, for fear of being told that he was a "show off". However, he writes, there are some ways out.

For example, these days construction work from is available private enterprises. However, most of the work is apparently done by foreign laborers. This money will flow out of the country without going through banks and without tax to the government.

The writer says he used to study the reasons why youth find it hard to find work after finishing high school. Some people are ready to work in construction if the state sector has the management and protection regulations in order to ensure that employers don't take advantage of them and disallow foreign labor to compete for a wage. The youth labor association should be established into a group or unit in each village, each district, and each province to search for work.

After that, the writer thinks Lao youth will not risk their lives and lose face and honor working across the Mekong River.

Souphaphone Mixab, *Pathet Lao*, January 6, 2003 (unedited).

If unemployment is only 2.4 per cent (in 1995) on the national level, the towns have markedly higher levels: 16–18 per cent in Paksé (chief town of Champassak province in the south), 12–18 per cent in Savannakhet; 8–11 per cent in Vientiane, Luang Prabang and Thakhek. The Asian crisis of 1997 made the problem worse (Bounthavy and Taillard 2000, 60–61, 68). While some managed to obtain a scholarship from a foreign government to study in Australia, Japan, Singapore, the United States or France, most young people have few opportunities after completing their studies. Migration to the towns or other provinces represents an uncertain option.[8] Crossing the Mekong to try one's luck in Thailand therefore remains a temptation.

National and regional integration of ethnic minorities

The introduction of the market economy in Laos and regional integration also affect people living in the highlands, comprising very largely ethnic groups referred to as minorities. Two direct consequences of the transformation of the economic scene affect the environment and ways of life of these peoples: on the one hand, there are the rural development policies, in particular relocation programs; and on the other, industrial deforestation. The people in the uplands are today caught in a trap between two inverse dynamics: relocation which makes them come down from the mountains, and the arrival of people from the plains and elsewhere, who inevitably, increase the competition for a space seen by those who do not (yet) live there as empty or underutilized.

Ethnic minorities: composition and policies

Laos is a country of great linguistic and cultural diversity. The different ethnic groups are either autochthonous—the speakers of the Mon-Khmer languages are generally recognized as being the first inhabitants of the land—or, more recent immigrants, those belonging to the Tai group of languages (of which Lao is one), Hmong-Mien (originally from southeast China) and Sino-Tibetan. Conventionally, the Lao population is divided into four general categories, each corresponding to an ethno-linguistic family. According to the most recent national census in 1995, the Tai-Lao family comprised 66 per cent of the population, the Austro-Asiatic family 23 per cent (divided between Mon-Khmer ethnic groups, 22.7 per cent, and Viet-Muong, 0.3 per cent), and Tibeto-Burman and Sino-Tibetan (or Hmong-Mien) families, respectively 2.7 and 78.4 per cent. The remaining 1 per cent is composed of "others", people of Vietnamese, Chinese or Indian origins, mostly living in the towns.

According to the system of classification and the criteria selected for distinguishing them, the number of ethnic groups in Laos can vary considerably. Whilst the most recent official ethnic classification of the population (1995) counted 47 groups, another study listed 236 (Chamberlain, Alton and Crisfield 1995). The Lao ethnic group does not constitute a overwhelming majority (52 per cent of the population in the 1995 census), unlike neighboring countries (Vietnam, China, Cambodia) where the dominant ethnic groups

Whose nation?

Citizenship is granted to all the inhabitants of the country without discrimination.[9] The constitution adopted in 1991 indicted that the "pluri-ethnic Lao people" are at the heart of the origins of the Lao nation and the center of the work in constructing the motherland.[10] Article 8, the only one explicitly devoted to ethnic minorities, stipulates that the state "applies a policy of solidarity and equality to the different ethnic groups [which have] the right to preserve and develop their good traditions, customs and cultures, as well as those of the nation." The article also emphasizes that "any act of division and discrimination among ethnic groups is forbidden". Lastly the state undertakes to ensure "all measures destined to develop and continually improve the economic and social levels of all the ethnic groups."[11]

No special state or treatment (economic, political or cultural) is envisaged for ethnic minorities. During the Vietnam War or after 1975, the authorities never promised to create autonomous zones exclusively set aside for certain peoples, unlike what happened in Vietnam for a time or in China.[12] The principle remains to integrate minorities into a single political, economic and social fabric.

politically and economically (respectively the Kinh, the Han and the Khmer) also dominate demographically. The Lao live mostly in the plains of the Mekong valley. Other lowland regions are inhabited by ethnic groups close to those speaking various Tai-Lao tongues. The Austro-Asiatic speakers are found throughout the country, both in the plains and the highlands. The Tibeto-Burman speakers are recent arrivals from southwest China, and the Hmong-Mien speakers live mostly in the northern mountains.

The fine image of a people both united and varied promoted by the authorities has inspired metaphors celebrating at the same time solidarity, community, and diversity. One of the best known is that of the garden, notably taken up by Kaysone Phomvihane, the late president of the Lao People's Democratic Republic: "Each ethnic group possesses a good and beautiful culture and belongs to the national Lao community [*vongkhananyat heng saat lao*], like all the kinds of flowers which thrive in a colorful garden and give off different scents."[13]

Followed by three words *heng saat lao* (equivalents of the adjective "national"), *vongkhananyat* is a term frequently used in official discourse and texts to designate the Lao nation. Strictly speaking, it can translate as "family circle". Each person has therefore his or her place in the family. More precisely, each has his place, since, continuing the analogy, everyone knows his place in the family, unlike a garden which is cultivated according to a precise arrangement. This hierarchy can be clearly seen in a work published by the Ministry of Information and Culture: "The large communities [the diverse ethnic groups] are unified and the population is united; this is the population of Laos, [and] the linguistic community of the Tai-Lao is the kernel of this multi-ethnic structure" (Ministry of Information and Culture 1996, 13).

Influenced by the writings of Marx, Lenin and Stalin, the authorities praise cultural diversity and a multi-ethnic society in which all ethnic groups have the same privileges.[14] The celebration of diversity itself is moreover controlled and selective, since, as in Vietnam, the authorities are careful to make the distinction between "good" customs and "bad" traditions. Among the first are songs, costumes or crafts. Among the second, some, like hunting or swidden farming, are called "destructive of the environment", others are seen as "retarded" such as certain religious rites which involve animal sacrifice.

A way of life and an environment ever more threatened

Movements of people are far from being a recent phenomenon: for centuries, certain ethno-linguistic groups practiced swidden farming which obliged them to move around. Others migrated to seek seasonal work. In the nineteenth century, with the French colonial presence came the first attempt to "fix" these peoples. The twentieth century wars caused dramatic displacements of thousands of families caught up in the different wars. After 1975 it was no longer exceptional circumstances that led to the relocation of people, but a deliberate government policy, written into its plans for rural development. The minorities today have to confront the desire of the authorities to settle them in the villages of the plains specifically designated to accommodate them.

Relocation is one of the government's responses to the conflict perceived between swidden farming and the interests of the state in the exploitation of forest resources. The forests constitute, as noted, an importance source of foreign exchange, thanks to timber exports. The increasing pressure on the groups living in the highlands is closely linked to the question of the management of natural resources

Swidden versus settlement

The general term for swidden cultivation in Lao is *het hay* but in fact there are two main types of swidden cultivation, rotational (*hay moun vian*) and pioneering (*hay leuan loy*), and it is only the latter which is environmentally potentially destructive. Both can be conducted in terms of human needs and if the density of population is low. Rotational agriculture with a fallow period of 10 to 20 years can even produce larger crops than irrigated rice fields in the plain. Densities of 12 to 15 persons per square kilometer allow this type of cultivation to be conducted, in that they do not lead to permanent degradation of the soil and allow the forest to grow again. It would seem that the difficulties linked to the government policy of stabilizing swidden cultivation are based in part on terminology. In practice the government adopts two different attitudes in relation to rotational and pioneering cultivation. Whilst itinerant cultivation is clearly seen as potentially destructive to the environment (this is the term used by the government in its five year plan and development strategy) and should be eliminated, rotational swiddens are more or less tolerated. The government seems to recognize that the objective of stopping swiddens in Laos is impossible. Consequently, the term "stabilization" has replaced "eradication" and the rotated fields are currently classified as "gardens" (*souan*) for non-rice cultivation.[15]

Even if these agricultural practices are tolerated, the authorities do not grant them the same status as perennial production, which should include inundated rice fields, a construction site (for a homestead), and a garden (according to instruction 02822/AF of August 1996 concerning the allocation of land and forests for their management and use, published by the Ministry of Agriculture and Forests). The difficulties of applying the policy of stabilization of swiddens seems to be induced by difficulties in communication between agricultural and forestry specialists at the center and those in the provinces and districts.

Sources: adapted from Chazée 1994; Lao PDR, *Socioeconomic development strategy from now until 2020.* Vientiane, 2001; World Bank, *Poverty reduction fund project, Lao PDR social assessment report*, Vientiane 2002.

which are being depleted, a phenomenon for which the ethnic minorities are in fact hardly responsible. This policy of relocation is officially legitimized in the name of the necessity of national development and collective good.

Another less explicit objective is the settlement policy: of integrating the minorities into the national culture by having these people leave their original habitats and forcing them to adopt a radically different way of life; in other words, to conform to the traditions of the Lao ethnic group. In fact, the displacement of the inhabitants of the forests to the lowlands requires them to change, among other things, their agricultural practices. In observing this, the anthropologists Carol and Randall Ireson noted that "relocation becomes another means by which ethnic minorities are being 'developed' and turned into Lao" (C. and R. Ireson 1991, 935–36). Because of the frequent divisions in the same village between those for and those against relocation, it is often difficult to know if migration to the plains is voluntary or not. It is nevertheless evident that these displacements systematically bring with them changes which are in part covered in a report published by UNESCO in 1997:

> Resettlement appears to be one of the major causes of cultural rupture in Laos today. It might be said that this is the best way of integrating ethnic groups into the national culture, without which they will remain marginalized. It must be remembered however that the Lao national culture is a multi-ethnic culture, as the government has constantly reaffirmed right up to the last international conference organized by UNESCO on this theme, and that it is necessary to safeguard the cultural heritage of the diverse ethnic groups which form the Lao nation.

Integration is occurring naturally across the young generations. Ideally this can be left to happen gradually, without confronting particular traditions or beliefs. What must be avoided is any dramatic change to the cultural symbolic fabric as this can always engender movements of a protest nature able to endanger integration itself (Goudineau 1997, vol. 1, 36).

Deforestation, the development of permanent cultivated land and the building of infrastructure have increased since the 1990s, causing a reduction in the natural habitat of the people living in the forests. More generally, forest products represent a very important source of food and income for rural people. A household of five

> ### The forest as a resource
>
> Non-wood forest products are chiefly food (game, fish, bamboo shoots, fruits, green vegetables and honey), fibers (*khem* grass used to make brooms, and mulberry bushes), spices and medicinal products (cardamom and malva nuts), substances used in chemical industries and perfumes (benzoin, *peuak meuak*, resins, oleoresins, *kisi*, and *lamxay*), bamboo, rattan and fuel.
>
> Source: World Bank, SIDA, Finnish MFA 2001, 11.

persons consumes an average of 280 dollars a year in forest products (including wood for cooking and heating). Consequently 800,000 families, or 4 million people, would consume the equivalent to 224 million dollars per year in forest products, or 40 per cent of the total revenue of the households and the equivalent of 20 per cent of the GDP. In addition, forest products contribute to nearly 55 per cent of the revenues of families living in villages close to the forests (World Bank (World Bank et al. 2002, 11).

Notes

1   Kaysone Phomvihane, *Rapport sur la situation de l'an dernier, les orientations et les tâches révolutionnaires dans la nouvelle étape et les orientations pour 1977*, quoted in Stuart-Fox 1982, 106.

2   Department of Religion, "Religion and society", in *Lao Sang Sat*, 1(1), 1998, p. 43.

3   Keyes, Hardacre and Kendall 1994, 5. In *Cultural Crisis and Social Memory*, Shigeharu Tanabe and Keyes (2002, 6) explain the crisis of modernity in Thai and Lao societies by the rupture between the present and the past, which created great tension between the desire for abstract rationality and the desire to resist in order to retain particular values and elements which formerly constituted certitudes.

4   It is however worthwhile pointing out that this popular religious fervor, taken up by the authorities, only effects a part of the population: more than one-third of the inhabitants of Laos are not Buddhist according to official statistics (National Statistics Center, Vientiane 1997).

5   Mongkhol Vongsamang, "Deputy Minister warns of dangerous urban culture", *Vientiane Times*, October 11, 2002.

6   Union of Lao Youth, Union of Lao Women, Ministry of Education, Vientiane municipality, and Save the Children (Great Britain) 1998, 45.

7   The adoption of the counter-corruption law by the National Assembly in 2005 nevertheless seems to indicate the government's willingness to improve the

management of the country's institutions and their credibility in the eyes of the international community.

8   We know of young unemployed graduates from Vientiane who went to live for a time in Sekong (a province in the southeast of the country, bordering Vietnam) to work, one in a garage, another with a transport company.

9   This is not the case, for example, in Thailand, where numerous ethnic minorities, in particular in the north, have uncertain status or live illegally, although some of them have lived in the country for several generations.

10 *Constitution of the Lao People's Democratic Republic.* Supreme People's Assembly, Vientiane, 1991, 1.

11 Ibid., 4–5.

12 Hardy and Nguyen 2004, 383–423.

13 Ministry of Information and Culture, *Pavatsaat lao* (History of Laos), Vientiane 1996, vol.1, 13. The Vietnamese authorities use the same metaphor. See Salemink, 2000, 136.

14 For more details on the influence of Marxist-Leninist theories and the writings of Stalin on the question of minorities and nationalism, see Pholsena 2002, 175–197.

15 Some three-quarters of all rice fields are cultivated combining many kinds of rice with a great variety of different plants, like maize, vegetables, fruit trees, tobacco, gourds, etc.

8 CONCLUSION

At the beginning of the twenty-first century, Laos is no longer a buffer state. Military and ideological confrontations have been replaced by economic competition. Former enemies Thailand and Vietnam, who exerted their rivalry over the territory of the Lao kingdoms and then an independent Laos, have ended their confrontation by proxy. Unimaginable ten years previously, the integration into ASEAN of Vietnam, Laos, and Cambodia in the second half of the 1990s truly marked the end of the Cold War and lastingly removed the threat of inter-state conflict in Southeast Asia. But, in finding its place among the community of nations, Laos also realized its economic weakness and its technological backwardness. The "cocoon" of the socialist bloc has been broken. Development has become an insatiable goal which makes the state realize the precarious nature of its current situation. A work in Lao published in 2002 entitled *Pathet Lao Nay Sankhom Nanasat* (Laos in the International Community) clearly expressed this feeling of vulnerability when confronted with regional integration:

> Isolation is no longer possible. But necessary coexistence is infused with competition of an intellectual order. Such a country with a better education system, and therefore of more competent people, will have the possibility of developing and strengthening itself in the economic and social spheres, of becoming richer and carving out a niche for itself in the world. On the contrary, an incompetent country will be relegated to the group of poor and backward states. This is the situation which confronts Laos today, and we believe that no Lao is satisfied when confronted with the humiliating position of his nation, a position accorded it by the international community. But we are forced to accept it, if only temporarily, or otherwise we will find ourselves

removed from the list of those aided, which will make us still poorer…
Let us accept this position, and work so that it is not prolonged, to the
point where it becomes a persistent habit and turns us into perpetual
assistance seekers. (Bounkhong Soukhavath, Vientiane, 2002, 157)

The end of the socialist economy and the beginning of regional
integration have made the Lao confront a harsh reality. The opening
of economic frontiers though should present new opportunities.
The gamble of placing Laos in the heart of the region as a trade
crossroads has an historical basis as well as being a current project.
At the beginning of the nineteenth century, the French colonial
authorities hoped to link Laos to Vietnam by a land bridge and find
a river route to China thanks to the Mekong. They failed. Today, the
project of the Lao government and funding agencies, particularly the
Asian Development Bank, of transforming the country into a regional
economic pivot has yet to become a reality. The economic and
technological means though are much greater and the determination
of neighboring counties, notably China and Thailand, to strengthen
economic integration in the region is stronger. It remains to be seen
if a genuine opening up of Laos will assist its inhabitants as much as
the economies of neighboring states.

Whatever happens, cross-frontier trade has not materialized with
the construction of highways and signing of trade agreements. The
routes taken by Chinese caravans existed before the arrival of the
Europeans. Boats continue to make daily crossings between the two
banks of the Mekong and traders daily cross the Lao-Chinese and
Lao-Thai frontiers with little state control. The history of trade
and smuggling cannot be separated from the desire of the political
authorities, whether they are proto-states, sultanates or kingdoms,
from controlling and extracting profit from these movements. The
volume and types of products imported and exported have changed,
though, as well as the routes used by traffickers.

The permeability of their frontiers has also contributed
to an increase of drug trafficking. Illicit products (particularly
methamphetamines or *yaa baa*) are believed to transit through
northern Laos from the northern border areas of Myanmar, destined
for the Thai market. States have renewed their policies of combating
illegal trade; they connect with and collaborate with the others,
with international organizations such as Interpol and the ILO (see
Tagliacozzo 2002, 193–200). GMS governments are thus facing a
highly challenging, if not paradoxical, task of trying to bring about

a borderless economic space but also retain the imperative of border control.

Migration to Thailand, though it is not a new phenomenon, begins to raise concerns. For a long time, Lao political authorities have sought to dissuade these movements into Thailand. But while a program of information coupled with a policy of preventing the trafficking of youths is favored by the government and foreign donors, the attraction of the big neighbor remains strong.

Migration does not constitute, though, a one-way flow. Located in the heart of Southeast Asia, Laos occupies a unique geographical position. In the north of the country, small provincial hamlets now receive a continual flow of Chinese, to the point where Chinese has become a lingua franca almost to the same degree as Lao. The capital and the towns of the south receive an increasing number of Vietnamese migrants, while the cultural and economic influence of Thailand dominates the urban areas and along the Mekong. Future studies on the regional integration of Laos should analyze these phenomena, which are essential to projecting the sociological evolution of the country.

Another factor to be investigated, essential for those who wish to better understand the country's future, concerns the people of Lao origin living abroad. After 1975 and the seizure of power by the communists, hundreds of thousands of Lao took refuge in neighboring countries, and elsewhere. This exodus lasted until the end of the 1980s and has led to the emergence of transnational Lao networks. As proof of the influence of the Lao diaspora, transfers of money from abroad now constitute the chief income of households in Laos. The return of some of this diaspora, mostly for very brief visits, is little documented. Will it play a major role in the economic take-off of the country? What will be the attitude of the government to the Lao exiles? Shall we see a reconciliation and healing of a fraught past or a continuation of the separation between the two "Laos" which time and space have forever distanced? These questions are not without importance in the matter of regional integration. But if for a country of some five million inhabitants the challenges to be faced are not without risks, they also bring real opportunities.

CHRONOLOGY

1353
Foundation of the kingdom of Lan Chang (or Lan Xang) by Prince Fa Ngum

Lan Xang stretches from Yunnan in the north to Sombor in the south, from Khorat in the west to Lao Bao in the east

1374–1427
Reigns of Sam Sen Thai (1374–1417) and Lan Kham Deng (1416–27), son and grandson of Fa Ngum. The death of Lan Kham Deng causes a serious succession crisis

1442–1479
After a decade of trouble, the last son of Sam Sen Thai, Saiya Chakkaphat, seizes power and reestablishes stability in the kingdom

1448
Muang Phuan (present-day Xieng Khouang in northeast Laos) becomes an administrative entity of the *Dai Viet*

1501–1571
The descendants of Saiya Chakkaphat succeed to the throne and restore the kingdom devastated by war

1548–1571
In the reign of Setthathirat, the That Luang was built (1566–67) in Vientiane, today it is the national symbol of Laos

1560
Setthathirat, to challenge the Burmese, allies himself with the kingdom of Ayutthaya

1563
First Burmese invasion
The capital is moved from Luang Prabang to Vientiane

1574
Lan Xang becomes a vassal of the kingdom of Pegu (Burma), marking the beginning of a troubled period

1638–1695
King Sourinyavongsa reorganizes the administration and the army. The first Europeans arrive. The Dutch trader Van Wuystoff and the Jesuit Fr Leria are both struck by the prosperity of the kingdom

1707–1713
Succession troubles; the kingdom of Lan Xang is split into three principalities: Luang Prabang, Vientiane, and Champassak

1767
Destruction of Ayutthaya, the Siamese capital, by the Burmese, allied to the kingdom of the principality of Vientiane

1771
Wars between the principality of Luang Prabang (allied to Siam) and that of Vientiane, which receives Burmese military support

1768–1782
Restitution and expansion of Siamese territory by General Taksin, made king

1778
Capture of the prince of Champassak by the Siamese

1779
Capture of Vientiane by the Siamese

Submission to the Siamese by Luang Prabang; all three Lao principalities become Siamese vassals

1802
Advent of the Nguyen dynasty in Vietnam (with Hue as capital)

1827–1828
Revolt of Chao Anou, Lao ruler of Vientiane, against Siamese authority. Vientiane is sacked and its inhabitants deported to the Siamese plateau of Khorat. Annexation of the principalities of Vientiane and Champassak by Siam

1828
Luang Prabang recognizes the suzerainty of Hue

1834–1847
The Siamese policy of deporting the Lao people on the east bank of
the Mekong and the Plain of Jars, in reaction to the incorporation into
Vietnamese administration of the region of Hua Phan (in the northeast of
present-day Laos) as far as present-day southern Laos

1847
Treaty signed between Bangkok and Hué establishing co-suzerainty over
the Plain of Jars. Relocation of thousands of Phuan families to the Khorat
plateau and inland areas of the kingdom of Siam

1859–1862
Military intervention of France in south Vietnam

1861
The French explorer Henri Mouhot dies near Luang Prabang

1862
Treaty of Saigon between France and Vietnam: creation of Cochinchina

1863
Treaty establishing the French protectorate over Cambodia

1866–1868
French expedition up the Mekong, led by Ernest Doudard de Lagrée and
Francis Garnier, who explore the river from Saigon to Yunnan in the hope
of finding a navigable route to China from Vietnamese territory under
French control

1887
Formation of the Indochinese Union under French domination; it includes
Tonkin, Annam, Cochinchina, and Cambodia

Attack on Laung Prabang by Ho and Tai bandits, led by Deo Van Tri, head
of the Tai grouping of Sipsong Chau Tai (the twelve Tai principalities).
The king of Luang Prabang, accompanied by Auguste Pavie, first French
Vice-Consul and future Governor of Laos (1893–95), flee the capital which
is sacked

1893
October 3. Treaty between France and Siam, the latter ceding all the
territory on the left bank of the Mekong to France.

1899

Administrative reorganization of Laos and nomination of a "Résident Supérieur" (High Commissioner)

1904

Anglo-French agreement: Britain and France signed the Entente Cordiale in which they recognized their respective zones of influence in the region

1907

Definitive Franco-Siamese treaty, delimiting and making official the present frontiers of Laos

End of 19th century–1937

Numerous revolts by mountain peoples, indicating popular discontent with the colonial administration

1930

Foundation of the Indochinese Communist Party, giving a fresh impulse to the anti-colonial struggle in Vietnam and the rest of Indochina

1936

Foundation of the Lao section of the Indochinese Communist Party

1940 (December)–1941 (January)

Brief military conflict between France and Thailand; loss to Siam (given Japanese support) of French territory on the right bank of the Mekong

1941

Agreement between Prince Savang Vatthana and the "Resident Supérieur": the kingdom of Luang Prabang is given the same status as Cambodia and Annam (north-central Vietnam)

Administrative modernization of the Lao kingdom

1945

March. Internment of civil and military members of the French colonial administration by Japanese forces

April 8. The Japanese grant Laos independence

August 27. Capitulation of Japan followed by the return of French troops

August–September. Coalition of Lao nationalists and formation of the Lao Issara (Free Lao), led by Prince Phetsarath

September 2. Ho Chi Minh declares Vietnam's independence

September 15. Proclamation of unity and independence of Laos by Prince Phetsarath

October 10. Prince Phetsarath is relieved of his functions as Prime Minister and Viceroy

October 12. Creation of a provisional government by the Lao Issara

1946
March 27. Battle of Takhek (southern Laos) between French troops and Lao-Vietnamese forces, who suffered a severe defeat

April–May. Retaking of Laos by the French

May 11. Adoption of a constitution; Laos becomes a monarchy in the French Union

Exodus, with difficulty, of Lao Issara government to Thailand

November. Thailand returns the right bank territories of the Mekong to France

1949
February. Souphanouvong forms his own political movement, the Progressive Organization of the Lao people, in the north of Laos

July 19. General Franco-Laos convention. The country becomes independent within the French Union

October 25. The Lao Issara government in exile dissolves itself. The Lao nationalists split up: moderate members of the government led by Prince Souvanna Phouma, Katay Don Sasorith and Phanya Khammao, return to Laos. Prince Phetsarath rejects the amnesty and remains in exile in Thailand, while Prince Souphanouvong definitely broke with Lao Issara and continues his alliance with the north Vietnamese communist movement, the Viet Minh.

Proclamation of the Chinese People's Republic by Mao Zedong

1950
February 6. Transfer of power to Royal Lao Government. France retains its right to extraterritoriality in the administration of justice and the control of internal security (the secret police)

March 22. Formation of the Royal Lao Army

August 13–15. Creation of the Neo Lao Issara (Free Laos Front) and the government of resistance of the Pathet Lao (Lao country) during a congress of the people's representatives in north Vietnam

1951
August. Souvanna Phouma forms his first government

1953

Offensive in Laos of troops of the Neo Lao Issara, together with Vietnamese "volunteers". The present provinces of Hua Phan and Phongsaly in the northeast pass under the control of Pathet Lao

October 22. Total independence of Laos

1954

May 7. French defeat at Dien Bien Phu, Vietnam

July 20. Signing of the Geneva agreements and withdrawal of France from Indochina. Vietnam is divided at the 17th parallel. The independence and territorial integrity of Laos and Cambodia are reaffirmed. Pathet Lao forces are allowed to regroup in the provinces of Hua Phan and Phongsaly while waiting for future integration into the political system of the country

September 8. Creation of the Southeast Asia Treaty Organization, a defensive alliance under American aegis; Laos is included

1955

Beginning of American aid to Laos; 120 million dollars are granted between 1955 and 1958, four times the amount spent by France in the preceding eight years

March 22. Creation of the Lao Communist Party, the Phak Pasason Lao (Party of the Lao People)

April. Afro-Asian meeting at Bandung. Souvanna Phouma reaffirms the neutrality of Laos (supported by France and China, but rejected by the United States and the Democratic Republic of Vietnam)

December 14. Laos is admitted to the United Nations

1956

March. Souvanna Phouma forms his second government

June. Agreement in Vientiane stipulating the formation of a bipartisan government of national unity with two members of the Neo Lao Haksat (formerly Neo Lao Issara), the demobilization of Pathet Lao troops (except for two regiments) and additional elections on May 4, 1958

November 18. Souphanouvong returns to Prince Savang Vatthana, representative of King Sisavangvong, the provinces of Hua Phan and Phongsaly. The civilian elements of the Pathet Lao are integrated into the Royal Lao Government

November 19. Formation of a provisional government of national unity: Souphanouvong and Phoumi Vongvichit are named respectively Ministers of Planning, and Religion and Fine Arts

1958

May 4. Success of Neo Lao Haksat in legislative elections. The American government suspends its aid, on which the country largely relies, which causes Souvanna Phouma to resign

June 10. Creation of the Committee for the Defense of National Interests, supported by the United States

August 18. Phoui Sananikone, anti-communist and pro-American, becomes prime minister in the new government. Neo Lao Haksat receives no ministerial post

The North Vietnamese communists begin their strategy of reunification by armed force; southern Laos becomes a strategic region as a point of entry into South Vietnam. The (communist) Democratic Republic of Vietnam stations two battalions of its regular troops there. Strong protests from Vientiane

1959

January. Phoui Sananikone obtains full authority to fight "against subversive elements"

July–August. The ministers Souphanouvong and Phoumi Vongvichit are arrested

October 15. Death of Prince Phetsarath

October 29. Death of King Sisavang Vatthana; his son Savang Vatthana succeeds

December 24. An attempted coup d'état by the extreme right fails, leading to the resignation of Phoui Sananikone

1960

May. Escape of Neo Lao Haksat elected representatives

April. The right wins fraudulent national elections

August 8. Neutralist coup d'état by Captain Kong Le. Half the army (led by General Phoumi Nosavan, pro-American) sets up in Savannakhet an anti-coup d'état committee including Prince Chao Boun Oum (a descendant of the kings of Champassak)

August 16. Souvanna Phouma forms his third government

Mid-November. Most of the armed forces of the Royal Lao Government support General Phoumi

December 16. After two weeks of violent clashes in Vientiane between the forces of Phoumi Nosavan, who has the support of the United States and Thailand, and the troops of Kong Le, the general seizes the capital

Kong Le and his troops retreat to the Plain of Jars, where Pathet Lao forces join them. This alliance strengthens the communists

End of December. Ten of thousands of Hmong are evacuated under the supervision of General Vang Pao, the only Hmong officer in the Royal Lao Army, from the Plain of Jars. Until the end of the war, the United States maintains a huge air bridge to supply food, medicines and arms to these Hmong

The Hmong guerillas led by Vang Pao attack communist forces and gain strength, thanks to massive logistic and financial aid from the CIA

1961

January 1. A neutralist government is installed at Khang Khai in the Plain of Jars, directed by Quinim Pholsena, minister of the interior and head of the neutralist left-leaning party Santiphab (Peace Party). Souvanna Phouma in exile in Cambodia

March 23. The president of the United States, John F. Kennedy, announces his "strong and unreserved" support for a "neutral and independent" Laos.

April 24. Favorable reaction from the Soviet Union which, with Great Britain, invited twelve countries (Laos and its six neighboring states, members of the Surveillance and Control Committee (CISC or CIC), Canada, Poland and India, to participate in an "International Conference on the Lao question" which is to be held after the ceasefire in Laos

May 16. Geneva conference, following a ceasefire

June. The three Lao factions meet in Zurich. Their representatives, the three princes Souvanna Phouma (for the neutralist government of Khang Kay), Boun Oum (right-wing government in Vientiane) and Souphanouvong (Neo Lao Haksat, communist) agree on the formation of a government of tripartite national union with Souvanna Phouma as prime minister

1962

May. Battle of Namtha (northwest Laos); the Royal Lao Army collapses when confronted with the Pathet Lao

June 23. Formation of a second coalition government: Souvanna Phouma is Prime Minister and Minister of Defense; Souphanouvong Deputy Prime Minister and Minister of the Economy; Phoumi is another Deputy Prime Minister and Minister of Finance. The government of national union meets in Vientiane

July 23. The second round of Geneva agreements reaffirms the integrity and neutrality of Laos, forbidding foreign bases on its territory and setting a timetable for the withdrawal of foreign troops

1963

A series of provocations and assassinations in Vientiane; a climate of terror and insecurity prevails

April. The staff of the Neo Lao Haksat leave Vientiane. The capital is in the hands of the right and General Phoumi Nosavan; pressure on the government

1964

Souvanna Phouma, now convinced of the indispensable support by Vietnamese troops for the Pathet Lao, authorizes the United States, supporting the guerillas of General Vang Pao, to freely use Lao airspace

Intensive American bombardments in the northeast and east of Laos on areas under Neo Lao Haksat control. The Thai army, allied to the Americans, fights in northeast Laos

1968

Fall of Nam Bac, the last pro-American outpost, to the north of Luang Prabang

1969

Escalation of the war: 200 to 300 daily American air sorties to the north and south of Laos from bases located in northeast Thailand

150,000 refugees escape the bombardments in the north

Popular consultative conference organized by Neo Lao Haksat. The party asserts itself over the royal government and the army

1971

Pathet Lao and Vietnamese troops take over the provinces of Attopeu and Saravane, as well as the Bolovens plateau

1973

January 23. Paris agreements between the United States and the Democratic Republic of Vietnam

February. Ceasefire in Laos; end of American bombardments

February 21. Agreement in Vientiane to confirm the establishment of a third coalition government

March. End of the retreat of American forces in South Vietnam

1975

April 17 and 30. Fall of Phnom Penh and Saigon

December 2. Abolition of the monarchy in Laos and proclamation of the

Lao People's Democratic Republic. Kaysone Phomvihane, Communist Party secretary-general, becomes prime minister of the new regime

The exodus from the country is unprecedented; between 1975 and 1980, 10 per cent of the population flees Laos; this was to continue in later years

1976–1977
Thousands of former army and police officers are sent to "re-education" camps, along with former civil servants of the Royal Lao Government

1977
Resistance movement in the north of Hmong recruited by the CIA during the war; brutal repression carried out by the Lao People's Army aided by Vietnamese troops

Imprisonment of King Savang Vatthana and his family at Vieng Xai (Hua Phan). The king dies in captivity at the beginning of the 1980s

July 18. Signing of a treaty of friendship and cooperation with Vietnam

1978
January. Laos recognizes the new regime in Phnom Penh under Vietnamese tutelage. The Neo Lao Haksat is transformed into the Lao Front for National Reconstruction, with the objective of building socialism

1975–1979
Failure of the policy of collectivization of the rural production system

1986
Adoption of the "new economic mechanism", based on decentralization, private initiative, and freeing prices; the beginning of reforms

1987–1988
November–January. Armed conflict on the northwest frontier with Thailand

1989
Withdrawal of Vietnamese troops from Cambodia

1990
Arrest of senior Lao cadres (Thongsouk Saisangkhi, member of the Communist Party and Deputy Minister for Science and Technology, Latsami Khamphoui, Deputy Minister for Economics and Planning, and Pheng Sakchittaphong, official in the Ministry of Justice) demanding multi-party regime

1991
Paris agreements marking the end of the third Indochinese War

August 15. Proclamation of a new constitution

1992
General Khamtay Siphandone is appointed Prime Minister on the death of Kaysone Phomvihane

August 6. Exchange of ambassadors between Lao PDR and the United States

October 20–21. First conference for the development of the Greater Mekong sub-region, organized by the ADB in Manila

1994
April 8. Opening of the Friendship Bridge between Laos and Thailand

First loans to Laos from the ADB for a project under the Greater Mekong sub-region; ADB provides 60 million dollars for the Theun Hinboun dam

1997
Entry of Laos into ASEAN
Asian financial crisis

1998
Signing of the framework agreement of ASEAN in Hanoi for easing the transit of goods

1999–2002
Summit meetings between the prime ministers of Laos, Vietnam, and Cambodia

1999
October 26. First demonstration demanding "authentic" democracy in Vientiane

December. Signing an agreement of cooperation for five years between Laos and Vietnam to consolidate at all levels in all areas the links between the two countries

2000
Hmong rebellion in the province of Xieng Khouang (northeast Laos); army intervention

A series of explosions in the capital which continue sporadically in 2001, 2003, and 2004 in Vientiane and in the south of the country (Thakhek and Savannakhet)

July. A group of some 60 "resistance" soldiers of Thai and Lao nationality cross the Thai frontier and seize the frontier post of Vang Tao in Laos. Six of the besiegers are killed

July. Visit of Khamtay Siphandone to China

November. Return visit of Jiang Zemin to Laos

December 23. Opening of the Kaysone Memorial Museum (at a cost of 8 million dollars)

2001

March. Seventh party congress. Bounyang Vorachit is named Prime Minister

April. The IMF grants a loan of 40 million dollars to Laos, spread over three years

July. Hanoi declaration by member countries of ASEAN; stated intention of assisting in the development of the efforts and resources of the most recent members of ASEAN (Cambodia, Laos, Burma and Vietnam)

2002

April 9. The fifth national assembly reelects for five years General Khamtay Siphandone president of the LPDR

February. Visit of Prime Minister Bounyang Vorachit to China

May. Visit of Khamtay Siphandone to Vietnam

July 18. Celebration of the 25th anniversary of the signing of the Treaty of Amity and Cooperation with Vietnam

September 18. Celebration of the 40th anniversary of the establishment of diplomatic relations between Vietnam and Laos

September–October. The parliamentary session approves the plans for the construction of Nam Theun II dam

Mid-December. The government announces its intention of declaring January 5 a public holiday in honor of King Fa Ngum and the celebration of the 650th year of the foundation of the kingdom of Lan Xang

2003

January. Inauguration of the statue of King Fa Ngum in Vientiane

February–August. A series of deadly attacks on the highway linking Vientiane with Luang Prabang, said to be by a group of Hmong rebels opposed to the government and the army

May. Amendments to the constitution; municipal elections will be held in the provinces for the first time since 1975

2004

February–March. Hundreds of Hmong rebels in the provinces of Luang Prabang and Xieng Khouang give themselves up to the Lao authorities following an amnesty and promises of land distribution

March 20–21. Working meetings between Bounyang Vorachit and his Thai counterpart, Thaksin Shinawatra, together with their ministers at Paksé; numerous agreements signed; the two prime ministers attend the foundation of the "second Lao-Thai friendship bridge" linking Savannakhet and Mukdahan, due for completion in 2005–2006

2005

March. World Bank grants financial and political risk guarantees in support of the Nam Theun II dam project.

September. Vietnam opens a consulate in Luang Prabang Province

BIBLIOGRAPHY

Acharya, Amitav. 2000. *Constructing a security community in Southeast Asia: ASEAN and the problem of regional order*. New York: Routledge.

ALMEC. 2002. *ASEAN maritime transport development study*. Jakarta: ASEAN Secretariat.

Amer, Ramses. 1999. "Conflict management and constructive engagement in ASEAN's expansion." *Third World Quarterly* 20 (5): 1031–48.

Andersson, Magnus. 2003. *Economic integration, trade and transport infrastructure: a case study of transport linkages between Thailand and Lao PDR*. Lund: Lund University, Department of Social and Economic Geography.

Anonymous. 2000. "Aspects of forestry management in the Lao PDR." *Watershed* 5 (3): 57–64.

Asian Development Bank (ADB). 2001. "Pre-investment study for the Greater Mekong Subregion East-West Corridor, Integrative Report." February.

———. 1998. "Cross-border movement of goods and people in the Greater Mekong Sub-Region." September .

———. 2003. *Key indicators of the Lao PDR*. www.adb.org/LaoPDR, Manila: ADB, October.

———. 1996. *Étude de la stratégie opérationnelle du pays pour la République démocratique populaire du Laos*. Manila: ADB, July.

Baker, Chris. 2003. "Ayutthaya rising: from land or sea?" *Journal of Southeast Asian Studies* 34 (1): 41–62.

Bakker, Karen. 1999. "The politics of hydropower: developing the Mekong." *Political Geography* 18 (2): 209–32.

Banomyong, Ruth. 2003. *Transit transport issues in landlocked and transit developing countries*. New York: United Nations Economic and Social Commission for Asia and the Pacific (ESCAP).

——— and Beresford, Anthony. 2000. "Freight transport modal choice in Lao PDR." In *Proceedings of the Logistics Network Conference (LRN)*, Cardiff University, 7–8 September, pp. 45–54.

Bezy, Pierre-Yves. 1996. *East-West Corridor study, Third Project Steering Committee Meeting Transit Facilitation*. Proceedings of Laos-Thailand-Vietnam meeting, Danang, 9–11 February, Economic and Social Commission for Asia and the Pacific (ESCAP).

Boisseu du Rocher, Sophie. 1998. *L'ASEAN et la construction régionale en Asie du Sud-Est*. L'Harmattan, coll. Logiques politiques: Paris.

Bouahong Phantanousy. 1994. "The experience of the shifting cultivation stabilization programme of the Department of Forestry." In *Shifting cultivation*, edited by D. Gansberghe and R. Pals. Vientiane: UNDP.

Bounkhong Soukhavath. 2002. *Pathet lao nay sangkhom nanasat* [Laos in the international community]. Vientiane: privately published.

Bounthavy Sisouphanthong and Christian Taillard. 2000. *Atlas de la république démocratique populaire lao: Les structures territoriales du développement économique et social*. Paris: CNRS-GDR Libergéo-La Documentation française.

Branfman, Fred. 1970. "Presidential war in Laos, 1964–1970." In *Laos: war and revolution*, edited by Nina S. Adams and Alfred W. McCoy, 213–80. New York: Harper & Row.

Brown, MacAlister and Joseph J. Zasloff. 1986. *Apprentice revolutionaries: the communist movement in Laos*. Stanford CA: Hoover Institution Press.

Burchett, Wilfred G. 1959. *Mekong upstream: a visit to Laos and Cambodia*. Berlin: Seven Seas.

———, Alton, Charles and Crisfield, Arthur G. 1995. *Indigenous people's profile*, Vientiane: CARE International for the World Bank.

Chazee, Laurent. 1994. Shifting cultivation in Laos: present systems and their future (unpublished).

———. 1999. *The peoples of Laos: rural and ethnic diversities with an ethnolinguistic map*. Bangkok: White Lotus.

———. March 2002. Executive summary, Smallholder Development Project, Rural Sociology. Unpublished.

Christie, Clive J. 1998. *Southeast Asia in the twentieth century: a reader*. London and New York: I.B. Tauris.

———. 2001. *Ideology and revolution in Southeast Asia 1900–1980: political ideas of the anti-colonial era*. Richmond: Curzon Press, pp. , 112–56.

Coedes, Georges. [1964] 1989. *États hindouisés d'Indochine et d'Indonésie*. Paris: De Boccard.

Condominas, Georges. 1980. *L'espace social à propos de l'Asie du Sud-Est*. Paris: Flammarion.

Culture Research Institute (in collaboration with Grant Evans). 1998. *Vientiane Social Survey Project, 1997–1998*. Vientiane: Ministry of Information and Culture.

Dommen, Arthur J. 1979. "Laos: Vietnam's Satellite." *Current History* 77 (452): 201–2, 225.

———. 1985. *Laos: keystone of Indochina*. Boulder, CO: Westview Press.

Donovan, D.G. 2002. "Globalization: A View from the Lao Hinterlands." In Kyoto Review of Southeast Asia, October. http://kyotoreview.cseas.kyoto-u.ac.jp/issue/issue1/index.html (accessed May 2003).

Dovert, Stéphane, ed. 2001. *Thaïlande contemporaine*. Bangkok: IRASEC/Paris: l'Harmattan.

——— and Treglodé, Benoît de, eds. 2004. *Viêt Nam contemporain*. Bangkok: IRASEC/Paris: Les Indes Savantes.

Durand, Frédéric. 1994. *Les Forêts en Asie du Sud-Est: recul et exploitation*. Paris: L'Harmattan, coll. Recherches asiatiques.

Economic and Social Commission for Asia and the Pacific (ESCAP). 2000. *Governance re-invented: the progress, constraints and remaining agenda in banking and corporate restructuring in East and South East Asia*. New York: United Nations ESCAP.

———. 2001. *Private Sector Perspective in the Greater Mekong Subregion*. New York: United Nations ESCAP, ST/ESCAP/2065.

Evans, Grant. 1988. *Agrarian change in communist Laos*. Singapore: Institute of Southeast Asian Studies.

———. [1990] 1995. *Lao peasants under socialism and post-socialism*. Chiang Mai: Silkworm Books.

———. 1993. "Buddhism and economic action in socialist Laos." In *Socialism: ideals, ideologies, and Local Practices*, edited by C.M. Hann, 132–47. London: Routledge.

———, ed. 1999. *Laos: culture and society*. Chiang Mai: Silkworm Books.

———. 1998. *The politics of ritual and remembrance: Laos since 1975*. Chiang Mai: Silkworm Books.

———. 2002. *A short history of Laos: the land in between*. St. Leonards, NSW: Allen and Unwin.

——— and Rowley, Kelvin, eds. [1984]. 1990. *Red brotherhood at war: Vietnam, Cambodia and Laos since 1975*. London: Verso.

Fall, Bernard. 1965. "The Pathet Lao: A 'Liberation' Party." In *The Communist Revolution in Asia: Tactics, Goals, and Achievements*, edited by R.A. Scalapino, 173–97. Englewoods Cliffs, NJ: Prentice-Hall.

Forbes, Andrew D.W. 1987. "The " CinnHo " (Yunnanese Chinese) Caravan Trade with North Thailand during the Late Nineteenth and Early Twentieth Centuries." *Journal of Asian History* 21 (2): 1–47.

Gansberghe, Dirk van, and Pals, Rio, eds. 1994. *Shifting Cultivation Systems in Rural Development in the Laos PDR*. Vientiane.

Goscha, Christopher E. 1995. *Vietnam or Indochina? Contesting Concepts of Space in Vietnamese Nationalism, 1887–1954*. Nordic Institute of Asian Studies (NIAS), Reports Series no. 28, Copenhagen.

———. 2000. Le contexte asiatique de la guerre fanco-vietnamienne: réseaux, relations et économie (d'août 1945 à mai 1954), vol I. PhD diss., École Pratique des Hautes Études, Paris.

Goudineau, Yves, ed. 1997. *Resettlement and social characteristics of new villages. basic needs for resettled communities in the Lao PDR. An Orstom Survey*, vol. 1 and 2. Bangkok: UNESCO-UNDP.

———. 2000. "Ethnicité et déterritorialisation dans la péninsule Indochinoise: considérations à partir du Lao." Autrepart. les Cahiers des sciences humaines, no.14, L'Aube, pp.17–31.

———, ed. 2003. *Culture minoritaires du Laos: valorisation d'un patriommoine*, Editions UNESCO, Coll. Mémoire des peuples, Paris.

——— and Vienne, Bernard. 2001. "L'Etat et les minorités ethniques: la place des 'populations montagnards' [chao khao] dans l'espace national." In *Thaïlande contemporaine*, edited by S. Dovert, 143–71. Bangkok: IRASEC/Paris: l'Harmattan.

Guerin, Matthew, Andrew Hardy, Nguyen Van Chinh and Stan Tan Boon Hwee. 2003. *Des Montagnards aux minorités ethniques: quelle intégration nationale pour les habitants des hautes terres du Vietnam et du Cambodge?* Bangkok: IRASEC/Paris: l'Harmattan.

Gunn, Geoffrey C. 1988. Political struggles in Laos (1930–1954): *Vietnamese Communist power and the struggle for national independence*. Bangkok: Editions Duang Kamol.

Hann, Chris C., ed. 1993. *Socialism: ideals. ideologies, and local practice*. London: Routledge.

Hardy, Andrew and Nguyen Van Chinh. 2004. "Gérer la question ethnique sur les hautes terres: un exercice d'équilibriste." In *Viêt Nam contemporain*, edited by S. Dovert and Benoît de Tréglodé, 383–432. Bangkok: IRASEC/ Paris: Les Indes Savantes.

Harris, Ian, ed. 1999. *Buddhism and politics in twentieth century Asia*. London: Pinter.

Hirsch, Philip. 1995. "Thailand and the new geopolitics of Southeast Asia: resource and environmental issues." In *Counting the costs: economic growth and environmental change in Thailand*, edited by Jonathan Rigg, 235–59. Singapore: Institute of Southeast Asian Studies.

———. 1998. "Dams, resources and the politics of environment in mainland Southeast Asia." In *The politics of environment in Southeast Asia: resources and resistance*, edited by Philip Hirsch and Carol Warren, 55–70. London: Routledge.

————. 2002. "Global norms, local compliance and the human rights-environment nexus: a case study of the Nam Theun II in Laos." In *Human rights and the environment: conflicts and norms in a globalizing world*, edited by Lyuba Zarsky, 147–71. London: Earthscan.

————, and Warren, Carol. 1998. *The politics of environment in Southeast Asia. resources and resistance.* London: Routledge.

International Labour Organization (ILO). 1998. *The social impact of the Asian financial crisis.* Bangkok: ILO.

———— /IPEC [International Programme on the Elimination of Child Labour]. 2003. *Lao PDR: Preliminary assessment of illegal labour migration and trafficking in children and women for labour exploitation.* Bangkok: ILO.

International Rivers Network (IRN). *Power struggle: the impacts of hydro-development in Laos,* www.irn.org/prgrams/mekong/namtheun.html (accessed September 2003).

Ireson, Carol J. and Ireson, Randall W. 1991. "Ethnicity and development in Laos." *Asian Survey* 31 (10): 920–37.

Karl, Deutsch Wolfgang. [1957] 1969. *Political community and the North Atlantic area: international organization in the light of historical experience.* New York: Greenwood Press.

Katay D. Sasorith. 1953. *Le Laos: son évolution politique, sa place dans l'union française.* Paris: Éditions Berger-Levrault.

Keyes, Charles F., Hardacre, Helen and Kendall, Laurel, eds. 1994. *Asian visions of authority: religion and the modern states of East and South East Asia.* Honolulu: University of Hawai.

Khien Theeravit, Adisorn Semayaen, and Thantavanh Manolom. *Thai-Lao relations in Laotian perspective.* Bangkok: Institute of Asian Studies, Chulalongkorn University.

Kraft, Herman Joseph S. 2000. "ASEAN and intra-ASEAN relations: weathering the storm?" *Pacific Review* 13 (3): 453–72.

Kusuma Snitwongse. 2001. "Thai foreign policy in the global age: principle or profit?" *Contemporary Southeast Asia* 23 (2): 189–212.

Langer, Paul F. and Zasloff, Joseph J. 1970. *North Vietnam and the Pathet Lao: partners in the struggle for Laos.* Cambridge MA: Harvard University Press.

LAO PDR. 2001. *Socioeconomic development strategy from now until 2020, 2010 and the Fifth Five-Year Socioeconomic Development Plan (2001–2005).* Vientiane.

Le Thanh Khoi. 1992. *Histoire du Việt Nam: des origines à 1858.* Paris : Sudestasie.

Lefèvre-Pontalis, Pierre. 1902. Mission Pavie Indo-Chine 1879–1895. *Géographie et voyages. Voyages dans le Haut Laos (et sur les frontières de Chine et de Birmanie).* Paris: Ernest Leroux.

Leifer, Michael. 1989. *ASEAN and the security of Southeast Asia*. London: Routledge.

———. 1993. "Indochina and ASEAN: seeking a new balance." *Contemporary Southeast Asia* 15 (3): 269–79.

Lyttleton, Chris. 1999. "Any port in a storm: coming to terms with HIV in Lao People's Democratic Republic." *Culture and Health* 1 (2): 115–30.

———, 2000. *Endangered relations: negotiating sex and AIDS in Thailand*. Bangkok: White Lotus.

——— and Amorntip Amarapibal. 2002. "Sister cities and easy passage: HIV, mobility and economies of desire in a Thai/Lao border zone." *Social Science and Medicine* 4 (February): 505–18.

———, Paul Cohen, Houmpanh Rattanavong, et al. 2004. *Watermelons, bars and trucks: dangerous intersections in northwest Laos*. Vientiane: Institute for Cultural Research.

Malee Traisawasdichal. 1997. "Rivers for sale: a contemporary account of socialist Lao PDR in transition to the 'marketplace'." Reuter Foundation Paper 78, Green College, Oxford.

McCormack, Gavan. 2001. "Water margins: competing paradigms in China." *Critical Asian Studies* 33 (1): 5–30.

Mayoury and Pheuiphanh Ngaosyvathn. 1994. *Kith and kin politics: the relationship between Laos and Thailand*. Manila: Journal of Contemporary Asia Publishers.

Mennonite Central Committee (MCC), Mines Advisory Group (MAG), and Lao PDR. 1994. *Summary description: Uunexploded Ordnance Project, Xieng Khouang, Lao PDR*. Vientiane: MCC-MAG-LPDR.

Michaud, Jean, ed. 2000. *Turbulent times and enduring peoples: mountain minorities in the South-East Asian massif*. Richmond: Curzon.

Milner, Anthony and Quilty, Mary, ed. 1996. *Communities of thought: Australia in Asia*. Melbourne: Oxford University Press.

Ministry of Information and Culture. 1996. *Pavatsaat lao* [History of Laos], vol. 1. Vientiane: Ministry of Information and Culture.

Ministry of Labour and Social Affairs. 2002. *Trafficking in women and children in the Lao PDR. Initial observations*. United Nations project. Vientiane: Ministry of Labour and Social Affairs.

Muni Sukh Deo. *China's strategic engagement with the new Asean: an exploratory study of China's post-Cold War political strategic and economic relations with Myanmar, Laos, Cambodia and Vietnam*. IDSS Monograph no. 2. Singapore: Institute of Defence and Strategic Studies.

Nguyen Vu Teng. 2002. "Viet Nam-ASEAN co-operation after the Cold War and the continued search for a theoretical framework." *Contemporary Southeast Asia* 24 (1): 106–20.

Osborne, Milton. 2000. *The Mekong: turbulent past, uncertain future*. St Leonards NSW: Allen & Unwin.

Parnwell, Michael J.G. and Bryant, Raymond L., eds. 1996. *Environmental change in Southeast Asia: people, politics, and sustainable development*. London: Routledge.

Pholsena Vatthana. 2002. "Nation/representation: ethnic classification and mapping nationhood in contemporary Laos." *Asian Ethnicity* 3 (2): 175–97.

————. 2004. "Le Viêt Nam et ses voisins de l'ex-Indochine." In *Viêt Nam contemporain*, edited by S. Dovert and B. de Tréglodé, 147–67. Bangkok: IRASEC/ Paris: Les Indes Savantes.

————. 2005. "Laos. 'Towards subregional integration': 10 years on." In *Southeast Asian Affairs*, edited by Chin Kin Wah and Daljit Singh, 173–88. Singapore: Institute of Southeast Asian Studies.

Reinach, Lucien de. 1901. *Le Laos* (Vol.I). Paris: A. Charles.

Reynolds, Craig J., ed. 1991. *National identity and its defenders: Thailand, 1939–1989*. Chiang Mai: Silkworm Books.

————. 1996. "Thailand". In *Communities of thought: Australia in Asia*, edited by Anthony Milner and Mary Quilty, 100–25. Melbourne: Oxford University Press.

————. 1998. "Globalization and cultural nationalism in modern Thailand." In *Southeast Asian identities: culture and the politics of representation in Indonesia, Malaysia, Singapore, and Thailand*, edited by Joel S. Kahn, 115–45. London: I.B. Tauris/ Singapore: Institute of Southeast Asian Studies Singapore.

Rigg, Jonathan, ed. 1995. *Counting the costs: economic growth and environmental change in Thailand*. Singapore: Institute of Southeast Asian Studies.

Roche, Jean-Jacques. 2001. *Théorie des relations internationales*. Paris: Montchrestien, Clefs/Politiques.

Rüland, Jürgen. 2000. "ASEAN and the Asian crisis: theoretical implications and practical consequences for Southeast Asian regionalism." *Pacific Review* 13 (3): 421–51.

Salemink, Oscar. 2000. "Sedentarisation and selective preservation among the montagnards in the Vietnamese central highlands." In *Turbulent times and enduring peoples: mountain minorities in the South-East Asian massif*, edited by Jean Michaud, 125–50. Richmond: Curzon.

Samrane, Paul. 2000. *Country report to the National Workshop on Illegal Labour Movements: the case of trafficking in women and children*. Vientiane: Ministry of Justice.

Scalapino, Robert Anthony, ed. 1965. *Communist revolution in Asia: tactics, goals, and achievements*. Prentice-Hall, Englewood Cliffs, NJ,

Skeldon, Ronald. 2000. *Population Mobility and HIV Vulnerability in SEA: An Assessment and Analysis*, UNDP South East Asia HIV and Development Project, Bangkok,

Southavilay, Thongleua and Castren, T. 1999. *Timber Trade and Wood Flow Study: Country Report: Lao People's Democratic Republic. Poverty Reduction and Environmental Management in Remote Greater Mekong Subregion Watershed (Phase I)*. Vientiane.

State Planning Committee and National Statistical Centre. 1997. *Results from the population census 1995*. Vientiane: State Planning Committee-National Statistical Centre.

Steinberg, David Joel, ed. [1971] 1987. *In search of Southeast Asia: a modern history*. Honolulu: University of Hawai'i Press.

Stern, Aaron. *Thailand's migration situation and its relations with APEC members and other countries in Southeast Asia*. Asian Research Center for Migration (ARCM)-Institute of Asian Studies, Chulalongkorn University, Bangkok.

Stuart-Fox, Martin, ed. 1982. *Contemporary Laos : studies in the politics and society of the Lao PDR*. Santa Lucia : University of Queensland Press.

———. 1986. "The first ten years of communist rule in Laos." *Asia Pacific Community* 31 (1): 55–81.

———. 1989. "Laos in 1988: in pursuit of new directions." *Asian Survey* 39 (1).

———. 1991. "Foreign policy of the Lao People's Democratic Republic." In *Laos: beyond the revolution*, edited by Joseph J. Zasloff and Leonard Unger, 187–208. London: Macmillan.

———. 1995. "Laos: towards subregional integration." In *Southeast Asian Affairs 1995*, edited by Daljit Singh and Liak Teng Kiat, 177–95. Singapore: Institute of Southeast Asian Studies.

———. 1995. "The French in Laos, 1887–1945." *Modern Asian Studies* 29 (1): 111–39.

———. 1997. *A history of Laos*. Cambridge: Cambridge University Press.

———. 1998. *The Lao kingdom of Laan Xaang: rise and decline*. Bangkok: White Lotus.

———. 1999. "Laos: from Buddhist kingdom to Marxist state." In *Buddhism and politics in twentieth century Asia*, edited by Ian Harris, 153–72. London: Pinter.

———. 2003. *A short history of China and Southeast Asia: tribute, trade and influence*. St. Leonards, NSW: Allen & Unwin.

Tagliacozzo, Eric. 2001. "Border permeability and the state in Southeast Asia: contraband and regional security." *Contemporary Southeast Asia* 23 (2): 254–74.

———. 2002. "Smuggling in Southeast Asia: history and its contemporary vectors in an unbounded region." *Critical Asian Studies* 34 (2): 193–220.

Taillard, Christian. 1989. *Le Laos, stratégies d'un Etat-tampon*. Paris: Reclus, coll. Territoires.

———. 2005. "Le Laos à la croisée des corridors de la région du Grand Mékong." In *Le Laos, doux et amer: Vingt-cinq ans de pratiques d'une ONG*, edited by Dominique Gentil and Philippe Boumard, 71–92. Paris: Editions Khartala et CCL.

Tanabe, Shigeharu and Keyes, Charles F. 2002. *Cultural crisis and social memory: modernity and identity in Thailand and Laos*. London: Routledge-Curzon.

Thayer, Carlyle A. 1982. "Laos and Vietnam: the anatomy of a 'special relationship.'" In *Contemporary Laos: studies in the politics and society of the Lao PDR*, edited by Martin Stuart-Fox, 245–73. St. Lucia, Qld: University of Queensland Press.

———. 1999. "Vietnamese foreign policy: multilateralism and the threat of peaceful evolution." In *Vietnamese foreign policy in transition*, edited by Carlyle A. Thayer and Ramses Amer, 1–24. Singapore: Institute of Southeast Asian Studies.

——— and Ramses Amer. 1999. *Vietnamese foreign policy in transition*. Singapore: Institute of Southeast Asian Studies.

Toye, Hugh. 1968. *Laos: buffer state or battleground*. Oxford: Oxford University Press.

Treglodé, Benoît de. 2000. *Un théâtre d'ombres: le Viêt Nam entre la Chine et l'Asean au lendemain de la crise asiatique*. Paris: Les Études du Ceri, n° 68.

Tubtim Kaneungnit, Phanvilay Khamla, and Hirsch, Philip. 1996. "Decentralization, Watersheds and Ethnicity in Laos." In *Resources, nations and indigenous peoples: case studies from Australia, Melanesia and Southeast Asia*, edited by Richard Howitt, John Connell and Philip Hirsch, 265–77. Melbourne: Oxford University Press.

Tumlin, Karen C. 2000. Trafficking in children in Asia: a regional overview. ILO-IPEC International Labour Organization, International Programme on the Elimination of Child Labour (ILO-IPEC), unpublished.

Lao Youth Union, Lao Women's Union, Department of Education, Municipality of Vientiane, and Save the Children (Great Britain). 1998. *Listening to the Voice of Young People*. Vientiane: UNICEF.

United Nations Development Program (UNDP). 2000. *South East Asia HIV and Development Project, HIV Vulnerability and Population Mobility in the Northern Provinces of the Lao People's Democratic Republic*, prepared by James R. Chamberlain, April.

——— 2003. *Rapport mondial sur le développement humain 2003*. Paris: Economica.

United Nations Indusrial Development Organisation (UNIDO). *Composition and evolution of Lao PDR's external trade*. Vientiane: UNIDO.

United Nations Inter-Institutional Project on Human Trafficking in the Mekong Sub-region. 2002. Overview paper of human trafficking in the Mekong Sub-Region. Vientiane, 23 February, unpublished.

Vienne, Marie-Sybille de and Napote, Jacques. 1995. "Laos 1975–1995: restructuration et développement." Geneva: Les Cahiers de Peninsule No. 3, Etudes Orientales/ Olizane.

Vipha Utamachant. 2001. *Phonkrātopkhongsānyawitānyoulaethorāthātkhamphromd aenrāwangthailao* [Impact of Thai-Lao cross-frontier radio and television transmissions], Bangkok: Chulalongkorn University Press.

Walker, Andrew. 1999. *The legend of the golden boat: regulation, trade and traders in the borderlands of Laos, Thailand, China and Burma.* Richmond: Curzon Press.

Wille, Christina. 2000. *Trafficking in children into the worst forms of child labour in Thailand: rapid assessment findings from four research sites along the Thailand-Lao PDR and Thailand-Myanmar border areas.* Bangkok: ILO, International Programme on the Elimination of Child Labour.

———. 2001. *Female labour migration in Southeast Asia: change and continuity.* Bangkok: Chulalongkorn University.

World Bank. 2002. Lao Logistics *Development and Trade Facilitation in Lao PDR,* Working Paper. Washington, D.C.: World Bank.

———. 2002. *Poverty Reduction Fund Project, Lao PDR. Social Assessment Report,* report prepared by Care International.

World Bank, Swedish International Development Agency (SIDA), and Finnish Ministry of Foreign Affairs. 2001. "Lao PDR Production Forestry Policy: Status and Issues for Dialogue". Vol. 1, Main Report, 11 June 2001, http://lnweb18. worldbank.org/eap/eap.nsf/Countries/Lao+PDR/ (accessed in September 2003).

Wyatt, David K. [1982] 2001. *Thailand: a short history.* Chiang Mai: Silkworm Books.

Zarsky, Lyuba. 2002. *Human rights and the environment: conflicts and norms in a globalizing world.* London: Earthscan.

Zasloff, Joseph J. and Leonard Unger, eds. 1991. *Laos: beyond the revolution.* London: Macmillan.

INDEX

ABOUT THE AUTHORS

Vatthana Pholsena is Assistant Professor at the Department of Southeast Asian Studies, National University of Singapore. She will join the Institut d'Asie Orientale (Lyon) in January 2007 as a CNRS research fellow. She is the author of *Postwar Laos: The Politics of Culture, History and Identity*.

Ruth Banomyong is Associate Professor and Head of the Department of International Business, Logistics and Transport Management at Thammasat University in Thailand. Since 1995, Ruth has been a Consultant for UNCTAD's Trade Logistics Branch in Geneva and UN-ESCAP's Transport, Communications, Tourism and Infrastructure Development Division in Bangkok.